THE PASSIONS

ISBN 0-87220-226-7 paperbound
ISBN 0-87220-227-5 clothbound
(formerly ISBN 0-385-09740-9)

ROBERT C. SOLOMON

The Passions

Emotions and
the Meaning of Life

Hackett Publishing Company
Indianapolis/Cambridge

99 98   3 4 5 6 7 8 9 10

Cover design by Robert C. Solomon

For further information, please contact

Hackett Publishing Company
P.O. Box 44937
Indianapolis, Indiana 46244-0937

Library of Congress Cataloging-in-Publication Data

Solomon, Robert C.
   The passions: emotions and the meaning of life/Robert C. Solomon.
      p.   cm.
   Originally published: Garden City, N.Y.: Anchor Press/Doubleday,
1976. With new pref.
   Includes index.
   ISBN 0-87220-227-5 (hard: alk. paper)
   ISBN 0-87220-226-7 (pbk.: alk. paper)
      1. Emotions (Philosophy).   2. Meaning (Philosophy).   3. Life.
I. Title.
B105.E3S65   1993
152.4—dc20   92-45228
                                                       CIP

The paper used in this publication meets the minimum requirements of
American National Standard for Information Sciences—Permanence of Paper for Printed Library Materials, ANSI Z39.48-1984.

CONTENTS

PREFACE TO THE HACKETT EDITION

The Passions was published in 1976, at a time when the topic of emotions was receiving virtually no attention whatever in Anglo-American philosophy and very little attention in the social sciences. The scene wasn't much more appealing in Germany and France, where the new scientism and structuralism had eclipsed phenomenology and existentialism, in which Max Scheler and Jean-Paul Sartre, for example, had once had some extremely interesting things to say about the more sentimental and passionate side of life. Western philosophy had so long thought of itself as the exercise of "pure" reason and dismissed the emotions as "irrational" that even the rich literature that already existed in works by Aristotle and the ancient Stoics, by Descartes, Spinoza, Malebranche, and Hume, for instance, were largely ignored. Socrates may have sung the praises of philosophy as *eros*, and the discipline was still called "the *love* of wisdom," but philosophy had become anything but erotic, and whatever passion may have been generated by certain philosophical disputes, this passion got no respect in philosophy and much less did the emotions warrant becoming the subject of the discussion. There was a hole at the heart of philosophy, and soon after graduate school, in the thrall of the existentialists despite my analytic training, I knew what I wanted to do with my life—put the passions back in philosophy.

The core of this book is a *theory*, however, not a polemic. It is a theory of emotions, and in a very short, perilous phrase, it is the theory that *emotions are judgments*. It is, even in that single phrase, an attempt to shift the emotions, from their traditional demeaning role as unintelligent distractions and intrusions into the life of reason, to essential features of reason itself. My thesis is that the emotions are themselves rational (and therefore sometimes irrational too). They are ways of seeing and engaging in the world, our ways of "being tuned" into the world, in Heidegger's delightful metaphor. The theory is not yet fully developed but rather is put forward in as uncompromising and persuasive terms as I could manage. If it oversimplifies the complexity of the notion of "judgment," excessively minimizes the role of physiology and feeling, and plays down the essential role of desire, for example, that was in order to push to its fullest what has since been designated as "the cognitive theory." Emotions are intelligent, cultivated, conceptually rich engagements with the world, not mere reactions or instincts. I wanted to get away as quickly as possible from the old appeals to indescribable "affect" and the dismissal of emotions from the realm of theory as uninteresting (in psychology, a mere pedagogical dangler in the standard topic, "motivation and emotion"). I wanted to get away from the then-prevalent idea, in both philosophy and the social sciences, that there was very little to say about the emotions, that they were insignificant if not "ineffable." One could express them, perhaps in words, and one could report ("incorrigibly") their presence, but the emotions themselves would best be left to the poets.

Emotions are not merely a "phenomenon," a curiosity of human psycho-physiology to be studied and understood. They are far more meaningful, moving, and essential than that. Thus the connection between the passions and the "meaning of life," a big question often swept under the rug by more modestly puzzle-minded philosophers. The great question of "meaning" is treated as a sophomore's confusion, a philosophical joke more suited to the comic pages than the seminar room. But if the philosophers have no answers, their silence itself provides one. That is, there is no meaning. They would not say, most of them, that life is "absurd," Albert Camus's classic response. But there may well be a candid admission that reason alone cannot answer such a question, whether or not religion can do better. Rational constructions, extravagant teleologies, appeals to science, and the vacuous utilitarian appeal to human happiness all have their merits, but none does the job. But if reason alone cannot answer the question, what about our impassioned (and by no means irrational) engagements in life? Thus I suggest that emotions are the meaning of life. It is because we are moved, because we feel, that life has a meaning. The passionate life, not the dispassionate life of pure reason, is the meaningful life. (The passionate life of reason is the passionate life in disguise.)

This view is directly opposed to certain ancient (and modern) Stoic answers, that life has meaning only insofar as we disown and "see through" our emotions, that the proper philosopher's response to the world is detachment, dispassionate contemplation, *apatheia* or apathy. It is also at least superficially opposed to the Buddhist ideal of "liberation," which urges us to free ourselves from our passions, although beneath that obvious disagreement there lies a more profound agreement on the connection between emotions, attachments, and meaning. Of course, *which* emotions make life meaningful remains an open question, but there is a partial answer to that question implicit in *The Passions*. On the one hand, there are those grand passions, what Nietzsche too timidly calls the life-enhancing *(lebensbejahend)* passions. I sometimes think of them as the emotions most worthy of majestic or intimate musical accompaniment. They are the driving force of a life well lived, life lived as a work of art, life that is filled with meaning and meanings. On the other hand, there are those emotions that Nietzsche calls the life-stultifying *(lebensverneinend)* passions, "which drag us down with their stupidity." They define our lives as petty and defensive. If one wanted to compose background music for these emotions, it would be in the style of *kitsch*. But stultifying passions can nevertheless be extremely clever, e.g. envy and resentment, and what makes them stupid is not their lack of intelligence but their philosophically restricted vision of life. All emotions make life meaningful, I wrote in what follows, but some meanings are demeaning.

A book on "the passions" is necessarily a personal matter, and I am delighted that my favorite of my books is about to be published by my favorite publisher. My very special thanks to Jay Hullett and his good colleagues for making this possible.

NOTE: In this edition of *The Passions*, I have strengthened the emphasis on the main line of argument about the nature of emotions and the meaning of life by eliminating the more speculative phenomenology that appeared in the Doubleday and University of Notre Dame editions. I have also cut the final chapters on resentment, self-deception, and self-realization, as they have been superceded by more recent publications. The result is a more streamlined and, I think, a better book.

Robert C. Solomon
Austin, Texas
September 1992

Conquer your passions and you conquer the world.

Hindu Proverb

Give me that man who is not passion's slave
And I will wear him in my heart's core.

Shakespeare (*Hamlet*)

Love, music, passion, intrigue, heroism—these
are the things that make life worthwhile.

Stendhal

PREFACE

"Life is absurd."

No, it is not.

But our retort is unconvincing. It lacks intellectual conviction. The complaint that "life is absurd" seems to be supported by the whole of human reason; our response is but a visceral reaction, the sense that something, something indefinable, is wrong, not with life, but with *the* life that finds itself absurd. Even when the complaint is our own, as it often is, it gives us that uncomfortable feeling of barely transparent fraud and self-deception. But the intellectual integrity of the complaint itself, all but the epigram of our modern sensibilities, goes unchallenged, however ignored or pushed to the perimeters of our existence by the ongoing habits and stubborn persistence of our everyday lives.

The problem is no less than a misconception of ourselves which has condemned us to the seemingly irrefutable conclusion, expressed in varying degrees of eloquence and despair by our best philosophers, that "life is absurd," that "man is a useless passion," that "ultimately, *nothing* has any meaning." But it is not a uniquely modern misconception; it is the same misconception that lies at the heart of two thousand years of equally self-demeaning attempts to ward off precisely that same sense of absurdity, to prove or postulate some divine, transhistorical, or utopian "meaning" of human life that stands outside of life itself.

The problem is often said to be our own "irrationality," our sometimes extravagant but always vain desires and expectations, our sometimes uplifting but more often disruptive and destructive moods and emotions. The problem, in short, is our *passions*, those shortsighted and self-indulgent less-than-wholly-human lapses in our objectivity and our knowledge of Reality. The answer, on the other hand, has always been thought to be that "spark of the divine" called "reason," which distinguishes man from the animals and allows him to transcend the petty indulgences and vain pretensions of personal self-importance of his passions. But the problem lies in the very realm in which we have always sought our answer—in the arrogant but emasculated concept of reason that has always pretended to provide our lives with the meanings we demand but has never succeeded. And the "answer" (though in fact the dissolution of the "problem") lies in precisely those visceral feelings that have as yet received no adequate and intellectually respectable defense. In short, the answer lies in our passions, so rarely understood and so little appreciated.

The thesis of this book is quite simply stated: to return to the passions the central and defining roles in our lives that they have so long and persistently been denied, to limit the pretensions of "objectivity" and self-demeaning reason which have exclusively ruled Western philosophy, religion, and science since the days of Socrates. Our passions have too long been relegated to mere footnotes in philosophy and parentheses in psychology, as if they were intrusions and interruptions—sometimes welcome distractions but more usually embarrassing if not treacherous subversions of lives that *ought* to be conceived in "higher" terms.

Our passions constitute our lives.

It is our passions, and our passions alone, that provide our lives with meaning.

But the defense of this thesis requires in turn a new look at the nature of the passions themselves—and their alleged antithesis with "reason." Our passions are not the animal intrusions and physiologically based disruptions that they have always been thought to be. Neither are they sporadic and "irrational" intrusions into otherwise meaningful and quite "rational" lives. The passions are not threatening or overwhelming "forces" that push us in this way or that, hopefully to be controlled by "the sweet light of reason." It is not as if the passions themselves (and thus our lives) were dirty little secrets that would best be left in the darkness untold. This approach to the passions, which I collectively entitle "the Myth of the Passions," is itself part and parcel of that system of denial and neglect that leads so directly and inexorably to the conclusion that "life is absurd." The Myth of the Passions, like all myths, is self-serving, and dramatized for the sake of our own self-image. It is the myth of passivity; the self-serving half-truth is the fact that we often suffer from our passions, submit ourselves to them, find ourselves carried away and foolishly behaving because of them. The purpose of the myth is evident enough—to cast ourselves in the role of helpless martyr, battling powerful and irrational forces within us. Arthur Schopenhauer's pessimistic philosophy, which cast our lot as victims of an all-powerful and irrational Will within us, was only an extreme and bitter variation of a theme that has been held by almost everyone, philosophers and nonphilosophers alike, for over two thousand years. So long as the "passions" render us "passive," the most important and vital attitudes and actions of our lives fall beyond the scope of our doing and our responsibility, and so we find ourselves with an elaborate and convenient system of excuses, for our feelings, for our behavior, for our Selves. "I couldn't help it; I was angry;" "She's not responsible; she's in love"; "Don't blame him; he was embarrassed": These are symptoms of a malady that cuts far deeper than a merely faulty theory of human nature. These are the products of irresponsible self-deception, attempts to place blame and responsibility beyond ourselves for what, I shall argue, is in fact the most our own. Our passions—our emotions, moods, and desires—define us, our selves, and the world we live in.

Our language and our thinking about the passions is riddled with this myth of passivity; we "fall in" love, much as one might fall into a tiger trap or a swamp. We find ourselves "paralyzed" with fear, as if we had been inoculated with a powerful drug. We are "plagued" with remorse, as if by flies or mosquitoes. We are "struck" by jealousy, as if by a Buick; "felled" by shame, as a tree by an ax; "distracted" by grief, as if by a trombone in the kitchen; "haunted" by guilt, as if by a ghost; and "driven" by anger, as if pushed by a prod. Our richest poetic metaphors, grown trite with overuse, are images of passivity. We are "heartbroken," "crushed," "smitten," "overwhelmed," "carried away," and "undone" by passion. The passions are said to emanate from the heart—spiritual animal sap pumped through our veins. Our hearts, beyond the reach of our wills, are contrasted with our "heads." While the latter struggles to maintain calm, the former suffers the fate of any butcher's victim—our hearts are cleft in two, as bruised and bloody flesh, hot or now grown cold, pounding, beating, breaking, bursting, gushing love, and "flesh rejoicing," hard as stone or soft with aching, stabbed and smitten, torn and tender. The poet can say, "Speak to me, O my heart!" but what philosopher need so address his head? Our feelings, unlike our thoughts, are "visceral"— akin to and not only involving stomach cramps and flushing pulse. Resentment is bile, and rage is from the spleen. We are made sick with grief or fear and our souls swell with rage. Anger is like riding a wild horse, wrote Horace, and ever since (and before) the picture has remained unchanged. The passions are our inheritance from a more primitive and animal part of the soul, originating in the body, unlike thought and reason, which are of "Divine" origin, "man's gift from the gods."

The passions have been generally agreed to be primitive and "natural," disruptive and irrational, lacking in judgment and purpose or reason, without scruples, and sometimes shockingly short of taste. Horace also wrote that "anger is brief madness," while his contemporary Sallust argued that "no mortal man ever served his passions and his interests at the same time." We all have learned that "love is blind." And a popular 1940s' song whined, "If my desire drives me a little insane, am I to blame?"

Our contemporary attitude is well summarized in a well-known bit of jargon from Freud's later psychoanalytic theories; the seat of reason is the "ego," the "I," or the "Self," while the home of the passions is that foreign cauldron of energies called the "id," literally the "it," what is *not* part of ourselves, rather the outside threat to the Self or ego and its social ally the "superego." This battle defines the life of the human spirit: "us" against "it," reason and civilization against the monstrous demands and aberrations of the passions. Controlling these wild beasts is the purpose of human society, religion, and reason. In our maturity we are held responsible for such control, no matter how difficult it may be. But there has been no suggestion that we might also be responsible for the passions themselves, which might need no "control" at all if we were to realize only that they are our own making in the first place.

In the place of this Myth of the Passions, I have sought to provide an alternative; perhaps an alternative mythology, I admit, but one which has the self-confirming virtue of bringing back to our Selves the control and recognition of responsibility for these systematically misunderstood phenomena which could not be more central to our lives. In place of the self-denying myth of the passions, I want to substitute a self-esteeming representation of emotions as our own *judgments*, with which we structure the world to our purposes, carve out a universe in our own terms, measure the facts of Reality, and ultimately "constitute" not only our world but ourselves. Rather than disturbances or intrusions, these emotions, and the passions in general, are the very core of our existence, the system of meanings and values within which our lives either develop and grow or starve and stagnate. The passions are the very soul of our existence; it is not they who require the controls and rationalizations of reason. Rather, it is reason that requires the anchorage and earthy wisdom of the passions. The passions are not irrational; they are in their very essence "rational," as Nietzsche wrote, "as if every passion did not contain its quantum of reason."[1] It is said that the passions are without judgment or at least without *good* judgment, but I insist that, to the contrary, they are themselves judgments of the most important kind. It is said that the passions are without purpose, that they conflict with our ambitions and distract us from our goals, that they distort our sense of reality, create illusions, and are "blind." But the passions are the very *source* of our interests and our purposes.* The passions, in short, are not those primitive ragamuffins and the refuse of our psychic life that Western rationalism has always warned us against with thinly veiled repulsion; they are the high court of consciousness, to which all else, even reason, must pay tribute. They are not intrusions or distractions, but rather the essential structures of our existence. The passions are judgments, *constitutive* judgments according to which our reality is given its shape and structure.

It is through our passions that we fill (not simply find) our lives with meanings, the same meanings that the "absurdity of life"

* Hume for example, says that only passion moves us; reason has no such power.

theorists have always overlooked, denigrated, or denied. But not all meanings are of equal worth, and our all-too-familiar sense of absurdity (of which the philosophy of the "absurdity of life" is a rationalization) is not a matter of lack of meaning so much as our own choice of the *wrong* meanings, the *wrong* passions. The use of such value concepts may seem wholly out of place in a discussion of the passions, but this, too, is symptomatic of the Myth of the Passions, as if a passion were simply a natural force, to which evaluations of "right" and "wrong" were utterly beside the point. But every emotion is a strategy, a purposive attempt to structure our world in such a way as to maximize our sense of personal dignity and self-esteem. And, as strategies, our emotions can be more or less successful, more or less direct, well or ill conceived, effective or self-defeating.

It is not uncommon for those who defend as well as those who attack the passions to consider "the passions" as a single class and of equal value. Thus, Hume says, "Reason is, and ought to be, the slave of the passions." But *which* passions? Love, sympathy, and respect, we would probably agree; but how about resentment, hatred, and envy? Some passions are to be striven for; others are to be avoided and overcome. But this seemingly Manichean dualism need not be based on any personal preferences on our part; it is intrinsic to the emotions themselves and to our individual outlooks on the world. We each seek that same sense of dignity and esteem and that same sense of mutual respect and hopefully painless intimacy with each other. The differences in the strategies of the emotions are to be valued precisely according to these universally shared goals and needs.

Every passion endows our lives with meaning, but every meaning is not ultimately meaningful, ultimately successful in maximizing our dignity and self-esteem and making possible the mutual respect and intimacy we desire. The "absurdity of life" is nothing other than our own unsatisfactory choices, typically the choice of defensiveness and resentment, competition and "meaningless" routines, when what we would really prefer is the trust and intimacy of love and mutual respect, co-operation and a sense of shared significance. The "absurdity of life" is but a philosophical camouflage for our own self-imposed dissatisfaction. But so, too, it is philosophy that is able to see through that camouflage, see through that dissatisfaction, and provide us with the ability to undo the damage we have always been doing to ourselves.

This book began as an essay on the emotions. It has obviously become much more than that. It is, I suppose, a "philosophy of life," although the pretentiousness of that expression makes me cringe. My methods are a peculiar amalgam of both my Anglo-American "analytic" training and my marked preferences for certain themes and temperaments in recent European philosophy. My manner, for example, is far more in sympathy with the polemical style of certain Continental favorites of mine; it consists in mercilessly hammering away with my central thesis, using every weapon of argument, metaphor, literary and philosophical allusion, irony, and sarcasm that I can call to my defense. I have tried to minimize yet retain the more technical and professional problems which have plagued recent philosophy; I hope the nonprofessional reader will bear with me through those (hopefully few) sections in which such technicalities are given central attention. For my purpose here is not to be scholarly or definitive, much less to restrict myself to the same often digressive problems that have kept the problems of the passions in a state of neglect for centuries; my aim is to overturn the too-well-ordered and self-deceptive categories of "reason" and "the passions," in which the latter always receives both second billing and unchallenged critical abuse. The Myth of the Passions is not only a philosopher's mistake or an academic psychologist's construction. It is embedded in our everyday conceptions of ourselves and lies at the core of our most common personal complexities. It is the source of our most powerful false ideals and our emptiest values. The Myth of the Passions is the tacit justification of our unbridled fetishism for "cool" and loveless rationality and defensiveness, and it is the ideological prod for the impersonal greed and pointless pursuit of counterfeit self-esteem that defines so many of our contemporary woes. (I try not to be too evangelical about all this, but I confess that I do not always succeed.)

AUTHOR'S NOTE

What is the use of studying philosophy if all that it does for you is enable you to talk with some plausibility about some abstruse questions of logic, etc., and if it does not improve your thinking about the important questions of everyday life.

Ludwig Wittgenstein[2]

This book is my first attempt to bring together a general philosophy that has been emerging piecemeal for several years in lectures, professional essays, and, more importantly, in my teaching, in conversations with friends, and in my own personal and private thoughts and worries "about life in general." Accordingly, I think of this book as part of a personal struggle, not a "theory" so much as the formulation of a world-view, a kind of "hardheaded Romanticism." While its source is undeniably my own concerns and those of my students, friends, and contemporaries, I hope that what has been projected from that source will have far more general and systematic significance. Appropriately, I expect considerable abuse from both sides—from my professional colleagues for not being impersonal and (what is the same thing) "professional" enough; from others for not being "straightforwardly personal" but rather cloaking my intimate concerns with a mantle of abstract philosophy. As if a writer on these subjects ought to suffer something of a burlesque, baring his soul for the entertainment of his critics! But however revealing, there is nothing autobiographical about the following doctrines. Whatever else they may be, they are not mine alone.

Any undertaking of this scope and ambition carries with it a number of personal and professional debts. First and foremost, there is my debt of gratitude to those many authors whose work and "influence" have so obviously inspired and directed my own theory. Specifically, there is Aristotle, Friedrich Nietzsche, Jean-Paul Sartre and Albert Camus, Philip Slater, John Barth, Henri

Beyle, and a dozen others, few of whom I have ever met or ever could meet. If I have presented the thoughts that follow as my own, then that pretention should always be measured against the often unspoken but obvious debts I owe to my philosophical colleagues, past and present. Then there are the various institutions that have made this project possible: the University of Texas for giving me a generous leave of absence in which to work; the University of Michigan, both for giving me my start in philosophy and for giving me support during the year in which I wrote this book; the Centre Universitaire International of the University of Paris, the Del Rio in Ann Arbor, Les Amis in Austin, and the Riviera in New York for providing me with facilities for free thinking.

But far more important than these conditions that have made the book possible are the many friends who have made its writing rewarding and even necessary. It is for them that I have written it, in the hope that they will recognize in the following pages the many things we have been arguing about and working through together for these many years. (Contrary to Nietzsche's famous dictum, the *best* readers are always one's friends.) It is they who have inspired these ideas, put up with me through them, and put me up in difficult times, who also put me down when my own glib intellectualizing belied the passions so apparent to those who know me. This book is first and foremost for them, and it is to them that it is dedicated:

For Frithjof Bergmann, who planted the seeds; for Jean-Paul Sartre, whom I've never met, who has so long been the model of philosophical and personal commitment; for Loretta Barrett, the most remarkable editor I've ever had, who encouraged the growth of a casual essay into a very personal book; for Benida and Ron Grant, in whose perpetually half-built house these ideas took their initial form; for David and Linda Obst, for their invaluable advice and criticism; for Zina Steinberg, who gave me sanctuary and so much more; for Bill and Sandra Mahan, who became friends just when they were really needed; for Judith Sanders, who defended the honor of psychology against my usually excessive sarcasm; for Molly Friedrich, Louisa Lawrence, and Claudia Haigler, who turned the usually tedious technical production of the manuscript into something of a party; for Andy and Jon

Solomon; for my parents; for Pat Steir, Robert Rosenblum, Melissa Jackson, Nick Partridge, Nancy Hart, David Zimmerman, John Storyk, Caroline Marshall, Jan and Sandy Weimer, Eleanor McLaughlin, Edwin and Joan Allaire, Mitch and Yvonne Ginsberg, and Larry and Lissy Sklar, all for being there; for K., the book's cause if not its object; and, ultimately, for Elke, who has always been my first and most critical reader.

R.C.S.
New York City
August 1975

INTRODUCTION: REASON AND THE PASSIONS

1. Philosophy?

This same philosophy is a good horse in the stable,
but an arrant jade on a journey.

Oliver Goldsmith, *The Good-natured Man*

Hang up philosophy!
Unless philosophy can make a Juliet.

Shakespeare, *Romeo and Juliet*

There is an air of paradox surrounding an attempt by philosophy to deal with the passions. For that matter, there is a certain irony that surrounds an attempt by philosophy to deal with the question of the meaning of life. In both cases, is not philosophy the problem? It is the bloodless abstractions of philosophy that would seem farthest from the stormy vehemence of the passions. A philosopher trying to understand a passion would seem like a cynic trying to understand the feelings of two people in love. And if there were no philosophy, many would argue, there would be no problem of the meaning of life; no question, and so no negative replies. That problem is, after all, the creation of philosophers, the product of several centuries of skepticism and a thinking that will not allow itself to be content with simple faith and simple feeling. Why not leave the passions to the psychologists and the poets? And why not leave well enough alone? Thus, the first problem of philosophy is philosophy itself; what can it do? Whom is it for?

Let me be outrageous and insist that *philosophy matters*. It is not a self-contained system of problems and puzzles, a self-generating profession of conjectures and refutations. It is not a rare and esoteric beetle that is cultivated and appreciated only by

a curious sect of respectable madmen, nor is it that detached and
cynical skepticism that Keats described in "Lamia":

> Do not all charms fly
> At the mere touch of cold philosophy?

We are all philosophers; the problems we share are philosophical
problems. What has been sanctified and canonized as "philosophy" is but the cream of curdled thought culled from the minds
of men rare in genius, but common in their concerns. Nothing has
been more harmful to philosophy than its "professionalization,"
which on the one hand has increased the abilities and techniques
of its practitioners immensely, but on the other has rendered it an
increasingly impersonal and technical discipline, cut off from and
forbidding to everyone else. Accordingly, most literate Americans
would be hard pressed to name a single living and active American philosopher and would admit without shame that they had
not the foggiest idea what contemporary philosophy is all about.
But this is tragic. Philosophy is nothing else than thinking about
life, the attempt to gear our inescapable expectations and conceptions to the material of our everyday world. "Why are we doing
this?" "Why did this happen?" "What is this worth?" "Who am
I?" All of us are philosophers; some are better trained and more
articulate, some have more of a sense of urgency, and some have
more of a sense of honesty. The only real distinction, however, is
between those who persevere and those who do not, between
those who get sidetracked or distracted and those who pursue
their thinking down through the fabric of their lives.

What does one do as a "philosopher" in a society that considers
the intellect the most useless as well as the most pretentious faculty of the human soul, a society that idolizes calculation of
means and unhampered efficiency, that prefers "entertainment" to
thought and programs to problems? One can play the "professor"
of an eccentric liberal arts subject within the unworldly confines
of our four-year intellectual ghettos for only so long. (That air is
meant to be breathed for only four months and eight terms at a
time.) One can submerge him(her)self in the "puzzles" of philosophy, score a point or two and be welcomed into the inner circles
of "professional" philosophy, feign the utmost seriousness (not

for the problems but for the profession), and pretend to be an ordinary human being, as if the twists and revelations of philosophy had not yet infiltrated his or her life. But this masquerade of professionalism, however rewarding from within, has reinforced just the objection that it ought to be fighting, the charge that philosophy is "irrelevant" to everyday concerns, inaccessible to ordinary intelligent people, a rare and exotic discipline to be enjoyed only by its practitioners. What is rarely argued, as if it were a breach of professional courtesy, is the fact that so many if not all of the professional "puzzles" emerged from gut-level ordinary questions, were elevated to their present levels of abstraction by some genius or other in the seventeenth or eighteenth century, and have remained in that high-flown orbit ever since. This is largely because no one has taken the trouble to re-establish communication between the proletarian question and the sophisticated technology of the answers.

But there is a crack in that tightly closed professional system, a constant flow of the uninitiated into the very heart of the game. It is our students who keep the profession alive. One may attempt to "profess" to them, but they teach in return, that philosophy is not a detached set of professional puzzles; it is rather a desperately needed discipline for straightening out confused lives. (I sometimes think that our educational system rather expects us to be cleaning shrimp—removing the nerve chord to make the product more palatable.)

In Europe, perhaps, the importance of philosophy would not have to be argued. Having seen revolutions and fascist dictatorships nourish themselves on Jean-Jacques Rousseau and Friedrich Hegel, no European would question the essential connection between philosophy and the passions, or philosophy and the vicissitudes of human existence. America has never learned any such lesson. Her students walk in after nineteen years of being taught how *not* to think and how not to worry. They are already stupefied with the stagnating advice that they should merely "be themselves," as if "being yourself" is not something you have to learn and as if the Self is not something that you have yet to *create*. Watching those faces, the bewilderment that explodes with simple questions, the confusion that emerges with small paradoxes, the gleams of resentment and gratitude and occasional hate and "thank you" letters that accompany the slightest quaking of their well-conditioned illusions and their poorly suppressed anxieties—one knows, as a philosopher, what has to be done. Less sure of its answers than science or religion, less sure even of the questions, philosophy can only be what it has always been, and the philosopher can only be what he has always been. He is a conscientiously persistent pain in the ass, a Socratic "gadfly" that pokes and nudges. He breaks free the crust of habits, throwing light on the more insidious passions, raising questions (even the wrong questions), and jostles the intellects of America's television-dazed children and hassle-tired adults until they become alive. If the languages of sophisticated logic and linguistics will not do this, or if the obscure phraseology of German metaphysics or French phenomenology will not be understood, then the language of philosophy will have to be *our* language, the language of a culture better educated in films than philosophy, more familiar with the language of the bedroom than the language of "Being." Philosophy belongs back in the streets, where Socrates originally practiced it.

It is ironic that every great advance in philosophical "method" has signaled a further step away from the problems that method was brought in to solve. Philosophy becomes increasingly abstract and forbidding; its problems are neglected and left in the hands of those least capable of dealing with them, adolescents learning to love and breaking free of their parents, depressed and frustrated fugitives from a society that forbids them to understand themselves, old men and women who find themselves in exile and finally are forced to face the now-retrospect questions of meaning. What began as nonsense has been made into truth, the claim that philosophy has no relevance to our everyday lives. The sophisticated irrelevancy of philosophy has often been defended as a matter of pride by many of my most likable colleagues. What can be argued? The battle is not with them. What must be done is to demonstrate that philosophy need not be detached from life, but rather serves life, co-ordinates and synthesizes the mess of material inconsistently drilled into us by others who were equally unclear about what they were doing. Philosophy is essentially an art. It is the art of living, the search for *wisdom*. (I have elsewhere called philosophy "conceptual sculpture," the shaping and developing of the intellectual structures within which we live our lives.) "Intellectually I know that, but emotionally . . ." We are used to contrasting the intellect with our passions. The mistake is in thinking of the passions merely as occasional *contents* of life. They are the defining *structures* of our existence, in fact, *identical* to the intellectual structures. This sounds odd only because we are so far away from that ideal harmony that emerges with this identity. And this is the point of philosophy I want to pursue here—to help make this harmony possible. Here we have (or will have) the resolution of our paradoxes: Philosophy and the passions ultimately provide *the same* structures of our existence, the one reinforcing the other; and the meaning of life is not a problem created by philosophy but rather that problem which gives rise to philosophy. And that problem is precisely the lack of harmony between the intellect and the passions that will be the main theme of this book.

How has philosophy gone astray, allowed itself to separate from its origins, even in the philosophy of Socrates himself? It is mistakenly believed that the meaning of human life, the forms and values which give it significance, is to be found "outside" of life itself, in the static realm of pure ideas. The many problems of philosophy ultimately boil down to a single barely articulate confusion. It might be summarized "*Why?*" It is the expression of the dull-witted shepherd boy in Raphael's "Resurrection," the brutal "*Por que?*" that appears in Goya's "Horrors of War." It begins in an instant; we find ourselves running for no apparent reason, wondering why we are doing what we are doing, puzzling over the fact that people are so nasty to each other. But no sooner does this philosophical attitude emerge than a fifty-skipped-steps dialectic carries us off to the far reaches of thought, to the borders of incomprehension and nonsense. The myriad of little earthy "whys" are incorporated into a single all-encompassing cosmic question, "Why anything?" That is, "Why is there anything, rather than nothing?" Facing this impossible but unnecessary question, God is frequently introduced, nominally as a reply, but in fact, of course, as an already accepted conclusion, independent of philosophical niceties. Or else, at this point, there is a shrug of the shoulders, perhaps a frown and some mumbling about "meaninglessness," and an uncaring return to the ongoing routines of the everyday. But the mistake in any case is the confusion of philosophical thinking with the posing of incomprehensible questions. It is possible to be philosophical without being incomprehensible. *The business of philosophy is not to transcend the human, but to illuminate it.*

At the risk of being simple-minded, I suggest that there are two kinds of philosophical thinking, what Gabriel Marcel called the "philosophy of the concrete" on the one hand and *denken überhaupt,* thinking about *everything* at once, on the other. Of course, a philosophy of the concrete can very quickly become universal; concrete questions about the passions, the workings of reason, the Self, and our relations with others soon become the structures of an answer to the question "What is man?" But that isn't really a very enticing question by itself; it usually receives, and deserves, only a one-phrase answer ("rational animal," "social animal," "thinking animal," the only animal that loves/thinks/wears clothes/talks/gets embarrassed, etc.). Concrete thinking remains faithful to the experience that initiates it; it refuses to let go of the little questions, "Why do I feel this way about her?" ("It has long been an axiom of mine that the little things are infinitely the most important"—Sherlock Holmes [Sir Arthur Conan Doyle, "A Case of Identity."])

Abstract thinking, *denken überhaupt,* on the other hand, is only too happy to be freed of such questions. It may require examples and illustrations, of course, but they might be drawn from anywhere, preferably not from one's own experience—particularly painful or confusing experiences. Abstract thinking may focus on a very specific problem, one well defined and carefully narrowed down over the course of centuries by other philosophers, but it is not thereby any less abstract. Traditional metaphysical questions are of this sort; they are very specific, yet not concrete in the slightest. In fact, metaphysicians have always boasted with pride of their ability to shake free of the concrete confusions of life. This has always been, in the words of one of its older proponents, one of the "consolations of philosophy": Fascinating and perplexing problems, often allowing us to escape from unhappy marriages and nasty afternoons, harrowing confusions about careers and commitments, a grief that will not pass or anger that rages unexamined below the clouds of abstract thought.

The key to concrete philosophy is the passions; to understand them is to understand the essential structures of human experience. Philosophy by itself can provide no such structures; it has no motivating power. But it is only with an understanding of *particular* passions that we in any sense understand ourselves. It is all well and good to accept or reject my thesis that passions are judgments, chosen, constitutive, and so on; but it is a very different matter to apply that thesis, as it was originally induced, to *this* love and *this* anger, *this* spite and *this* sorrow. Thus, the passions do not fall beyond the domain of philosophy, but rather provide it with a subject matter.

So long as the question of the meaning of life is posed in its abstract form, "Why anything?" it will escape every attempted answer within our experience. To every such attempted answer, there will be a further question, "Why that?" This "absurd reasoning," which I discuss in the following chapter, is either hopeless or a mere excuse to slip in a bit of religious proselytizing. (This is not to hold anything against religion or God, but only to insist that *this* is not the way into such beliefs, in spite of the rich history of such arguments.) What gives our lives meaning is not anything *beyond* our lives, but the richness *of* our lives. And that richness is predominantly a product of the passions, which thereby become our answer to the problem of the meaning of life. The business of philosophy is not to find or invent transcendent meanings, but to illuminate the meanings *in* life.

But why illuminate them? If philosophy doesn't have to find meanings, if we've already got them, then what is the point? Are we not now just creating another set of philosophical "puzzles," for which we already have answers? What is the point of philosophy? Why should our lives require "illumination" if they are already richly endowed with meanings? Is not philosophy at best an intellectual gloss over an already preordained fact—an impotent observer who might report and editorialize, but who is incapable of adding anything, who is possibly a distraction or a nuisance, a cynic and a killjoy?

It is the key to the philosophy defended in this book that there is no ultimate distinction between reason and passion, that reason and passion together are the means of "constituting," not merely understanding, the world. And this means that to understand a passion is to be in a position to change it. To "illuminate" the darker passages of the mind is to change the climate from fog to daybright, from seething resentment to noontime love. I have already indicated that I shall argue that all passions are not equally acceptable, and it is in the light of reflection that their differences become evident. My purpose here is a radical one: not only to understand but also to change people, or rather, to let them "become who they would be." And with a change in people, no doubt, the world will change as well. Marcuse: "A radical change in consciousness is the necessary first step towards radical social change."

We have all had the experience of watching ourselves in the midst of an absurd political argument, and thinking, "I should be above all of this." And we have all had an experience similar to this: We are sitting in the main lobby of the Port Authority Bus Terminal in New York at morning rush hour, observing the throngs of sleepy hassled commuters grumpily rushing to and from buses to work, silently cursing each other and the world and deftly pushing each other aside, and we think, "Man must be more than this!" "Man must be more than this"—more than this zoo of frustrations and hassles, disappointments and petty successes, desperate leaps of affection and nasty displays of mutual defensiveness.

The unexamined passion may not be worth having; a passion examined must *earn* its place in our personality. A change in society might change the passions as well. In a society with equal distribution of goods and without social classes, such desperation and defensiveness would be unnecessary.* Unnecessary, perhaps, but not impossible; most of us have all seen our little utopias—com-

---

* All forms and products of consciousness cannot be dissolved by mental criticism, by resolution into "self-consciousness" . . . but only by the practical overthrow of the actual social relations which give rise to them" (Karl Marx, *The German Ideology*, p. 28). But how is this revolutionary attitude itself made possible if these "actual social relations" are still effective? (And if they are not, then their overthrow is unnecessary.) Only through the "No!" of the subjectivist rebel, the Romantic demand for autonomy.

munes and friendships, love affairs and families—fall apart without the aid of the usual social and economic pressures. It is the basic structures of our lives that need changing, not simply the superstructures of political economics. Those basic structures are the passions, and the passions do not depend on sociology; they depend on philosophy, the conceptual constitution of whatever world we live in—socialist, capitalist, democratic, or authoritarian. It is not capitalism that teaches greed and alienation; it is our greedy and alienated conceptions of ourselves that lay the foundation for capitalist ideology. We must change ourselves before we change society; and we must understand ourselves in order to change.

> The important thing
> is to pull yourself up by your own hair
> to turn yourself inside out
> and see the whole world with fresh eyes.
>
> Peter Weiss, *Marat/Sade*

2. The Myth: Reason versus the Passions

Since the earliest of Western thinking, the meaning of human existence has been sought first in the calm reflections of rationality. In Aristotle:

> the function of man is activity of the soul which follows a rational principle. . . . If reason is divine, then, in comparison with man, the life according to it is divine in comparison with human life . . . reason, more than anything else, *is* man.

In Shakespeare:

> What is a man,
> If his chief good and market of his time
> Be but to sleep and feed? a beast, no more.
> Sure, he that made us with such large discourse,
> Looking before and after, gave us not
> That capability and god-like reason
> To fust in us unus'd.

In Goethe, "That glimmer of divine light—man calls it Reason."
And in Immanuel Kant:

> Our existence has a different and far nobler end, for which
> reason, not happiness, is properly intended. . . . Reason issues
> its commands unyieldingly, without promising anything to the
> inclinations, and, as it were, with disregard and contempt for
> their claims, which are so impetuous.

The passions, on the other hand, have always been treated as
dangerous and disruptive forces, interrupting the clarity of reason
and leading us astray. "What reason weave/By passion is undone"—Alexander Pope, *An Essay on Man.* Or Hamlet: "The
very torrent, tempest, and, as I may say, whirlwind of your passion." Even love is not freed from this judgment. To the contrary,
every tragedy from *Medea* to the present bears out Oscar Wilde's
cruel claim, "each man [or woman] kills the thing [s]he
loves." In Aristotle the passions were allowed their place, but always subservient to reason. In his *Ethics* he virtually excluded the
possibility that a young man could lead the "good life," "so ruled
is he by his passions." In most of Christianity the passions in general were denied even a subservient place; they were distractions
from belief, "temptations of the flesh," spurs to Sin. Certain
selected passions survived, of course—faith, naturally, and a
peculiarly emaciated and universally expanded notion of "love."
Augustine, for example, summarizes the case in his *Confessions:*
"Thou hast created us for thyself, and our heart cannot be
quieted till it may find repose in Thee." Fifteen hundred years
later, Nietzsche sarcastically recapitulated: "Thus it is ever, only
the emasculated man is the good man" (*Twilight of the Idols*).
In Kant's philosophy not even faith and love are left to the passions; faith becomes a species of "practical reason" in his second
Critique, and the love he supports from the Scriptures is explicitly
distinguished as "rational love"—not the "pathological" love of
the passions. Even David Hume, one of the few defenders of the
passions, found it necessary to defend a naïvely optimistic and
truncated theory of human nature; the "passions" to which he appealed were "sympathy" and "sentiment"; with little mention of
resentment and envy, greed and hatred, the violence that comes of
rage and jealousy.

The wisdom of reason against the treachery and temptations of the passions has been the central theme of Western philosophy. It has defined ethical theories, from the "rationalist" theories of Aristotle and Kant to the antithetical "naturalist" and "emotivist" theories of David Hume, John Stuart Mill, Bertrand Russell, and the logical positivists. But underlying that theme has been another, less often argued because so frequently assumed—the *distinction* between reason and passion, based upon an archaic "faculty" psychology of the human soul. Reason is that part of the soul that is most our own, the only part of the soul that is completely under our control. The passions, however, belong to that part of the soul that is inherited from the animals, an "inferior" faculty that must be mastered. These invading forces must be contained, as emissaries of the devil or malicious tricks of bored or vengeful demons. What has always linked us to the gods has been our ability to reason ("the fact that we can do sums," quips the wry Lord Russell). What has always tied us to the beasts and kept us from divine wisdom has been our inability to control our passions. Consequently it has always been thought to be the main business of philosophy to develop the powers of reason to enable us to control the raging forces "from below." Such were the ambitions of Socrates, Plato, and Aristotle, Augustine and Aquinas, Kant, Spinoza, and Schopenhauer. Speculative thinking, far from being the free play of the imagination that is now mocked by many more "hardheaded" philosophers, was the one anchor within reach to save us from being carried away by the torrent, tempest, the whirlwind of passion.

Against this repressive conception of rational control of the passions, there has always been a "counter-culture" to point out the "unnaturalness" of damming up nature's torrents. Plato and Aristotle refer to such "Romantics," and every period of history that finds the balance of power favoring the side of suppression has responded with a similar reaction. Against the hyperrationalism of the Enlightenment, against the dull daily "business as usual" of the "Reaction," against the mechanical conception of the universe in Isaac Newton and the mechanical conception of man in current technological double-think, a renewed stress on the passions and the irrational is the predictable response. But even the "Romantics" did not disagree with the underlying assumption of rationalism—that reason and the passions are firmly opposed. Even the very best of Romanticism has fallen prey to the Myth of the Passions, equating passion with "letting go," submerging oneself in the powerful forces that nature has excited within us. Look at a painting by Eugène Delacroix or listen to the overture of a Wagnerian opera. If Delacroix followed Rousseau and Wagner Schopenhauer, the result is the same: the submersion of human reason in the violent churnings of irrational will; the *Death of Sardanapalus*, a whirlwind of destructive fire and blood-red murder; the opening lines of *The Flying Dutchman*, sweeping us away in sound. Accordingly, the Romantic artists, despite their genius, have always been prone to maximize the nature of their "mysterious gift of genius" and minimize the all-too-classical conceptions of "control," "education," and "discipline." They celebrate the frenzied creative energies burning inside of them and take for granted the exhausting labors and planning that is necessary for their genius. Romanticism shares with the repressions of rationalism the essential distinction that I am attacking. They have not changed the myth, only shifted its priorities.

3. The Meaning of Life

What is it for? What does it lead to? At first it seemed to me that these were aimless and irrelevant questions. I thought that it was all well known, and that if I should ever wish to deal with the solution it would not cost me much effort. . . . The questions, however, began to repeat themselves frequently, and to demand replies more and more insistently; and like drops of ink always falling on one place they ran together into one black blot.

Leo Tolstoy, A *Confession*

The idea that life is meaningless, "absurd": Where does this idea come from? From thought and philosophy, from that very divine and God-like light called "reason." And yet it is held that that "gift" of thought is itself the meaning of human existence, its definitive attribute, and the source of all virtue. What can this paradox mean?

Most of us know that sense of absurdity that clouds over our involvement in otherwise meaningful tasks, routine housework and assignments, casual conversations and playful games. This sense often appears as a feeling but always has its origins in thought. It is that distaste created by reflection, wrenching us away from a life full of petty meanings to re-examine them *all*. "Why this?" and "Why that?" and ultimately, "Why anything?" We expect an answer, but there is silence. "There is nothing!"—a thundering inference from mute premise. This is what Albert Camus has called "the Absurd." It is, he says, the defining sensibility of our age. It emerges at the end of a ruthless and "absurd reasoning," the last step of which, the "therefore," is that "life is not worth living." But the steps to that "therefore" are often difficult to follow, not only because they are almost infinite in number. One "why" leads to another, and that to yet another, and there is inevitably an end to the answers.

This "absurd reasoning" is the most dramatic of all examples of *denken überhaupt*, thought which attempts to encompass everything at once. It is the quest for the ultimate justification of human experience, the search for a meaning which lies outside of that experience. And, of course, within our experience, no such meaning can be found. At this point, one is tempted to "leap" beyond experience as a matter of faith, to reject the rational demands that initially brought us to this desperate precipice. Camus labels this "leap" "philosophical suicide," and he rightly chastises it as a form of self-deception and lack of courage. Or, in equal desperation, one might try to hide the traces of thought that have led us to this abyss and "fall back" with a renewed compulsive vigor to the everyday tasks and involvements in which we had been occupied. But this, too, is a form of self-deception, the conscious denial of a truth already recognized. How is it possible, then, to live in the face of such knowledge? Camus's answer is no more satisfactory than those he rejects: *scorn* and *defiance, rebellion* and *pride*. We stay alive through our stubbornness, unwilling to submit to meaninglessness but equally unwilling to deny it. Camus claims that we stay alive through our *passions*, but they are often the wrong passions, the passions of self-degradation, resentment, and spite. What, then, is to be our response to "the Absurd"?

To refute, not just deny, the Absurd, one need only reject the kind of philosophical thinking it embodies, *denken überhaupt*.

One need not thereby reject either philosophy or thinking. Because human thought has found that it is *capable* of breaking away from the confines of experience, escaping from the commitments and passions of everyday life for an abstract realm of "pure" ideas and "pure reason," it has mistaken that liberty for freedom, childishly supposing that these hitherto inaccessible realms were "more true" and meaningful than the experience and passion-torn lives that thought has left behind. It is, to borrow Kant's favorite simile, like a dove who thinks that, because flight is so much easier in the lighter atmosphere, it should be easier still with no air at all. Against this conception of "pure reason," *denken überhaupt*, we must learn the limitations of living thought. Thinking must be anchored to experience, and the search for meaning must be geared to the source of meaning, namely, our passions—our emotions, our moods, and our desires. The fact that reason *can* get away from them does not entail that it *ought* to. In the realm of pure mathematics, such thinking may be delightful. In response to the questions of concrete philosophy, such thinking is disastrous. It results in a crisis of reason, the conclusion, according to the best of arguments, that life is meaningless. With this absurd conclusion we may well expect a new invasion of Romantics and hedonists, fascists, fanatics, and fools of all sorts, all of them willing to fill the vacuum of meaning that reason has created with their own often inhuman nonsense.

4. The New Romanticism; Passions and the Meanings in Life

Is life worth living?—it is a question of the Liver.

Anon., *Punch*, Vol. 73

To be in a passion you good may do,
But no good if a passion is in you.

William Blake, *Songs of Innocence*

The position I wish to defend might well be interpreted as a new version of Romanticism, a thesis to the effect that human life has its meaning in our passions and nowhere else. But I insist on a clear distinction between the "old" Romanticism and the "new": The role of passion as the source of meaning may be the same, but the nature of the passions has changed as much as imaginable. In my thesis the passions are not to be separated from reason; they are to be welded together into a single unit. I should like to view all of our acts as Shelley envisioned dreams, as "passion-winged ministers of thought." One might reverse a phrase aptly invented by Iris Murdoch to describe Sartre's philosophy, "Romantic rationalism"; and call my philosophy a "rational Romanticism."

The core of this "rational Romanticism" is the thesis that *emotions are judgments*, not blind or irrational forces that victimize us. Emotions are the life force of the soul, the source of most of our values (not all; there is always hunger, thirst, and fatigue), the basis of most other passions. Moods are but generalized emotions; and many desires, including all of those which are considered exclusively human—ambition and a sense of duty, wishes and hopes, and even love and lust—are based upon the emotions. Emotions are said to distort our reality; I argue that they are responsible for it. Emotions are said to divide us from our interests and lead us astray; I argue that emotions create our interests and our purposes. The emotions and consequently the passions in general are our reasons in life. What is called "reason" is the passions enlightened, "illuminated" by reflection and supported by a perspicacious deliberation that the emotions in their urgency normally exclude.

It is our passions, not our reason (and surely not "nature"), that constitute our world, our relationships with other people and, consequently, our *Selves*.

It is the *differences* between the various emotions that will occupy me, the differential analysis of the self and world views of a remarkably sophisticated family of judgments which together define our world, as promising or pessimistic, as happy or absurd, as threatening or friendly, as demeaning or as edifying, as worth living in or dying for. But before I can do so, I shall introduce what may at first seem like a new view of the world, a parallax in which all is viewed differently even while remaining the same. It is the view that all passions share in common, a view that all of us in fact adopt at a great many moments in our lives, particularly those, as you might imagine, which are defined by the passions, by love and fear, anger and envy, pride and shame, hope and vanity.

5. My World and Reality; "Subjectivity"

> Do you think that the things people make fools of themselves about are any less real and true than the things they behave sensibly about?
>
> G. B. Shaw, *Candida*

I am in love, and my world glistens with the reflected light of love. The telephone screams expectations at me long before it rings; she might call. An old wineglass sparkles despite its cloudy surface; she used to drink from that. The world around me announces her absence at every moment, and her briefest appearance—even in a daydream—obliterates the random facts of the world in the dazzle of that one magical fact of her seeming presence.

Of course she won't come; my world is a packet of illusions and false hopes, exaggerated meanings and falsified memories. I have lost "my sense of reality"; I've "lost touch." My emotion has "carried me away," distorted my view of the world, and pushed me into a temporary state of benign madness. But what is this "Reality" which I've lost? Why are my visions "illusions," my hopes "false"? Why is my love-bright world any less "real" than the dull gray world of "Reality"? Why is it that every time I'm happy someone attempts to deflate my world and give me a "truer" view of Reality? Has anyone ever attempted to do so on one of those bleak Monday mornings when I'm late for work, behind on my assignments, sick in both my stomach and my head, and rushing for the subway? Is that the paradigm of Reality? Why not my happier world as well?

What is Reality? "Everything that is real," you might say. But my world is a happy world; yours is the world of a man who is angry; his is the tasteless world of his cynicism. Is the happiness real?—or the objects of your anger?—or the bland transparencies of his cynicism? How can Reality be happy, offensive, and bland all at the same time and for each of us? "Reality is none of those things," you say; Reality is just what it is, "the facts"; those other things are "in us." But it is not just I that am happy—my *world* is bright and gay, populated by singing birds and bright colors. And your world: Is not the most real thing in it the offense, the insult that commands your anger? The singing of the birds in your world is disturbing noise and distraction. In his world, however, that same singing is only sound, with pitch and frequency but no melody, a monotonous repetition of meaningless whistles. Which of these are "the facts," and which are falsehoods and illusions imposed by us? How can you say that the world of the cynic, devoid of delights and significance, is "real," and dismiss my happiness and your anger as "illusions" and distortions? And if you are right, then who needs "Reality"?

It is not only philosophers who hold this view of "Reality." "Realists" of all persuasions join them in stripping the values and meanings from Reality as if it were so much unnecessary and distracting chrome hammered loosely onto an old Cadillac by an overzealous teen-ager. The idea that there is one "Reality," itself but a "totality of facts,"† free from values, is a view that is accepted almost universally in our society. It requires no flair for metaphysics, only the easily accessible view that Reality is "out there," something other than our experience, which is a reasonably accurate "representation" of that Reality. Except, that is, when we let our perceptions get distorted by the passions, caring about matters that are "really" of no importance and becoming involved in nasty situations which are "really" "just the way things are." Of course, each of us has our views of Reality, variously distorted by our own concerns and involvements. But Reality is Reality, the same for all of us; in fact, the same whether it is "for us" or not. "There are many truths," wrote Friedrich Schiller, "but there is only one Truth." And so we contrast that

† Ludwig Wittgenstein, in his *Tractatus Logico-philosophicus*, defended this view explicitly in the early part of the century; his conclusion was, inevitably, that values were unreal, and thus he founded that most bloodless school of thought—logical positivism (that is, ethical negativism).

"one Truth" with the illusions that accompany my being in love, and my love appears as it "really" is, a distortion and a daydream.

This lifeless conception of "the one Truth" and "Reality" as the arbiter of all disputes makes proper understanding of emotions impossible. Reality is impotent, for all its natural powers. Reality has no values. Thus the "realist" is able to attack all concerns as "idealistic" and foolish, as "really" without values and "just the way things are." I will not argue against Reality as such, for that would only be nonsense. But there are problems to which Reality is incapable of providing answers—problems of meaning and value. It is undeniable that there is "only one Reality." But the source of that Reality is not simply our experience, nor is it simply the world that we find before us, free from our values and our interpretations. "Reality" is a very sophisticated concept that has emerged with a very special kind of thinking: "scientific thinking" or "objectivity." Adopting this mode of thinking, which defines "rationality" in most areas of our society, it follows that there is but one Reality. To know this Reality is to be purged of all personal illusions and fantasies, myths and prejudices. The hallmark of objectivity is the "scientific method." The goal and rule is to measure all claims as anonymously as possible. It is the attempt to weigh all the various perspectives and experiences and balance them with as much impersonal data and controlled experiments as possible before coming to any conclusions about the "nature of Reality."

This "objective perspective" is the hallmark of human knowledge, the framework of the greatest achievements of science, humanity's most powerful weapon against ignorance and stupidity. It would be a grotesque mistake to attack it as such, as so many recent writers of a "Romantic" persuasion have felt compelled to do. What is necessary is only to realize that it is a "perspective" and not the whole of human experience. Even Kant, an enthusiastic advocate of Newtonian science, took his primary task in philosophy to "limit the pretensions of knowledge to make room for faith." My thesis, similarly, is that the very conception of Reality and "the world" is the product of an "objective" viewpoint, one that has its obvious benefits but one that *must* not be allowed to encompass the whole of human experience. If it is given that all-inclusive domain, then our passions will indeed look like distortions, and our values—all our values—will appear to be so many pretentious vanities tacked onto the indifferent and passive structures of Reality. It is this all-encompassing objectivity which sets in motion that "Absurd reasoning" which renders the world and our lives meaningless, mere grains of sand in the infinity of the universe.

In contrast to this notion of "objectivity," I want to introduce a conception of "subjectivity," a world view which harbors no pretenses of a single Reality and finds ridiculous that objective humility that reduces all human life—in particular *my* human life—to a spot of nothing enduring only an instant of eternity. It is a perspective in which values are real; and they are not just "in our minds" but "out there" in our world. It is within this subjective viewpoint, with its tolerance for differences and all-important *self*-concern, its "existential" emphasis on *my life* (whatever that life might look like to an objective observer from a distant planet), and its concern for what is of value, that the passions play a central role. From the objective standpoint, the passions are merely distortions, "pathological" if you like. But the passions are uniquely subjective, although they sometimes pretend to have a certain objective status (more of that later). They are not concerned with *the* world but with *my* world. They are not concerned with "what is really the case" with "the facts," but rather with what is *important*. Of course, it will have to be shown that subjectivity, so conceived, does not *deny* the facts, does not deny *Reality*. Ideally, subjectivity acknowledges all and only the facts of Reality. (In practice, of course, we are always ignorant about something or other.) What distinguishes subjectivity from objectivity is not a denial by the former of "the facts" of the latter; rather, subjectivity *adds* to Reality a personal perspective and values. I shall call the result of this addition *surreality* (literally from the French), "reality plus." The passions, the bearers of values, constitute *our* world, our *surreality*. *Reality* is not the world of concern in this book. My concern is with the world we *live* in, not the lifeless complex of facts and hypotheses that one finds so elegantly described, without a trace of passion, in the pages of our best science textbooks.

It is important to stress, even in this introduction, that the standpoint of "subjectivity" does not in the least require the first-person *singular*. To say that the passions are essentially subjective and *self*-concerned is *not* in the least to say that they are necessarily "selfish" or self-indulgent. In fact, many, if not nearly all, of our emotions *essentially* include other people, not only as their objects but as a contributing source of their values and as shared subjects in what is called *intersubjectivity*. It is often said that the passions are antisocial and oblivious to the feelings of other people; but to the contrary—the passions are precisely those structures which commit and bind us to other people, in anger and resentment as well as in love and hate, in the calm intimacies of friendship as well as the defensive stalemates of resentment and mutual distrust and insecurity.

The thesis of "subjectivity" which I defend owes much to the researches in "phenomenology" that have been so vigorously pursued in the past half-century, particularly due to the tremendous efforts of the German-Czech philosopher Edmund Husserl (1859–1938), and his most illustrious student, Martin Heidegger (1889–1976), whose name will appear many times in the course of my arguments. I have attempted to avoid the now impossibly cumbersome jargon of that school, however, and substitute my own concept of "subjectivity" in order to avoid many of the polemics and disputes that are now associated with phenomenology and to start the investigation afresh.

6. Reflection and Innocence

> Know thyself!
>   Delphic Oracle (Juvenal)
> He that increaseth knowledge increaseth sorrow.
> ("Ignorance is bliss.")
>
>   Ecclesiastes

If the passions were but impersonal "forces" inside of us, like the gas that erupts after a cabbage meal, self-knowledge regarding them would be no more than a physician's commentary, describing certain goings on and perhaps being amused or embarrassed by them but surely having no effect on them whatsoever. If, on the other hand, our passions are subjective judgments, forms of interpretation of ourselves and our world, then what we have to say *about* them would indeed make a difference. Our judgment, unlike our physiology, is surely influenced by what we know about ourselves.

The Myth of the Passions is often accompanied by a second myth, "the Myth of Innocence," a typically Romantic fantasy that finds much that is admirable and even enviable in the cruelty and sadism, naïveté and ignorance, insensitivity and self-indulgence of children. If the passions are "natural," it is argued, then it is oppressive and "unnatural" to confine and constrict them in the process of "growing up" and becoming "civilized," that is, repressed. With more than a hint of despair, Freud employed such a myth as the key to his social philosophy, particularly in *Civilization and Its Discontents*. And without his mixed feelings, generations of rebellious Romantic thinkers before and after Freud have voiced similar arguments, usually in the name of "nature" and "freedom" together, forgetting those persuasive Kantian arguments to the effect that there is nothing "free" in nature. In the Myth of Innocence self-examinations and attempts at self-knowledge are at best useless pretensions; much worse, they are damaging structures and artificial attempts to fetter man's "natural goodness" for the sake of the arbitrary and degrading conventions of "civilized" society. That reflective self-awareness that sees through and is abashed by the shameless indulgences of childhood is considered by the proponents of this second myth to be just so much repression—"crimes against nature." They refuse to see or at least to condemn the brutality and insensitivity, so concerned are they for the supposed "freedom" they have lost.

In a society in which the forces of "education" and "civilized behavior" are so far out of line with the demands of self-esteem, of course there must be a reaction in defense of the passions, which in turn defends self-esteem against imposed degradation and foolishness. But the resolution of this conflict cannot be a Rousseauian "return to innocence," only a renewed attempt to coordinate the demands of reflection (which degenerates into repression only when it has lost touch with passion and life) with the prereflective demands of the passions (which are neither "natural" nor "free" prior to their scrutiny in reflection). The confusion is a familiar one; the fallacious inference from the abuses of reflection and education is coupled with the generalization of praise from a small set of emotions (for example, Rousseau's "natural sympathy") to the passions as a whole, including all forms of hostility, greed, envy, spite, hatred, and resentment. Reflection need be neither an impotent observer of the passions nor an oppressive tyrant which attempts to subdue them altogether. Reflection is part and parcel of the passions, participating in their constitution of our world and giving them advice and direction that, because of their sense of immediacy and impatience, they often would not have on their own. Innocence, by way of contrast, is nothing other than irresponsibility and a refusal to be self-critical. It tends to protect passions already established, a psychic status quo, without questioning the origins or the purposes of the sometimes self-defeating and often defensive and hostile attitudes it celebrates as "natural." Innocence is not only ignorance: It is a refusal to know oneself, a refusal to change.

The Myth of Innocence, like its companion Myth of the Passions, has its charms; it, too, is a self-serving system of *excuses*. In innocence, a passion is a passion, to be acknowledged without criticism and without question. It is only with reflection that we find ourselves horrified by our own attitudes, ashamed of our anger, guilty about our guilt, embarrassed by our love. In innocence, that often painful reflection is dismissed as irrelevant; those passions, though mine, are not my responsibility. "You'll just have to accept me the way I am" (defensive, hostile, petty, unreasonably angry, unfair, joyless, and offensive).

The Myth of Innocence has a second and related benefit: Without self-consciousness, the question of the "meaning of life" is out of the question; a sense of absurdity is itself an absurdity. Prior to critical self-reflection, there is no problem "who I am," no problem of choices or of values. My world simply presents itself to me; every passion is a categorical command; every opinion is an unquestioned truth.

It is easy to see how a person who is disgusted with life, discouraged and confused with the conflicts between self-indulgent temptations and the cold commands of conscience, could be tempted by this myth. But, in any case, a return to innocence is impossible: Once self-consciousness has arisen, it cannot be suppressed.‡ It must be worked *through,* such that the apparent "givens" of the passions are now affirmations of one's own self-image. One might still continue to be cruel and sadistic, insensitive and self-indulgent, in short "childish," but that person is now so *by choice.* One can continue to be resentful and spiteful, envious and righteously indignant, hateful or angry, jealous or guilty, but these passions cannot now be treated as other than one's own responsibility. Having *adopted* a certain attitude toward the world, toward oneself, and toward other people, a person has *chosen* to act this way. There are many reasons to pity a man, but his passions are not among them. What one "feels" is what one chooses and accepts. Whatever the situation, there is no one and nothing to blame but oneself. "It is senseless to think of complaining since nothing foreign has decided what we feel, what we live, or what we are"—Sartre, *Being and Nothingness.*

7. The Point . . .

> . . . to burn always by this hard gemlike flame . . .
>
> Walter Pater, *The Renaissance*

What everyone forgets is that passion is not merely a heightened sensual fusion but a way of life which produces, as in the mystics, an ecstatic awareness of the whole of life.

> Anaïs Nin, *Diary,* Vol. 5

It is often hard to take the problem of the "meaning of life" seriously.* It is not difficult to see why; the question as it is usu-

‡ In a famous argument in his pamphlet *Utilitarianism,* John Stuart Mill attempts to compare the life of a dissatisfied Socrates with the life of a pig. The first is preferable, according to Mill, because Socrates has experienced both kinds of life and he yet *chooses* the former. But in fact, Socrates has no more choice in this matter than the pig. Once his faculty of critical reflection has come to life, he is no more capable of the innocent piggishness of the pig than the pig is capable of appreciating the arguments of the *Protagoras.*

* After seven years of searching, the young man finally arrived

ally posed is unanswerable, if not nonsensical. More importantly, it is suspected that if one does not already *know* the meaning of life, philosophy will not be able to tell him. In a sense, this is true. Despite the pretensions of philosophy and reflective thought, the "meaning of life" is not to be found in those lofty heights but in the supposedly subphilosophical swamps of our passions. And if the passions are not giving our lives meaning, what then could be gained in the extravagances of reflective thought? (Here again is the Myth of the Passions; as if the passions could not be influenced—even determined or created—by our reflection.) But this much is true: The meaning of life is to be found in our passions, or it can be found nowhere.

The sense that life is meaningless is not really the problem, but only the abstract symptom of a concrete spiritual malaise. The source of that seemingly passionate sense may in fact be the *lack* of passion, the suffocation of the soul by that withered and joyless imposter that so often passes for "wisdom." (Thus the French aphorist Nicolas Chamfort quipped, "His passions make a man live, his wisdom merely make him last.") And, seduced by those who themselves lack passion, some of us are duped into ignoring the importance of our own passions. Like Nietzsche's man of "bad conscience," people learn to despise what is best in themselves, to admire and even worship the very impotence that is the source of their self-contempt.

The sense of meaninglessness may be based on the unadmitted domination of certain *degrading* passions, dragging us down and constituting our world in self-demeaning shades of distance and defensiveness. Accordingly, my purpose will not be to answer the "problem of the meaning of life" so much as to diagnose the mal-

---

upon the doorstep of the world-renowned but reclusive wise man, high in the mountains. He was forced to wait outside for seven weeks, but his perseverance finally earned him an audience:
"What is the meaning of life?"
"What?"
"What is the meaning of life?"
"Life is like a wheat field. . . ."
"Life is like a wheat field!?"
"You mean life *isn't* like a wheat field?"

ady from which this problem arises, that unmistakable and often passionate dissatisfaction and disillusionment with our world and with ourselves. Life is never "meaningless" when you're in love, but it often seems so when you are depressed. There is a sense in which all passions and all lives might be said to be equally meaningful. But a life of love is not the same as a life of envy, and a life of heroic ambition is not the same as a life of self-stultifying resentment. The problem is not that life lacks meaning but that certain meanings are *demeaning*.

Even the long history of "rationalism" and the worship of reason is infiltrated by an undercurrent of thought that clearly recognizes the vital importance of the passions. For Aristotle, the ideal of wisdom and the good life was not lack of passion, but the harmony of the passions with reason. Hegel, usually known as a super-rationalist, is well known for the phrase "Nothing great has ever been accomplished without passion." What is less well known is the fact that he borrowed that phrase almost verbatim from super-duper-rationalist Kant, who had written in his *History* that "nothing great has ever been accomplished without enthusiasm." (The phrase appears again and again, for example, in Benjamin Disraeli, who writes that "man is only truly great when he acts from his passions.") But in every case, the dualism remains, and the passions are slipped through a back entrance into conceptions of life that would sooner do without them.

I want to replace the Myth of the Passions with the thesis that men and women are not divided souls, half immortal thought, half beastly passions, the image that haunts Christ and Faust and everyone who has tried to find in himself "something more" than the merely human. To get rid of the supposed "meaninglessness of life," I shall examine in detail those passions which provide the meaning *in* our lives. Against the alleged passivity of the passions, I shall defend the theory that our passions are our own *doings*, and thus our own responsibility. And in place of that familiar lack of discrimination which takes all passions to be of equal value, I shall attempt to identify those passions with which I believe people can live *best*, in the light of reflection, and with the unhesitating acceptance of responsibility for the world we are thereby creating for ourselves.

My goal, in other words, is to break down and destroy the

debilitating and unnecessary conflicts between reason and passions, to bolster our appreciation of the passions without thereby
denying our "reason." My purpose is not only to understand but
to *realize* in ourselves that conception of harmonious strength
that used to be called "wisdom," whose ideal is nowhere better
formulated than in Plato's definition of "justice" in *The Republic*:

> not mere strength, but harmonious strength, desires and men fall-
> ing into that order which constitutes intelligence and organi-
> zation. . . . not the right of the stronger, but the harmonious
> union of the whole.

CHAPTER 1: LIFE AS THE PROBLEM

1. The Absurd

> There's not even a film.
> There's nothing . . . just nothing
> What the hell's "sincerity" anyway?
>
> Fellini, 8½ (1963)

> "Mr. Natural: what does it all mean?"
> "It don't mean shee-it."
>
> ZAP comics (1972)

Is life worth living? A familiar mistranslation of Socrates says that the unexamined life is not. But is the examined life worth living? What could it mean to answer no? What would it be to answer yes?

Once we have begun examining our lives—once the philosophical question of "meaning" has been raised—we must be prepared for an unwelcome answer. One shouts into the abyss, not expecting an intelligible reply. Yet we once were certain of an answer, that is, until we asked. Having only heard the question mentioned we knew: "Of course life has meaning—there is happiness and one's fellow men, love, and life's little pleasures, art and entertainment, a party downtown this weekend. . . ." But as we ask, we step back from living, as we might step back from love, and there is that quiet ominous sound like the ripping at the seams of a tightly fitting fabric. We immediately recognize what we have done. Our step backward has severed that intimacy which once served to answer our question, before it had been asked. We are like Pierre le Fou, changing his mind after he has tightly strapped and ignited the explosives around his head. That final "why" has undermined everything. Our involvements seem like childish games: our struggles vain gestures. Everything remains as before, but deadened, emptied of meaning. The world is no longer ours: We observe it, cynically, the hues of vitality shadowed by a cloud of our creation. The old habits keep us moving, robotlike, through the paces of life, but we are not wholly there. The "why" has no answer, and that is the singular fact that now defines our existence. That fact is called "the Absurd."

"The Absurd" received its classical formulation from Albert Camus in the early years of World War II. I believe that it is still the dominant philosophical conception of our time. It is not a philosopher's invention. It follows with merciless logic from our most everyday thinking. Our expectations of fairness and our demands for understanding, our ruthless pragmatism and our insistence on purposefulness—all lead us more or less directly to the Absurd. Whether by that dramatic name or not, the Absurd is well known to us all. Yet it has not been understood, and its usual formulation—even that provided us by Camus—is so misleading that the Absurd has been tolerated and accepted by most of us as irremediable. Camus even insists, in the name of a curious sense of philosophical integrity and defiance, that we "keep the Absurd alive." But the point is to go beyond it. Can philosophy, which has brought us to the Absurd, carry us through it as well?

2. "Life is cheap in Casablanca."

Reality never seems to live up to my best fantasies.

Morgan

The ruby roach racing across my floor in aimless panic: Its life could not lack meaning; it seems so through my eyes only, as it anonymously scurries to the molding to protect its tiny scrap of garbage. Absurd! But it is *my* life that I am judging, contrasting my own scurrying and my own garbage with that of a roach. Underlying the contrast are the obvious comparisons, and they do not escape my awareness.

My cat finds her life richly endowed with meanings. At the moment, she is too hot to be curious or to notice that I am watching her with a benignly hostile envy. She is draped across my desk like a melted candle, slightly hungry but content and confident that, after eight years, she will be fed upon command. She does not know it, but tonight she gets a medicinal bath. She will be upset in the extreme, her wetless world dampened and disoriented. But her life will not lack meaning; it will only be momentarily unpleasant, and she will not bear it graciously. Only I suffer from that cold, damp, sterilizing sense of pointlessness, which I cannot help but carry with a certain quiet dignity. I have done it to myself. Thinking has deprived me of the very meaning which it demanded. Philosophy has demonstrated for me the hopelessness of a life within which I was tolerably satisfied. Thus, a defense of philosophy becomes a defense of life, for those for whom it now requires defending.

The Absurd is intolerable, though not painful as such, somewhat like a fingernail accidentally bent over backward. Because it is undeniable that thought created the Absurd, the common reaction to the Absurd becomes a hostility to thought, an appeal to innocence and the passions. Philosophical questions are dismissed as jokes or postponed until later. (They are "too heavy" to be considered in our present state of mind.) The problem of life is replaced by life's little problems. Bureaucratic absurdities replace the Absurd, and legal formalities take on newly motivated "seriousness." A rise in the cost of vegetables spurs moral indignation formerly reserved for criminal executions. There is an air of desperation about us, as if we were trying too hard to take ourselves seriously. Meanwhile, the intellect refocuses its attention on subsidiary questions—how to explain certain emanations from space, how to resolve certain inconsistencies in Leibniz's logic, how to improve this and that. If the Absurd cannot be answered, it can be avoided. Or so we would like to think (that is, by not thinking).

If "the Absurd" were only a philosopher's sound, a mere idea, it would be no more worthy of our attention than any number of other impressive puzzles that have plagued thinkers from Plato to Wittgenstein. But the Absurd, though created in thought, will not contain itself as "an idea." It poisons our everydayness and gives our every experience a tinge of desperation, "nausea," Sartre calls it. Our jokes take on the cast of gallows humor, a distracting playfulness, or a welcome viciousness. We find ourselves desperately trying to move more quickly, nowhere; or we try to slow down to a crawl, "entertaining ourselves." Camus's conception of "keeping the Absurd alive" is perhaps nowhere better illustrated than in our new generations, the mutant freaks of the counter-culture, who, between television and drugs, have learned the lesson we forced upon them—ultimately, there is nothing worth doing.

3. Great Expectations: A Genealogy of the Absurd

"No graduating class has ever known such a promising future."

Richard M. Nixon (June 1956, June 1957, June 1958, June 1959, June 1960, June 1969, June 1970, June 1971, June 1972, June 1973, June 1974)

"We want the world and we want it *now*."

Anon., Berkeley (1964)

The Absurd is not, as many moralists would have it, an aspect of the "human condition." It is, perhaps, *our* condition, the threat that accompanies our peculiar ways of rationalizing our actions and our feelings. It was not always so, nor need it be. It may be, in fact, that this, the Age of the Absurd, which not incidentally accompanies the breakup of traditional religions, family structures, moralities, and national loyalties, is soon to pass, soon to be a historical curiosity to our successors for whom the "meaning of life" will be once again a presupposition rather than a question. But meanwhile, we have to live the question and understand its curious role in our lives.

The Absurd as we know it has made its appearance only in the past 150 years. There have always been absurdities, of course, and, looking back over the religious massacres of earlier centuries, we might well read our conception of the Absurd into them. But the Absurd is a product of a modern and sophisticated intelligence and an experienced imagination, an intelligence that demands, but does not find, justice from persons, from God, and from the universe itself. The Absurd requires a proud rebellious spirit that will question everything, that takes skepticism as the sign of a healthy intellect and cynicism as an equivalent of wisdom and worldliness. Of course there have always been isolated individuals with such attitudes, but today we find them throughout our society, torn by timidity, shrinking away from the demands of the Absurd, and groping blindly and desperately for whatever opiates will subdue the skepticism and replace the cynicism with hope. The opiate can be religion of any kind, nationalism at any cost, hero worship, and hedonism, drugs, and various "fetishisms"—dehumanizing idols—absurd totems and magical rituals of every grotesque and familiar shape.

The beginnings of the Age of the Absurd might be mapped out with almost startling precision. By the turn of the nineteenth century, the French *philosophes* had completed their creation of a new man-and-reason-centered ideology, one which replaced authoritarianism with popular rule, social inequity with at least nominal egalitarianism, God's laws and man's fate with the principles of Newton's physics and the rules of efficiency and profit of a burgeoning middle class. The French Revolution substantiated that ideology; the King was superseded by "the people," God was evicted from Notre Dame in the name of "Reason," and the universal promise of "liberty, equality, and fraternity" provoked a revolutionary fervor that knew no bounds. This was a totally human world, and it did not seem unreasonable to anyone at the time that man could totally change himself, his institutions and his hopes, his personality and his universe, all at a stroke. In these early years of unlimited hope and terror, the British poet William Wordsworth commented that there had never been such a time, never such expectations, such promises, and François René Chateaubriand, "it was bliss to be alive, but to be young was very heaven." From a safe distance, the oppressed nations of Europe, still struggling under antiquated monarchs and medieval customs, watched the rapid changes in France with awe and wonder, more than a bit of envy, and a comparable amount of fear. Then, into the traumatic vacuum of uncertainties in France appeared Napoleon, a foreigner who cast France in the role of a Divine model for Europe. To the people of Europe, Napoleon did not appear as a threat but as a promise. With Napoleon as its instrument, the revolutionary spirit and expectations of France invaded Europe. The wars and massacres were tragic but necessary and heroic means to

universal human self-realization. Never were earthly expectations
and hopes and fears goaded to such extravagance. The old life was
already buried, and every new act, even the simplest daily routine,
became a revolutionary performance. Everything was possible!
But extravagant expectations are doomed by their very extravagance. Men used to expect justice from the Lord, whose "mysterious ways" made it possible to endure any worldly injustice. But
these newly "Enlightened" men expected visible and immediate
justice, as if the universe owed them natural harmony and happiness. But the French Revolution soon collapsed into murder and
chaos; Napoleon became disappointing ("What? Is he, too, just
an ordinary human?" screamed Beethoven as he ripped apart his
dedication to the Eroica Symphony) and finally defeated.

Following a quarter century of war, the politics of Europe, dictated by Metternich, was peace at any price, the restoration of the
old ways and inequalities, as if to smother the revolutionary expectations which had grown to such extremes throughout Europe.

This was the period of "reaction," in which the people of
France and the German principalities, Italy, Spain, Austria, and
Prussia, found their newly inflamed desires and hopes censored
and suppressed by old realities. The only outlet, for many
suppressed revolutionaries, was a fanciful and obscure style of ar-
tistic expression, "Romanticism." It provided an escape from the
vulgar and oppressive political realities of the period and became
an underground cult of the imagination, keeping the hopes and
imaginations of Europe alive, saving the demands and expectations
of the revolution for a time when they might again receive political substantiation. But the revolutions that followed (at fifteen-
year intervals in France, less predictably in Germany and Italy),
even when politically successful, did virtually nothing to fulfill the
aggrandized hopes that had developed a generation or so ago. In
retrospect, the age of Napoleon and revolution could be viewed as
a Golden Age, though no one wanted it repeated. Then, life had
been a matter of hope and survival; now it was a problem of despair and boredom. The revolution had raised human expectations
to cosmic heights; its collapse left them without a promise in Reality. Thus, the divorce between cosmic expectations and Reality,
without the age-old hope of Divine intervention, was born. The
post-Napoleonic period, of "Romanticism" and "Reaction,"

might properly be called the beginning of the Age of the Absurd. Never had people expected so much; and never had they been so disappointed.

It is virtually a platitude among historians and churchmen that the anxieties and despair of the present age can be traced back to the crumbling of religious institutions and religious faith following the Enlightenment and the revolution. But the truth is something more than that. It is not the loss of faith in Divine grace alone that accounts for our sense of absurdity, but also and equally the extravagant *gains* in faith in human justice and the potentialities of human efforts. We may lament the loss of religion, but it is difficult if not inhuman to regret the compensating gain in our own self-confidence that has replaced it. The Absurd was born, not of loss of religion, but of gains in humanism. The more we thought of ourselves, the less we thought of our Reality. There was no one else to blame.

To the bloated and deflated expectations of nineteenth-century Europe, America added a "dream" of its own: unlimited desires and ambitions, incessant dissatisfaction as a goad to unending progress. First the freedom, then the "frontiers," then power, the world, the heavens. We have learned to expect everything and be satisfied with nothing. Raised in a world where dinners could be defrosted and served in minutes, we have learned to expect revolutions overnight, changes in human nature itself in weeks. Admittedly, the turbulence and disappointments of the past decade pale in comparison to the French Revolution and its aftermath, but its phenomenology and metaphysics are identical. And as the dream collapses (although it has never been defined), we find ourselves in the waves of a new "reaction," a new cynicism, a new Romanticism, complete with return to gothic horror stories, ill-directed political terrorism, esoteric religions of every variety (even a new Christianity), and renewed celebration of the occult, the mysterious, the foreign, and the transcendent. Our confidence in ourselves has grown beyond bounds, and we find ourselves in a world of our own creation, without satisfaction, without hope, frantically seeking "self-realization" and "entertainment" (which often amount to the same thing), pursuing a ruthless pragmatism that has no ends other than its own power, a hopeless hedonism that has no end but its own distraction. We self-righteously complain about corruption in government and watch with unabashed glee as the principle wrongdoers are publicly humiliated; but we neither work for nor entertain serious hopes for change. We carve out our own increasingly isolated and desperate lives, trying to ignore the fact that we know that they amount to nothing. We teach our children to do the same, and not to ask why. Our philosophy is a rationalization of despair, a glib philosophy of "the Absurd." But we do not take it seriously, of course. For we still have our expectations.

We were all spoiled children. Some of us were raised comfortably, others extravagantly, some of us not at all, in poverty and violence. But we were all similarly pampered, all taught the same absurd and unlimited hope and sense of infinite possibility. Nature was already conquered, a charming savage who delivered her wares without limit, on command, and at no cost. Our futures were sequences of promise, many with guarantees. We were all goaded to ambition, force-fed with promises of success, and we believed them. A few of us seemed to have made it, but the more success we achieved, the more this myth was nourished, the greater our hope and our expectations; and, inevitably, the greater the crash. Who can be surprised when it is the most "advantaged" children, the most "promising"—and therefore the most "promised"—who sometimes become the most violent and embittered revolutionaries? So it has been throughout the Age of the Absurd. In 1840 the great cynical Schopenhauer spoke to today's parents when he muttered: "It would be a great advantage to a young man if his early training were to eradicate the idea that the world has a great deal to offer him. But the intended result of education is to strengthen this delusion." We have been taught in childhood, as the philosophers of the French Revolution had not been taught until middle age, that the world is ours. And what less, then, could satisfy us?

4. Camus's Myth

THE MYTH OF SISYPHUS

The gods had condemned Sisyphus to ceaselessly rolling a rock to the top of a mountain, whence the stone would fall back of its own weight. They had thought with some reason that there is no more dreadful punishment than futile and hopeless labor.

You have already grasped that Sisyphus is the absurd hero. He *is*, as much through his passions as through his torture. His scorn of the gods, his hatred of death, and his passion for life won him that unspeakable penalty in which the whole being is exerted toward accomplishing nothing. This is the price that must be paid for the passions of this earth.

If this myth is tragic, that is because its hero is conscious. Where would his torture be, indeed, if at every step the hope of succeeding upheld him? The workman of today works every day in his life at the same tasks, and this fate is no less absurd. But it is tragic only at the rare moments when it becomes conscious. Sisyphus, proletarian of the gods, powerless and rebellious, knows the whole extent of his wretched condition: it is what he thinks of during his descent. The lucidity that was to constitute his torture at the same time crowns his victory. There is no fate that cannot be surmounted by scorn.

Camus, "The Myth of Sisyphus"

The modern sense of the Absurd is best captured in an ancient parable, restated in contemporary terms by Camus. In his book of the same title, "The Myth of Sisyphus" becomes a representation of us all, showing the gross disparity between our extravagant hopes and expectations and the cold "indifference" and meaninglessness of Reality. Sisyphus' futile task represents the futility of our own struggles; his tragic consciousness is our own recognition of the meaninglessness of our lives. His scorn and defiance are our only hope, our only happiness, our only honest passions.

This grand sense of absurdity must not be confused with the particular absurdities of everyday life—a broker running through the New York Stock Exchange wearing nothing but a mustache and sneakers, a young president shot down in the street, the sense-less slaughter of a thousand Bengalis. Such absurdities, no matter how tragic, presuppose a contrast with complimentary reasonable hopes and expectations. *The* Absurd, however, involves our lives as wholes. The hopes and expectations that it finds frustrated con-cern our very existence, not any particular instances. Camus's last novel, *The Fall*, introduces "John the Baptist" Clamence, highly respected and successful lawyer and lecher, blessed with every ad-vantage of health, wealth, achievement, and social position imagi-nable, who sees through it all as so much pretense and fraud, amounting to nothing. Similarly, the philosopher Schopenhauer, despite a long life of fine dinners, good wines, sporadic if not wholly satisfactory affairs, and a somewhat belated but then ex-travagant literary success, complained as well that it all "amounts to nothing." Any self-conscious creature, whether Sisyphus, "the Proletarian of the gods," or the gods themselves, whether the emi-nent Clamence or the axle-man proletarian of the Renault assem-bly plant in Lyons, is subject to this all-encompassing sense of ab-surdity. From moment to moment, we cannot imagine a greater difference than that which separates the toil of Sisyphus and the equally repetitive labors of another "absurd hero," Don Juan ("1,001 in Spain alone"). But from that philosophical perspective in which we demand that our lives have meaning, the erotic and dashing affairs of Don Juan amount to no more than the daily efforts of Sisyphus, that is, they amount to—nothing.

The Absurd requires this philosophical expanse, a view of the whole, and consequently a certain leisure in life, a certain luxury of distance. It is thus true that the Absurd must be judged a *bour-geois* malady; it is a malaise that does not affect the hungry, the threatened, or the desperate. Life is not absurd to a Mexican peas-ant; it is only cruel. It is not absurd to a fugitive, only ominous. It was not during the invasions of Napoleon that the Absurd was born in Europe, but after, during the tedium of "the reaction," when lives were safe but life was boring. It was not during the en-thusiasm of the 1960s that the Absurd was reborn, with all those explicit and televised absurdities, but after, in that desperate calm when there seems to be "nothing to be done." The Absurd is a breach in cosmic expectations, a leap from life to a view of life, from the things of the world to the "worldhood-of-the-world" itself. The absurdity of life is not a single untoward event, breaking the surface of an otherwise calm and transparently meaningful life, filled with thousands of tiny meanings appearing one after the other in rapid succession. Nor is the Absurd a whirl that throws us about in senseless turbulence. The Absurd is rather that absolute silence and calm itself, that homogenous but viscous translucency that Camus describes as the seeming "indifference of the universe."

"At any street corner," Camus writes, "the feeling of absurdity can hit a man in the face." A momentary break in our chain of daily gestures and adventures—"rising, streetcar, four hours of work in the office or factory, meal, streetcar, four hours of work, meal, sleep, and Monday, Tuesday, Wednesday, Thursday, Friday, and Saturday according to the same rhythm— . . . But one day the 'why' arises and everything begins with the weariness tinged with amazement." Once the "why" has arisen, that "moment of lucidity" that marks all of philosophy, we wrench ourselves away from our everyday tasks and successes, our duties and our failures, our embarrassments and achievements alike, and we watch, as if from another room or from a distant nebula. We detachedly observe another couple making love; it is an absurd, an obscene performance. Even our own love-making seems absurd and obscene. Camus describes a man talking on the telephone behind a glass partition; we cannot hear him, but we see "his incomprehensible dumb show; you wonder why he is alive." We find ourselves in a political argument, view ourselves from a distance, still talking; we hear our words, but they lack conviction. The performance is pure vanity, and we wonder, without breaking the flow of our argument, why we are alive. We similarly separate ourselves from every human performance, including our own, from our feelings and our thoughts and even from our thoughts about our thoughts. The world becomes a screen of colorless movements and sounds, without meaning. And every act becomes a Marcel Marceau mime, a comedy whose only significance lies in the speechless familiarity of its senseless gestures.

What response can there be to this self-inflicted loss of meaning? We might try to return to our former involvement in our everyday tasks, perhaps voluntarily committing ourselves to extraordinarily tedious and compulsive tasks. But we are watching, always as if from that critical distance, commenting and mocking ourselves. Our response is a sham and a pretense. We are only distracting ourselves.

5. The Metaphysics of the Absurd*

"Gentlemen, you must excuse me for philosophizing."

Dostoevski, *Notes from Underground*

According to Camus, the Absurd is "the confrontation of man and universe," our expectations, and our "reason" against the infinite indifference and "inhuman silence" of Reality. But *why* *these* expectations, and is there really any such confrontation? The metaphysics of Camus is man and his reason on the one side, stark physical reality on the other.† But are there any such "sides" to the matter, or are not man and his universe a single unity, the one defining the other?

"The inhuman silence of the universe"—surely that is not our experience. Reality *screams* at us every second—commands and orders, duties and warnings, dangers and desires. What is Camus listening *for*, that he hears only silence? What is his conception of

* Some of these considerations have been clarified by Herbert Hochberg, "Albert Camus and the Ethics of Absurdity," *Ethics*, 1964–65.
† We recognize this as the metaphysics of Descartes. But where Descartes trusted and attempted to prove that God was the beneficent mediator between the two, Camus denies God, thus abandoning the hope of a reconciliation. Where Descartes affirms, Camus denies. Camus, like Descartes, is an extreme rationalist, fully in the tradition of Plato and the scholastics. (This sounds odd only because Camus has so long been grouped with that inscrutable class of "irrationalists" and "existentialists," both of which he vigorously rejects.) According to this ruthless rationalism, there can be no affirmation, no meaningfulness, except under the auspices of reason. But where Plato and Descartes find it, Camus does not. The Absurd, for him, is a strictly *rational* conclusion, and it is in the name of *reason* that he will not attempt to deny or transcend this Absurd.

"the universe," so distinct from ourselves and "indifferent," as if Reality were simply *given* to us value-free, investment-free, ego-free. Sisyphus alone with his rock and his task: is that what our lives are like? Surely not. But where does it come from—this metaphysics of rational consciousness versus the cold, not cruel but indifferent, world?

Sisyphus' world is not, as it first appears, his rock, the mountain, and his futile labors. His salvation, Camus tells us, is his "scorn for the gods." Similarly, Camus celebrates the virtue of *defiance*; but defiance against what? He is an atheist; he has no gods to scorn. Or Clamence, in *The Fall*, had committed no major crime (except, perhaps, receiving stolen property); yet he, too, is "condemned." For what? Camus tells us that we should live "without hope, without appeal"; but why? Camus (like Clamence) would seem to have every reason to hope—for peace in Algeria and Europe, a sunny day, a new love, some justice in the post-Occupation trials in France. Yet he clearly thinks of himself as hopeless, as condemned, as a tragic ("absurd") hero in a meaningless world.

But now a diagnosis begins to emerge—a metaphysician's diagnosis. The metaphysics here is not only the dualism of the psychical and the physical; it is, more importantly, the traditional Christian metaphysics of guilt and redemption. The "appeal" to which Camus refers is the Christian sense of "appeal"; the object of his scorn is indeed a god—or the shadow of a god—who has abandoned us. Or rather, Camus has abandoned God, but he has retained the whole of the Christian order of the passions, sin and guilt, condemnation and redemption. But now, while guilt and condemnation remain, redemption is impossible. Thus "John the Baptist" Clamence guzzles but does not taste Dutch gin in the seedy bars of Amsterdam, having given up a once eminently successful life with the realization that "no one is innocent." He has rejected the judge, but he has taken the judgment upon himself, as a "judge-penitent," defensively projecting his own sense of guilt and resentment upon mankind as a whole. "We all want to appeal against something! Each of us insists on being innocent at all cost, even if he has to accuse the whole human race and Heaven itself." *Ecce homo!*

Camus (and not only Camus) is a traumatized atheist, taking

upon his own quixotic shoulders the weight of Divine judgment.
We now expect of ourselves what we hoped for from God. The
"absurd hero" is a very Christian hero who absurdly seeks absolution from unspecified sins—like Kafka's Joseph K—in a world
where there is no longer absolution. Christianity, whatever else it
has done, has taught us the meaning of that objectless and self-
demeaning guilt, guilt by virtue of our very existence. Hitherto, it
also offered us the hope of salvation. But the basis of the guilt and
the hope were one and the same; having given up the latter, we
could give up the former as well. But we have taken the Sin upon
ourselves, and so kept the guilt as well. Underlying the metaphysics of the Absurd lies the ghost of a much older metaphysics;
but underlying that is a familiar but often undiagnosed malady of
passion, a bitter and defensive view of the world in which the passions of self-demeaning guilt and despair play a leading role. The
Absurd is but their rationalized façade.‡

It is this syndrome of resentment, the "passions of Sisyphus,"
that *constitutes* the Absurd. Camus took this passion, which he en-
nobled as "defiance," to be a "consequence" of the Absurd. This
sleight of hand is not infrequent in philosophy; one "ra-
tionalizes" his prejudices, arguing "objectively" and persuasively
on neutral ground, drawing the distortions of his biases from this
incontrovertible base. But the "objective" arguments presuppose,
not entail, the passions of the Absurd which form their support.
The absurdist *begins* with a passionate and resentful view of man
as inferior, as impotent, as persecuted and unfairly treated. He
then finds an "objective" viewpoint from which to develop and
formulate his resentment in a philosophically suitable manner. He
begins with his view of life as degrading and insignificant, and

‡ It is important to insist that the Absurd is not, even so explained, a conception that is absent from religious thinking. It is the
enormity of the guilt and the universe and the sense of our own
smallness that is the key to this conception, a sense that is as at home
in Christianity as in Camus. Kierkegaard, for example, whose piety
stands above doubt, retained a sense of the Absurd at least as keen as
Camus's, and his whole-hearted devotion to God did nothing to reduce, but only made more tolerable, that extreme sense of personal
absurdity.

then, balanced by his desperate need to salvage some self-esteem, projects his own sense of insignificance on the universe as a whole.

6. *"Absurd Reasoning"*

> Gradually it has become clear to me what every great philosophy so far has been; namely the personal confession of its author and a kind of involuntary and unconscious memoir; . . . In the philosopher, there is nothing whatever that is impersonal; and above all, his morality bears decided and decisive witness to *who he is.*
>
> Nietzsche, *Beyond Good and Evil*

Camus prefaces *The Myth of Sisyphus* with a reference to "an absurd sensitivity that is widespread in our age." What he gives us, however, is an "absurd reasoning," a ruthless pursuit through logic. In Camus's clumsy Cartesianism, the "logic" in fact is often lost. But the arguments are familiar enough. In fact, we probably rehearsed them in grade school. Properly formulated, they are, perhaps, irrefutable. They leave us speechless. They are, however, also irrelevant, like those philosophical puzzles that convince us that we can never know with assurance whether in fact we are asleep or awake.

There are at least two sets of such arguments; both turn on the notion of infinity, and both are to be found, more or less, in Camus. The first is quite simple: Compare puny man to the infinity of the universe. Or compare our brief lifetimes to the span of eternity. Or think of our meager actions within the context of galactic collisions. Or compare our infinitesimal finitude to the Divine Infinity of God. Or consider, whatever we do, we are going to die. The upshot is obvious; we are virtually nothing, our actions and feelings insignificant. But the visceral reaction is as inevitable as the argument is irrefutable; "not to *myself* I'm not." (An immortal god may only be infinitely bored.)

The second argument is as familiar as the first: To every human desire, there is the "why" of justification. "Why should you want that?" and "What will that get you?" and so on. And to every answer, there is a further "why" and then another, *ad infinitum, ad absurdum.* "The ultimate 'why' has no answer," Nietzsche warns us. Of course not, for there is no ultimate "why." The chain of justification is never completed, never attached, and so all of our desires and our values remain unsupported, unjustified, mere vanities, and—absurd. But the childish response is as appropriate here as in the last instance: "but not to *me.*" The problem in the following chapter, and in the rest of this book, is to give some philosophical credence to that innocent response, even in the face of the sophisticated irrefutability of its antagonists.

We might begin with the following analogue: The problem is the *meaning* of life. But what is "meaning"? For Camus and in both of the above sets of arguments, as well as for many others, "meaning" means "reference beyond itself," external "appeal" (in Camus's terms). Thus Morris Cohen, an American logician and contemporary of Camus, defined "meaning": ". . . anything acquires meaning if it is connected with or indicates or refers to something beyond itself, so that its full nature points to and is revealed in that connection" (*Preface to Logic*). It is clear that this is the sense of "meaning" that Camus has in mind for "the meaning of life," whether or not it is God that we find beyond." (It is not clear what the other candidates might be.) "Is it possible to live without appeal?"—that is, without meaning? As if the meaning of life can be found only outside of life itself. ("Don't you think life is for living?" "It's hard to think of what else one would do with it!"—Noel Coward.)

But the demand is incoherent: As a thoroughgoing "rationalist," Camus insists that only the meanings *within* our experience are allowed us—no unwarranted "leaps," no mystical "insights," no external "appeal." ("My rule is to get along with the immediate evidence.") But coupled with his notion of meaning, namely, a reference to some meaning-endowing source beyond our lives, *of course* it emerges that our lives are demonstrably meaningless, that is, Absurd.

It is worth noting, by way of analogy rather than argument, that the above notion of meaning has since been discarded by a great many philosophers, linguists, critics, and poets, particularly since the work of the later Wittgenstein. It has been increasingly evident, if not conclusively so, that the attempt to characterize meaning as "reference beyond itself" is applicable—if at all—only for very small units *within* a semantic system. But the system itself does not "have a meaning," nor, however, is it meaningless. (The word "loquacity" has a meaning *in* English, but what sense would it make to say that the English language has a meaning—or that it does not have one?) Similarly, Camus's self-stultifying quest for a meaning of life can be countered with the thesis that life can have no meaning, except insofar as it is considered (as it is in the above arguments) to be part of some larger system—of nature or of Divine creation. But subjectively, "for ourselves," this is not how we consider our lives. Life itself, in this sense, has no meaning. But so what? "What are the meanings *in our lives?*" is the only question.

A fair judgment of life can be obtained only within life itself. When philosophers and scientists pretend to examine the significance of our lives as if they were examining a bacillus under a microscope, they have already built into their examination that disdain for human existence that they pretend to draw as a conclusion. And when Camus insists upon a blanket meaningfulness for human life, he already condemns us to the seemingly awful judgment that there is none. Accordingly, he dismisses the distinction between meaningful and meaningless lives, even meaningful and meaningless moments in life. ("There are differences only in quantity; . . . There will never be any substitute for twenty years of life and experience.") No room for the choice of an Alexander or a Solomon—a short life and a heroic one, an average life and a wise one. It is at this point that we find ourselves forced to rebel, not against the Absurd, but against Camus's absurd metaphysics. We want to insist that life has meaning, not *of* it but *in* it, that these meanings are constituted by us through our passions. It is these meanings that do—or do not—make our lives worth living.

7. The Passions of Sisyphus

Why does Camus's myth strike such a responsive chord in so many readers? On the slightest philosophical examination, premises vanish and arguments dissolve, conclusions evaporate as whispy prejudices and concepts become mere shadows. Why are readers so impressed with these empty notions of "absurdity" and "appeal," "defiance" and "rebellion," "condemnation" and "heroism." What is it, in Camus and in ourselves, that renders us so receptive to his seduction, where "reason" is no more than a stamp of authority, supporting bad arguments and personal confusions under a limp but elegant façade of poetry?

Camus is not one of those philosophers, despite his occasional pretensions, who lead the reader from doubtless premise step by step by faultless inference. Yet his readers share his fallacies, make his unsound leaps along with him, obviously sharing something else besides his casual lack of concern for logic. The "something else," of course, is the impassioned world view behind those glib fallacies, not merely a metaphysics—a cold construction of concepts once written in Latin—but a passion, or a set of passions, that we, too, share. We, too, want to know "whether we can live without appeal," in the face of "the Absurd." But why should we feel the need to "appeal" in the first place, and why do we, too, hold on so tenuously to the conclusion that "life is absurd"? The evidence is in the passions, the prereflective sources of the meanings we find—or claim not to find—in our lives. And this is nowhere more evident than in Camus's own writings. Sisyphus is ultimately characterized in terms of neither his punishment nor his obedience, but in terms of his passions; "He *is*, as much through his passions as through his torture."

What are the passions of Sisyphus? "His *scorn* of the gods, his *hatred* of death, and his *passion for life*. . . ." He is without hope, without power, "*wretched*" but "*rebellious*." Yet he feels a "silent joy," Camus tells us, and "one must consider Sisyphus *happy*." A strange "happiness" indeed.

Sisyphus is the absurd hero because of his passions. But these passions, removed from their supposedly heroic context, display a defensive syndrome that is all too familiar. It is precisely that syndrome that projects our world in an absurd perspective, a syndrome of great expectations and consequent bitterness, helplessness and consequent resentment, hopelessness and consequent scorn, silent defiance and that consequent "sour grapes" self-satisfaction that tries to pass as "happiness," the spiteful joy of "negating the gods," that desperate last-ditch strategy of *accepting* and even celebrating a hopeless and futile life. Only one

ingredient is missing from this degrading portrait of human existence, the passion of *guilt*, supplied by Clamence from his barroom
pulpit. "It is not our tasks or our failures that are degrading, but
our very existence; not our crime that condemns us, but our very
being." Sisyphus has the emotional advantage of being "condemned" by the gods. We, on the other hand, condemn ourselves.
Camus's literary genius enables him to paint this ghastly scenario
in heroic colors; but we must see it for what it is. It is a degrading,
spiteful, and hopeless version of the Christian denigration of man
—as petty and helpless, virtually crushed by the weight of his guilt
and his punishment, virtuously salvaging his last crumb of self-
respect through resentment, scorn, silent defiance (but not refusal). This is humanity at its low ebb, man at his worst, casting
himself as an inferior being in a universe that has already defeated
him. But it has done *nothing*: nor has he, that is, except to project overwhelming powers of judgment upon a universe that no
longer has the Divinity to employ them. Not "indifferent" at all,
Camus's universe is animated by the projected powers of moral
judgment.

Why is Sisyphus "happy"?* Why should we be so sympa-
thetically struck by that final fiction as well as by his portrayal as
"absurd hero"? Because we all know about that perverse form of
glee and self-satisfaction which accompanies the last-resort self-
saving two-faced deference we allow ourselves just before total an-
nihilation. Having lost nearly everything—our pride, our sense of
dignity, our honor, our ability to love, to laugh, even to hate or be
angry—we turn, like a world-worn squirrel cornered by a playful
hound, baring our teeth in a hopeless display of defiance, and surprisingly, win the battle, though only because our all-powerful op-

* This strange conception of happiness, typically linked with the
concept of death, infiltrates all of Camus's novels. *The Stranger* ends
with Meursault awaiting death, when he "opens his heart to the benign indifference of the universe" and is happy. The last phrase of
The Plague, appropriately, is "a happy death." And Camus's first
novel, published in English in 1972, is entitled *A Happy Death*.
Only Clamence holds out, but even he, at the end of his monologue,
confesses to a resentful happiness, the same resentful happiness we
find in condemned Sisyphus. And there is a sense in which we surely
do not understand. (More tragic, there is a sense in which we do.)

ponent has lost interest in the contest. The happiness of resentment is the sense of relief upon our salvaging a last bit of dignity. Sisyphus' joy, Camus's happiness, a happiness he shares with every one of his pitiful and condemned characters and now with us, is the bittersweet refreshment of childish vindictiveness, a vengeance that need give itself no limits ("no rules of conduct"), as it has no effects other than its own smug gratification.

Once Sisyphus' mock heroism has been unmasked, revealing the distorted face of resentment, Camus's bitter conception of the Absurd becomes far less persuasive. In scorn and defiance, Sisyphus and Camus can curse the gods, "accuse the whole human race." Clamence carries on "the prosecution of others in his heart." But if resentment is intrinsically vicious, it is also essentially impotent, and the unbridled fury of its vindictiveness is balanced by its sense of total ineffectiveness. Yet it is a very short distance—and only one of temperament and consistency—from Camus's innocent defiance to the gleeful and perverse cruelty of the Marquis de Sade. A century and a half before "The Myth of Sisyphus," the infamous Marquis projected and cursed the same indifferent universe. But where Sisyphus limited himself to silent and obedient scorn, the Marquis saw his real and fictionalized acts of rape, murder, buggery, and "sadism" as the logical consequence of the same emotional premises. Sartre could represent Camus as one of France's great moralists, as "the Cartesian of the Absurd who refused to leave the sure ground of morality." But morality as well as cruelty, as Nietzsche once argued, can be the fruit of resentment. The more we dig under the surface of Camus's heroic Absurd, the more the *passions* resentment, "scorn and defiance" become the basic issue. Thus the theme of this book, which begins with the "meaning of life" and the problem of "the Absurd," becomes a philosophy of the passions.

Camus's "passion for life" is a desperate passion, the last grasping of a condemned or dying man which emerges when all of the substantial passions of life—love, hate, anger, and even sorrow—have been lost to him. This "passion for life" is like that burst of emotion one feels for a lover who is just stepping out the door for the last time. Even Camus admits: "I know, to be sure, the dull resonance that vibrates through these days. Yet I have but a word to say: that it is necessary." But that is not enough for us. Having learned to see through that degrading metaphysics that has defined humanity for so many centuries, we can now learn to see through those more secular self-imposed degradations that rationalize themselves as "the Absurd." "The point is to live," Camus tells us. But it is not enough to live out of stubborn defiance, like an unwelcome guest in life. Our image must not be that of scornful Sisyphus but that of the equally ancient legend of what Nietzsche called "the eternal recurrence." It does not aggrandize the repetition of despair, but rather it uses repetition as the ultimate test of meaningfulness:

> *The greatest stress.* What if some day or night a demon were to sneak after you into your loneliest loneliness and say to you, "This life as you now live it and have lived it, you will have to live once more and innumerable times more; and there will be nothing new in it, but every pain and every joy and every thought and sigh and everything immeasurably small or great in your life must return to you—all in the same succession and sequence—even this spider and this moonlight between the trees, and even this moment and I myself. The eternal hourglass of existence is turned over and over, and you with it, a dust grain of dust." Would you not throw yourself down and gnash your teeth and curse the demon who spoke thus? Or did you once experience a tremendous moment when you would have answered him, "You are a god, and never have I heard anything more godly." If this thought were to gain possession of you, it would change you, as you are, or perhaps crush you. The question in each and every thing, "Do you want this once more and innumerable times more?" would weigh upon your actions as the greatest stress. Or how well disposed would you have to become to yourself and to life to *crave nothing more fervently* than this ultimate eternal confirmation and seal?

> *Joyful Wisdom*

CHAPTER 2: THE NEW ROMANTICISM

1. The Passions and the Absurd

> All passions have a phase when they are merely disastrous, when they drag down their victim with the weight of their stupidity. . . . In view of the element of stupidity in passion, war was declared on passion itself, its destruction was plotted; all the old moral monsters are agreed on this; *il faut tuer les passions*. . . . *Destroying* the passions and cravings, merely as a preventive measure against their stupidity—today this itself strikes us as merely another acute form of stupidity. We no longer admire dentists who "pluck out" teeth so that they will not hurt anymore.
>
> Nietzsche, *Twilight of the Idols*

The answer to the Absurd is the passions. There will always be absurdities, of course, bitter gaps between our expectations and Reality—the death of a young friend, the murder of a president, "unrequited" loves, frustrating bumblings in the bureaucracy. So long as we have values and expectations—and to live *is* to have values and expectations—there will be no escaping these absurdities, no matter how one strives to deny their importance under one of the many banners of "Stoicism," Christianity, Zen, "realism," "cool," or Schopenhauerian cynicism. But *the Absurd*, the absurdity *of* life, is avoidable. It is a refusal to accept the passions and subjectivity as sufficient to give our lives meaning. *The Absurd* is the product of that bloodless and desperate "objective" reasoning that insists on going beyond all passions, beyond subjectivity, and thus beyond life. It demands that *something else* supply the significance of our lives. Even Gabriel Marcel, with his "philosophy of the concrete," falls prey to this demand. "All philosophies of immanence have had their day," he argues.[1] But there are *only* immanent meanings, and even the Absurd—that is, that sense of *lack* of meaning—must be accounted for "immanently," *within* our lives, *subjectively*. When the meaningfulness of life is in question, it is our personal dissatisfaction with the meanings *in* life—our passions—that is in question, and nothing else. Heidegger says that the passions (*moods* in particular) are our way of "being tuned into the world." An apt phrase, stressing again that Reality is never simply there for us but is always filled with chores and tasks, attractions and repulsions, matters of importance and things of value. And we, too, are never simply *there* but, to continue the electronic metaphor, "turned on" as well. My passions tie me to the moments of my life—that is, I tie myself to the moments of my life with my passions—with a sense of secure yet transient permanence. Those are the meanings of life, whether over a period of four hours or forty years. To wrench away and break those bonds, to sever the temporary meaningfulness of life, is to face—if only for an instant—the threat that those meanings will not be replaced. That *Unknown*, not what might happen but rather what might not, is the most terrifying prospect of our lives. I leave a dull party, and I am halfway to my car when I am struck by the temptation to go back. "What is there ahead of me?" It is a temporary weakness; it passes quickly. The specter of the Absurd often rises in such moments. The involvements of the past few hours have been slashed; in retrospect, they are meaningless. Standing nowhere, in between meanings, on the sidewalk at 1 A.M., life is meaningless. And so we make every effort to avoid those moments. We have ambitions and projects, books to write, jobs to do. We make ourselves a "home" which always confronts us with chores and values and a constant supply of meanings. We remain in a relationship, however unsatisfactory, which is filled with meanings and passions—even envy and resentment, hatred and indignation. Any meanings are better than possibly none. We cram our lives with appointments and schedules, so that the prospect of meaninglessness has no time to appear, except by appointment (a philosophy class, a "new wave" movie, an occasional evening alone in a bar).

When we find our lives absurd, the absurdity in question is neither Camus's grand conception of *the Absurd* nor the absurdities in life. The first is a philosopher's myth; the second the price of being alive. The absurdity we find in our lives is rather those moments of detachment, broken bonds in the past, nothing yet in the future. But are they really "moments of detachment," moments without meaning? Or are they more like those periods of estrangement at the party, not without meaning but with a very special kind of meaning—a sense of being excluded, of being somehow "inferior" or of not existing at all, of utter "dispensability"? There are moments following the severing of bonds—which seem in retrospect like bondage—which are characterized by wholesale relief and joy, despite the absence of any concrete future prospects. And absurdity appears often in those moments of intense bonding, in the midst of a great passion, a stormy rage, a violent scene, a time of grief. And so we begin to suspect, as Camus never did, that the source of absurdity is not meaninglessness at all, but a certain *kind* of meaning. The object of absurdity is not a "confrontation," with an "indifferent universe" or a man talking soundlessly in a telephone booth. The object of absurdity is our Self. Absurdity is a self-demeaning view of ourselves. It never appears in love; it almost always appears in depression and resentment. All are equally "meaningful"; in fact, depressions and resentments are often far more absorbing than the calm of love and friendship. The difference is *within* the meanings, and the meaninglessness of life is in fact a projection of our own sense of worthlessness onto the world. Camus's Absurd, projected onto the universe as a whole, is a *refusal* to accept himself, an attempt to compensate for his own sense of inferiority with a sham nobility and defiance against forces that can be blamed and safely despised at a distance.

There is a peculiar passion which is called "passion for life." Often, this notion is used to describe those happy and always welcome people with a contagious vitality and enthusiasm for whatever they do and wherever they find themselves. But there is another sense of "passion for life," employed by Camus in his attack on the Absurd, which is the very antithesis of an enthusiasm for life. It is the desperate attitude of a condemned or dying man, who senses that he is, for all passionate purposes, already dead. It is before his execution that Camus's "stranger" discovers this passion, as he "opens his heart to the benign indifference of the universe." But the universe had never before been "indifferent" to him, and the peculiar happiness he now describes is symptomatic of a loss of *living* that permeates the whole of Camus's philosophy. Only at the edges of life, bordering death, can one be "happy." This so-called passion for life is in fact a longing for life already lost, like the passion one feels for love lost—not love but loss. The problem of the Absurd arises only because one refuses to accept the passions and meanings of everyday life. This peculiar "passion for life" with which Camus answers the Absurd shares with the problem this same dissatisfaction and refusal. Both problem and answer are of similar origin; both share a *contempt* for life. To "love life itself," but not to find meaningful the contents of life, is an empty and lifeless philosophy, a vain search for meaning which begins by rejecting all possibilities. That is the Absurd. To rebel against it is already to miss the problem, to treat the Absurd as something *outside* oneself, when it is in fact but a projection of an emptiness *within*. Enough of Camus's "ruthless rationalism"; I prefer the "Romanticism" it seemingly opposes.

> MARAT: Citizen Marquis
> is your own lack of compassion
> What you call the indifference of Nature
>
> Weiss, *Marat/Sade*

2. Romanticism

> Passion is the element in which we live.
> Man, being reasonable, must get drunk;
> The best of life is but intoxication.
>
> Byron, *Don Juan*

There are as many characterizations of the old Romanticism as there are discussions of it, and few of them, even the most academic, are free from passionate partisanship. Irving Babbitt, in a classic study—or should we say "diagnosis"—of the Romantic movement, states his purpose as "stripping idealistic disguises from egoism, in exposing . . . sham spirituality." Arnold Hauser accuses the movement from a Marxist perspective of escapism and childishness, irresponsibility and irrationality.* Goethe said that Romanticism was "sickly," and Dominique Ingres called it "the cult of the ugly." In its defense, Stendhal characterized Romanticism in terms of the contemporary as opposed to the archaic; Victor Hugo equated Romanticism with the love of liberty. More recently, Jacques Barzun has called it nothing other than "the need to create a new world on the ruins of the old," and Sir Herbert Read has, like Hugo, equated Romanticism with freedom. The dispute between Romanticism and its archrival, "Classicism," has always been bitter. In Paris in the 1830s, Théophile Gautier marched around in a flamboyant red smoking jacket, expressly in order to "exasperate the Philistines." Theater openings were typically more exciting on the audience side of the footlights, with wild verbal and sometimes physical battles between impassioned opponents.

What is Romanticism? It is best known as a movement in the arts. Some scholars trace it back to medieval Christianity; a few even carry it back to the Greeks. As a self-conscious attitude and explicit philosophy, however, it is best restricted to modern times, in particular to the nineteenth century in Europe (and America) in which "Romantic schools" of music and literature, painting and poetry were most in evidence. One thinks immediately of William Blake, Lord Byron, and Percy Bysshe Shelley, Théophile Géricault and Eugène Delacroix, Victor Hugo and Alexandre Dumas, Hector Berlioz, Johannes Brahms, and Richard Wagner, John Constable and Joseph Turner, Novalis, Caspar David Friedrich, and August and Friedrich Schlegel, Ralph Waldo Emerson and Henry David Thoreau. But Romanticism, like all cultural movements, had its deepest roots in ideas, in philosophy, which in turn was but the expression of the fundamental attitudes of the age. The philosophical grandfather of Romanticism is universally agreed to be Jean Jacques Rousseau, whose sentimental naturalism

* "Romanticism; irrational and escapist . . . a fear of the present . . . childish . . . escape to utopia and fairy tale, to the unconscious and the fantastic, the uncanny and the mysterious, to childhood and nature, to dreams and madness, . . . all disguised and more or less sublimated forms of the same feeling, the same yearning for irresponsibility and a life free from suffering and frustration" (Arnold Hauser, A Social History of Art, Vol. 3).

inspired revolutions in philosophy and the arts as well as in French politics. He was the strongest single philosophical influence on Kant, and consequently on Fichte, Hegel, and several generations of German Romantics. He was among Goethe's favorite authors; Maximilien de Robespierre, Napoleon, Beethoven, and Delacroix were all enthusiasts. Although the Romantic interpretations seriously distorted his ideas, their essential theme remained constant: "Man is born free; and everywhere he is in chains"; "natural" man has an independence and sense of virtue which the arbitrary fashions and conventions of contemporary society have taken from him. Trust natural sentiment, not artificial reason. The message was soon overstated. It became a war between reason and the passions, a war with ideological and consequently political implications which the years following the French Revolution would make only too clear. But the truth of Romanticism, which I shall continue to defend, is precisely this emphasis upon the passions (but not to the exclusion of reason). "New Romanticism" is the thesis that it is the passions that give our lives meaning.

Although Romanticism surfaced most visibly as an aesthetic and philosophical theory, it existed primarily as a widespread human attitude, a reaction to the times, and a view of contemporary life. Superficially, romanticism manifested itself in slick sentimentality, "melodrama" and histrionics, forced emotionalism, hopeless love affairs, hapless suicides, a demand for happy endings, and adventure in the novels and plays of the period. Even Victor Hugo's friends were embarrassed by the "melodrama" of some of his productions. Heinrich Heine, a Romantic in many ways, complained of Goethe's Romantic *Werther* (which initiated an epidemic of sentimental suicides), "its effeminate dreaminess, barren sentimentality." Happy and hopeless endings served the same purpose of invoking the depths of feeling, which alone made life worthwhile. Medieval adventures and magical love affairs—preferably both—were the fantasies of whole populations, given substance by such popular authors as Sir Walter Scott in England, Victor Hugo in France, Goethe, Friedrich von Schiller, and many others in Germany.

Beneath this façade, however, which still tends to give "Romanticism" a bad name and a sickeningly sweet smell about it, evolved sophisticated systems of philosophical perspectives, not only in the complex metaphysics of Fichte and Friedrich Schelling, Hegel and Schopenhauer, but in the everyday thinking of everyone. For over a century, the "Enlightenment" had ruled men's attitudes with its stress on order and mechanism, universal reason, and peaceful progress. With the French Revolution and the "Terror," with the violence of the Napoleonic Wars and the ultimate collapse of France, that mode of thinking had been discredited. If reason had begotten so much bloodshed, how comparatively safe were the flights of fancy of Romanticism, the passionate love triangles which only rarely ended even in a duel, much less a suicide, the idealistic adventures that would occasionally cost the life of but a poet or two in foreign lands.

In this new way of thinking, it was the *irrational* forces that were given their due, both in the universe and in man. The world was no longer viewed as predetermined and orderly; it was an aimless rush of possibilities, and the imagination of a man could not stretch far enough to envision the future insanities that might lie in store. But man tried, and Romantic art quickly identified itself with the mysteries of the Middle Ages and the occult, the mysterious new religions of the Orient and more mysterious workings of man's unconscious. The Romantics worshiped beauty, but they worshiped the ugly, the grotesque, and the Gothic as well. (Walter Pater once defined Romanticism as "the addition of strangeness to beauty.") Life was an adventure, one which might end in any tragedy, death, or madness as easily as in victory or love. The universe was no longer the orderly and predictable mechanism it had been for Newton and Laplace; it was a throbbing, pulsating organism, itself rushing madly toward who-knew-what. Schopenhauer had only formulated, not created, this popular view in the intricacies of his Kantian metaphysics of the Will, that irrational cosmic force that was carrying us off to nowhere. Schelling and Hegel had only formulated the happier side of this same picture, that—despite the "slaughterbench of history" and human suffering—this living "world spirit" was indeed progressing toward unity and internal harmony.

Personally, the Romantics admired passion and imagination above all other human attributes. Accordingly, they worshiped genius above all, with its exceptional vision and self-driving power.

A "cult of genius" pervaded Europe, though few of its members were actually geniuses. Every man suspected genius in himself and so followed the Romantics' advice to "ignore all rules" and to follow *yourself*. "Inspiration" became the watchword in art, "conscience" replaced the moral rules in ethics. An intense individualism resulted, an individualism which not infrequently manifested itself in the eccentricities of a Byron or a Novalis, yet this individualism was always tempered with an intense universalism, an apparent contradiction on the surface, but the very essence of Romanticism on further examination. How could a movement which worshiped personal freedom endorse nationalism in Germany? How could a movement which worshiped genius construe itself as a movement of the "common man"? The answer lay in the passions, in a curious amalgam of subjectivity and intersubjective humanism that has often confused aesthetic and political critics for the past century. The freedom defended by the Romantics was ultimately a freedom *within* a community, not a society bound by the arbitrary fashions attacked by Rousseau, but a community developing "naturally," according to its own needs and temperament, on the basis of mutual intimacy and trust. And genius, no matter how eccentric, was but the avant-garde of general human development; "the poet holds the lantern for mankind," wrote Victor Hugo. Thus, Romanticism often carried with it a strong political ideology, of nationalism and socialism in Germany, of liberation and revolution in France. (How far from the "escapism" alleged by so many critics!)

The key to Romanticism, in all of its various manifestations, was a renewed awareness of *life*. ("Life is life's greatest purpose," wrote Fichte.) Against the dehumanizing and lifeless mechanism of Isaac Newton's universe, the Romantics urged an organic conception of a living universe. Against the promises of the Enlightenment for peaceful progress, which had ended in slaughter and disillusionment, the Romantics urged a spirit of adventure; no promises, only human effort and striving. Against the cold and calculating efforts of reason to organize society, the Romantics urged the hot-blooded and unpredictable surges of passion and "sympathy." And against the archaic codes and eternal verities of classicism and the Enlightenment, the Romantics urged experiment and change, development and evolution.

Today, when the universe has once again become dehumanized and man has "reduced the infinite creative music of the universe to the monotonous clatter of a monstrous mill" (Novalis, *Hymn to the Night*), when promises of progress have left us bitter and disillusioned, when the calculating "pragmatics" of American politics have exploded in stupidity and corruption, when archaic rules serve only to divide us and weaken us, a "new Romanticism" is in order.

It is worth emphasizing again and again that Romanticism is a movement of peacetime. In war, passions are at such a pitch, and so plentiful, that no philosophy is needed to remind us of their importance. When survival is at stake, no renewed emphasis on "life" is needed. Life never seems without meanings in the absurdities of war. It was during those peaceful years in England, when the Industrial Revolution was already displaying its worst tendencies toward exploitation and dehumanization and already filling the skies of Manchester and London with the black aura of progress, that Romanticism caught hold, as a form of protest. It was in France *after* the fall of Napoleon, during that retrograde and oppressive time known as the "Reaction," that Romanticism flourished as a protest against the vulgar commercialism of the bourgeoisie and the static boredom of the times. It was in Germany, following the collapse (with Napoleon) of their first major bid for national unity, that Romanticism had its heyday, as a protest against the impotence of the middle class and the unadventurous spirit that had made German liberation so far impossible. In short, Romanticism and the Age of the Absurd are contemporaries. Romanticism is a call to arms, a protest against a stagnant and dehumanizing world. Classicism, its supposed antithesis (really its complement), finds its place in times of great passion— for example, immediately before and during the French Revolution—when passion abounds but unity and discipline are lacking. Romanticism stirs up the spirit, gives meaning to once dreary lives. It is essentially a bourgeois movement, one that begins, not in terror or in battle, but in boredom, in the daily and lifeless routine that has become intolerable. It may consequently be a force for revolution or a force for conservatism (as in France and Germany respectively); but, in any case, it is a force. It *moves* us and renews our sense of vitality. It gives our lives meaning in times when "absurd reasoning" is mistaken as "rationality" and "realism," when the valuelessness of values is accepted as a foregone conclusion.

3. Rational Romanticism

Le coeur à ses raisons, que la raison ne connaît point.

Pascal, Pensées

As if every passion did not have its quantum of reason.

Nietzsche, Will to Power

It's often been said in philosophy and elsewhere that reason must *rule* the passions; it has been said by David Hume that reason "is, and ought to be, the slave of the passions." Both of these views are dangerous. To divide the human soul into reason and passion, setting one against the other in a struggle for control, one to be the master, the other the slave, divides us against ourselves, forcing us each to be defensively half a person, instead of a harmonious whole. There is no problem of reason *versus* the passions. There is only the problem of *who* we are and would be through our passions and on reflection. There are no different "faculties," only differences in scope and perspective.

Without the guidance of the passions, reasoning has neither principles nor power. Cut off from our "sentiments," we can justify or show that one cannot justify anything. Hume made this point powerfully but brutally when he insisted that it was not "irrational" (that is, against the dictates of reason) for him to prefer the slaughter of a hundred thousand Orientals to the painful pricking of his little finger. Reason makes contact with human values only through the passions. It is only a *particular* form of reason—*objective* reasoning—that is free of personal values and passions. And it is so neither by "nature" nor by logic, but by virtue of great effort, methodologically stripping itself of all personality and subjectivity. Objective reasoning has its place (even in self-consciousness). But objective reasoning is not the whole of reason. Reason itself is not devoid of ideology and personal commitment because of its abstractness and its appeal to universal principles, nor is it free of personal prejudice and preferences. Reason is articulate and hopefully expansive in its scope, but it is thereby no less subjective, whatever may be its objective pretensions, and no less personal, however "universal" it may claim to be.

From the other side, the passions cannot be cut off, even in logic, from reason and reflection. Of course, not all, in fact, only a few of our passions are reflective and fully articulate. Nietzsche was right in saying that the passions are often "stupid," despite their sometimes uncanny ability to "intuit" a situation which reflection does not yet even suspect. For example, we "find" ourselves suspicious and defensive with a fellow who, at the moment, exhibits no "reason" whatsoever not to be trusted and admired but who later proves to be a villain. But without reflection and articulation, the passions lack that critical scope and perspective that would allow us to see past our noses. Our passions can be obsessive and often, if not typically, myopic. They see but an inch in front of themselves, never bothering to look back or around, or even ahead. They often fail to understand the nature of their objects: grasping onto whatever lies immediately in front of them. We become angry at an innocent bystander, just because he or she is "standing by"; we fall in love without ever asking ourselves precisely (or even imprecisely) what we want or expect from or are willing to give to the other person. Reason and reflection provide the scope and perspective that allow for such understanding, a more adequate self-consciousness that sees past the immediate to longer-term needs and the welfare of others. But this reason and reflection are not something "added on" to our passions, the dictates of another "faculty" imposed upon them in order to "rule" or even "direct" them. Reason and reflection are but the articulate expression and expansion of the passions themselves. Reason is nothing other than perspicacious passion. And what is usually identified as the "stupidity" of the passions is also the narrowness of our reason, that is, our limited awareness and understanding of our world.

We often contrast the "spontaneity" of the passions with the "ponderous deliberations" of reason. And it is true that we often "find ourselves" in a passion. But this appearance must be explained. The fact that we "find" this to be the case does not entail nor even suggest that we are not ourselves responsible for them. And we all know so well the many times we "catch ourselves," not *in* a passion, but deliberating—even ponderously—in an effort to *build up* a passion, "working ourselves into a rage," "making ourselves feel guilty," or rehearsing the virtues and possibilities of a prospective "date" until we virtually *push* ourselves into the dubious abyss into which we allegedly "fall" when we "fall in love." There is nothing "spontaneous" about such emotion. And even when our passions are unquestionably spontaneous in that sense, it remains to be seen whether they are not so only because they have been used in similar circumstances so many times before and have already been so often practiced and finely developed. Like the apparently "spontaneous" genius of a Nicolò Paganini, a James Whistler, or a Thomas Mann, our passions are "spontaneous" only in the sense that they can benefit from many years of hard work and painful development; and the present masterpiece seems to emerge as if on its own.†

It is worth noting that reason, too, is often if not usually "spontaneous" in this sense. An idea just "comes to us"; we have a "flash of insight." And our most successful reflections are not always ponderous deliberations on the state of our souls. As often as not, they, too, "just appear" as if we "find" them in ourselves. Yet no one would be tempted to deny their rationality. Once again, the alleged differences between reason and the passions, prodded in the slightest, turn out to be no differences at all.

The passions, like the judgments of reason (I shall argue that our emotions are also judgments), are *conceptual* structures. They are not, as we usually say, "feelings." They are typically prereflective, but they are not essentially so. A passion rendered articulate and reflectively self-conscious is thereby a reflective passion, and no less a passion. Our passions—and in particular our emotions—are the structures of our world. They are what we have called our surreality and the structures of our Selves in that world. All emotions, whatever their putative objects, are *self-conscious*, and they take one's Self as a source of concern. But if every emotion is al-

† "It is not the strength but the duration of our sentiments that makes great men" (Nietzsche, *Beyond Good and Evil*).

ready, by its very nature, conceptual and self-conscious, it is obviously a small step—but often a difficult one—toward becoming articulate and reflective. Prereflective is not preconceptual. And the difference between conceiving and articulating is at most a matter of "expression," or, many psycholinguists would argue, a matter of degree.

It comes as little surprise to anyone to learn that some of our best poetry was first inspired and drafted in periods of passionate rapture, even in a state of despair or frenzy, when objective thought and reason were at ebb tide. (One thinks of T. S. Eliot scribbling "The Wasteland" in a Swiss flophouse.) Nor does it come as a surprise that a gifted poet may be a remarkably dull-witted human being. The explanation is usually doled out in terms of "feelings," as if the poet is distinguished from other men in his exuberance of them. But, then, "How does he translate these feelings into words?" we want to know, and we are answered in terms of "his gift." But in his state of rapture, "How does he translate the untranslatable, describe the indescribable?" And in answer to this nonsense, a great many modern poets deny the role of "feeling" altogether, as if poetry were strictly a *rational* (though still creative) enterprise. But the very problem turns on a false view of the passions, as if the passions were nothing but a feeling or a sensation, literally indescribable and, if this term makes sense at all, untranslatable. If an emotion is already a conceptual scheme, however, a world view and a system of metaphors (its "mythology"), then the poet's task is literally one of "expression" and articulation, not translation or description. (This is not to deny in the slightest the need for skill and "inspiration," special "talents" indeed. But the skill and inspiration are not a move *from* the passion *to* the poem, but rather they exist already in the very passion itself.)

The usual attitudes toward passion, reason, and brutality can be similarly reviewed. The familiar picture is this: Passion induces violence, virtually as a matter of course. Reason bypasses violence ("Let's be reasonable" *means* "Let's not fight"). But then there is the diametrically opposed Romantic-Rousseauian portrait: Man left to his "natural sentiments" is peaceful. It is "civilized" man, with his *rational* beliefs and property rights, that fights over land and love and initiates wars between nations and hatred between groups. But both theories are, needless to say, simplified if not simple-minded. There are both brutal and nonbrutal passions, hatred and vengeance as well as love and respect. Reason's role, however, is complex. It is a matter of fact that violence is, in most cases, self-defeating, and, therefore, reason is (that is, perspicacious passions are) generally against it. Most of our more brutal passions are also our more stupid passions, short on vision and closed to "rational considerations." But history makes clear that "rational considerations" are not always on the side of peace. A peace of reason might well be merely a matter of strategy, whereas a peace of mutual respect will endure. But one shouldn't speak of either reason or passion in exclusion. There are violent passions; there are reasons for violence. And then there is also the inability to adequately *express* our passions. Thus, Herman Melville's Billy Budd was led to violence, not through his passions or his reason, but because he found himself incapable of expressing his anger in any other way.

It has been suggested, following the Greeks, that the passions are rude eruptions, whereas reason is calm and enduring, even "eternal." One of the most common mistakes, however, is to think of the passions only in their moments of crisis, when anger "boils over" and jealousy "erupts" in violence. There are such "eruptions," of course, and it is often *through* them that one comes to recognize an emotion. The nature of our passions does not require these explosive manifestations. One can love for years, never once bursting into frenzy or despair. Such moments are more likely before the establishment of love or just preceding its imminent demise. In fact, as a structure of the Self and the world we live in, a passion—or at least the passions in general—would *have* to be calm and enduring. It is a serious error to think that a passion is powerful and "real" only when it is in jeopardy; thus, the Romantics, in their novels and in their sometimes histrionic lives, intentionally threw their passions to the test at every opportunity, laboring under the fallacy that passion was "true" only in crisis.

We can "harbor" our anger for years, anchored peacefully in a sanctuary of personal offenses and defensiveness, running amuck and causing a squall only on those rare occasions when an offense is agitated or defensiveness threatened. It is commonly thought that such squalls "let out" the anger, as if, to continue the usual fluid (I shall call it "hydraulic") metaphor, it were "bottled up" during all that harboring. But one of the consequences of my thesis, perhaps among its most "practical" corollaries, is that such squalls, quite the contrary of "letting the anger out," only serve, through increased thought and agitation, to increase its intensity. The anger is not the squall, and the result of the squall will most likely be to anchor our anger more securely (in the stream of consciousness?).

It is important to remember that reason, despite its hypertrophied characterizations in terms of "eternity" and "the divine" in traditional philosophical literature, has more than its own share of stupidity. The many varieties of "objective reason," for example, however brilliantly they might perform in their own quarters —in mathematics and scholarship, in theoretical biology or in bridge or chess matches—are often profoundly inept at dealing with life. Most of us know near-geniuses who have trouble deciding which shoe to put on first, and none of us is particularly surprised. "Intelligence has nothing to do with life," we often hear, and the early Romantic celebration of the "common man" certainly played this theme to the hilt. Of course, this is not even plausible once one remembers that reason can be "practical" as well as "theoretical." And modern theorists have seriously challenged the legitimacy of even this distinction. Surely there are few "practices" that do not require some degree of theory, and perhaps there are no theories that wholly succeed in removing themselves from the realm of their practical applications. But this much is clear, that pure theoretical reason is as intimately related to the day-to-day problems of life as good taste in wine to the task of cleaning out the cat litter.

But before we allow ourselves to extol without qualification the virtues of "practical reason," as Kant did, we must remind ourselves just how often this "reason" is nothing more than a "rationalization"—not a rationalizing—of the passions. We hear ourselves going on about the virtues of charity, when we realize that we are moralizing only in order to soothe the embarrassment of our having been gouged by a local fund for a small fortune this afternoon. Alternatively, we sermonize on the virtues of a hard day's work, significantly and soon after encountering a group of begging

gypsies. It can be argued‡ that the entire rational edifice of abstract systems of morality, such as we find in Kant and in Christianity, are nothing but such rationalizations of deep-set and unacceptable passions, notably envy and resentment. But, again, it
must not be supposed that such instances are a *subversion* of
reason by the passions, somewhat like the take-over of a radio station by guerrilla marauders. Reason is no more than *the thinking
of the passions,* and any attempt to break away from the passions,
to become purely "objective," is already to leave behind all question of value and of meaning.

The distinction between reason and the passions, in short, is
based upon a series of faulty paradigms: a model of the passions
as disruptive explosions in crisis situations and a model of
"reason" that limits itself to "objective" and impersonal reason,
appropriate to intellectual and technological problems but in-
humanly cut off from day-to-day reflection. There are no two
"faculties"; there is no distinction. There is only the reason of the
passions, more or less articulate, more or less perspicacious. There
is, in short, only *rationality,* and the only Romanticism worth
defending is what we have called "rational romanticism," in
which the "reason-passions" distinction plays no part.

4. *The Function of Reason*

> The function of reason is to allow expression of certain passions
> at the expense of others. A morality is a set of principles which
> restricts passions; a successful morality is one which restricts only
> the life-stultifying passions, which may be fatal, where they drag
> their victim down with the weight of their stupidity.
>
> Nietzsche, *Twilight of the Idols*

Nietzsche may be forgiven for backsliding into the Myth of the
Passions in return for his distinction between two kinds of passions, "life-enhancing" (*lebensbejahung*) and "life-stultifying"
(*lebensverneinung*). The distinction is oversimplified, but it un-

‡ For example, by Nietzsche in *Genealogy of Morals* and *The An-
tichrist.*

derscores an insight which is typically ignored by the old Romantics and by virtually all rationalists as well: that the passions play
varied roles in our lives, that "reason" is neither "for" nor
"against" the passions, and that the function of rationality is to
distinguish among the passions rather than react to them as a
class, an invading force from the "id" or an untoward disruption
of our lives. Every passion, even the most stupid and life-denying,
"has its quantum of reason" (also Nietzsche). But some reasons
(paradoxically) are more rational than others.

Philosophy is (literally) the "love of wisdom." "Wisdom" is a
word not heard very often today. But of course not. It is a concept
that has been emptied of the passions, as if wisdom were reserved
for old men, their lives all but finished, looking back on experience with that calm and assurance that come only with retrospect.
But wisdom is nothing of the sort; it is rather a matter of living
both thoughtfully and passionately, bringing understanding to
bear on every passion and forcing every passion into the light of
reflection. Wisdom and rationality have too long been distinguished from passion and enthusiasm, as if the "wise man" were
one who refuses rather than invites involvement, as if the "rational man" has no passion, never gets angry, prefers convenience
to love, and sees his world only in the cold steel-gray of "Reality."
Instead, think of Socrates, enjoying his drunkenness and the pleasure of his students as much as their conversations. Or T. E.
Lawrence, who incorporated similar pleasures and fanatical dedication, self-inflicted hardship and torture, among his various "pil-
lars of wisdom." Even Goethe, that paragon of rationality and
"good citizenship," enjoyed a variety of Roman orgies and
mistresses, in his unequaled sense of discipline and "freedom
within limitation." The function of reason—whose result is wisdom—is nothing other than the selection and encouragement of
what Nietzsche called the "life-enhancing passions"—the maximization of personal dignity and self-esteem.

In place of "wisdom" and as an excuse for rationality, modern
man seems to prefer what he calls "common sense." (It is sometimes called "horse sense"; the comparison is apt.) It is not a matter of personal experience and reflection; surely not a matter of
passion and involvement. It is rather a substitute for experience, a
matter of proper training and agreement with the "common"

fund of accumulated prejudices (most of them prudent, few exciting) of *das Man*. Borrowing from a long-misunderstood passage from Aristotle (who in fact argued that you couldn't do too much of a good thing[2]), "common sense" dampens passion with advice, "nothing to excess" and "everything in moderation." But life is excess and exuberance, following Oscar Wilde rather than pseudo-Aristotle, "Anything worth doing is worth doing in excess." "Common sense" is the origin of so many empty lives of little experience and no adventure, nominal subjectivity, and, above all, little passion. Here is another source of the Absurd, in this impersonal and "common" fund of prudent and "rational" boredom and resentment. But there is nothing "common" about wisdom, as Socrates proved in his ultimate sacrifice, courageously acting on behalf of the very principles according to which he was "commonly" condemned.

All passions have the same end—personal dignity and self-esteem. But each passion, though tied by its own logic to all the others, tends to become obsessed with its own objects and outlook. Each follows what it takes to be an optimal strategy; but from a more inclusive view it is evident that these individual strategies conflict and interfere with each other. These are strategies that are virtually always disastrous (like running backward in football). It is the business of rationality to eliminate or modify them, to organize the passions in a co-ordinated effort, joining them together toward a common goal (which means, however, that some of them will have to spend most of their time on the bench). Moreover, it is possible that even a co-ordinated strategy will be less than optimal, even disastrous. Thus, I shall argue that rationality is the search of the passions for optimal strategy for achieving self-esteem. What is called wisdom is the attainment of this optimal strategy, the "harmony of the soul" that was so celebrated by the Greeks, harnessed from the enthusiasm and chaos so encouraged by the Romantics. It is what Aristotle called *eudaimonia*, "living well," surely not devoid of passion, but not devoid of reason either. Indeed, it is only when this insidious distinction begins to disintegrate that the ideal of "self-esteem," "wisdom," and classical "harmony of the soul" will begin to make any sense for us.

CHAPTER 3: THE MYTH* OF THE PASSIONS

> Passion: the state of being subjected to or acted on by what is external or foreign to one's true nature.
>
> Webster's Third New International Dictionary

> Passion: Souffrance, série de tourments . . . Mouvement, agitation que l'âme éprouve . . . Émotion: trouble, agitation de l'âme.
>
> Dictionnaire Petit Larousse

1. The Passions

"Passion" originally referred to *suffering* (as in "the Passion of Christ"). Its meaning has expanded considerably, but the basic image—that in passion something *happens to us*—remains the same. The passions render us passive, the happy passions of joy and love as well as the painful passions of grief, guilt, and despair. And so, in an important sense, we think of ourselves as suffering the passions, even joy and love, and the gloomy connotations of crucifixion still linger in the very term.†

Various passions "strike" us, "overwhelm" us, "consume" us, "paralyze" us; we "fall" into them, "give way" to them, and we at-

* "Myth has been shown to be an effective truth-preventive edifice that can be of significant value when used in a conscientiously applied program of oral poetry and regular professional care." (Jon D. Solomon)

† Paul Ricoeur, the most important and durable of contemporary French academic philosophers, insists that "all passions are unhappy" in his massive work, *Freedom and Nature: the Voluntary and the Involuntary*, Vol. I (Evanston, Ill.: Northwestern University Press, 1966). In terms of the dualistic title of that volume, the passions clearly fall on the side of the "involuntary."

tempt to "hold them down," "keep the lid on," "maintain control," and "suppress" them. Insofar as the passions are thought to be actions at all, they are merely *reactions* to events beyond our control. (See the two dictionary definitions above.) The entire history of human thought (Eastern as well as Western) has tended to view the passions as forces in some sense "outside" us, beyond our control, eruptions from an unconscious Freudian "it" or Cartesian "animal spirits" sapping the strength of Reason. And whether the passions are consequently viewed with alarm or derision or rather, as in German Romanticism, with the enthusiasm of a small child with a new surfboard viewing a powerful wave, the upshot is the same—as if passions are disturbances, breaking the calm of contented objectivity.

The word "passion" is now somewhat dated, at least in English, conjuring up Victorian memories of overwhelming sentiments and semihysterical outbursts. It retains something of that usage in French literature, where it is often contrasted with the milder form of "*émotion.*"‡ ("*Sentiment*" is the more general term, usually encompassing both.) The German "*Leidenschaft,*" like the English "passion," has explicit connotations of "suffering," whereas "*Gefühl,*" the near equivalent of "emotion," has much milder and laudatory overtones (like so many German words that refer to the personality; contrast this with its derivative, Yiddish, whose psychological vocabulary consists almost entirely of terms of pathos; again, etymology anticipates ethology).

It is because of this history of the word "passion," embodying within it everything I wish to argue *against* (look at those dictionary entries again), that I have chosen it as the generic term to cover the entire range of those phenomena (a neutral word for the moment) that may be said to "move" us. The other side of this traditional image is the idea that, were it not for the passions,

‡ See, for example, Théodule Ribot, *Essai sur les Passions* (Paris: Alcan, 1912): "A passion is an emotion prolonged and intellectualized; passions are *explosive.*" See also J.-A. Rony, *Les Passions* (Paris: Presses Universitaires de France, 1961): "passions [are] violent emotions . . . incapable of adaption and obsessive." But compare M. Pradines (*Traite de Psychologie*) who, following Rousseau, contrasts the violence of both emotions and passions to calmer "sentimentality."

men would remain forever in a state of sloth. Freud canonized this myth in the name of science (first as the "Constancy Principle," later as the "Nirvana Principle"), arguing throughout his career that the "psychic apparatus" has a natural tendency to *inertia* (the principle is also called the "Law of Inertia"), as if God created man in order that he might sleep.* But why this supposition? And if physical models are preferred, why not "momentum" instead of inertia? Are we ever bodies at rest? And apart from our passions, do we have any personalities at all? Or even any consciousness?

My intention was to begin with an analysis and a critique of traditional philosophical theories of the emotion, especially in Aristotle, the Stoics and St. Augustine, Descartes, Hume, Spinoza, Hobbes, Rousseau, Whitehead and Sartre. I quickly found, however, that such an intention was bound to absorb my entire project, which, after all, was to get clear about "the passions" for myself, and share my thoughts with my readers. I also found, although I expected to find, that theories of the passions occupied at best a secondary role in the works of the great philosophers, usually dependent upon theses and doctrines that they had developed elsewhere, and rarely complete as analyses of emotion. This was true, for example, even of those few philosophers who chose to write separate "treatises" on the passions and gave them an important place in their over-all philosophy—Descartes and Hume most importantly. And when I started to describe the various analyses provided by Aristotle, whether his general account of the passions in *De Anima* or his specific analyses in the *Rhetoric*, I found myself qualifying and excusing, trying to explain the fact that Aristotle shared few of our psychological concepts and lacked any sense of what we call "subjectivity." Yet, at least superficially, his analysis of the passions as "activities" is nominally identical with our own—except that what he means by "activity" is very different from what we mean. The same is true of the Stoics, who argued, in a fashion, that the passions are *judgments*, again anticipating our own thesis, at least nominally. But I found myself

* Cf. Nietzsche: "Sleeping is no mean art; for its sake one must stay awake all day" (*Thus Spake Zarathustra*).

caught in academic scholarship and forced to choose between historical inaccuracies and a purely historical book. I chose to do neither. And again, my attempted studies of Descartes and Hume turned into small "treatises" of their own. Nietzsche's views on the passions are so varied and complex that it would be a short volume to separate them out, despite the fact that his actual suggestions occupy only assorted fragments and aphorisms. And Sartre, whom I have analyzed elsewhere,† surely deserves no less than a complete study of his own.

Accordingly, I have preferred to save these analyses for another publication and use this study as a forum for my own theory. I shall occasionally refer to those aspects of traditional theories with which I most strongly disagree—for example, Kant's infamous statement that the passions are "pathological" in contrast to "Practical Reason." But I otherwise leave it up to my colleagues to recognize the agreements and disagreements I have with previous thinkers.

2. Emotions, Moods, and Desires

There are three fundamental species of passions: (1) emotions, (2) moods, and (3) desires. There are any number of related expressions of zeal and enthusiasm, motivation and psychological attitudes, ranging in intensity from "attitudes" and "preferences" to "manias" and "obsessions." These might also be included as passions, but they are not of particular concern here. What all passions have in common is their ability to bestow *meaning* to the circumstances of our lives. Our emotions can turn routine and humdrum encounters into dramatic tragedies and farces. Our moods "tune us in" (in Heidegger's phrase) or "turn us off" (in more contemporary idiom) to the bland facts of the world. Desires convert mere "things" into goals and instruments, mere "facts" into conquests and frustrations, mere "possibilities" into

† "Sartre on Emotions," with questions to Sartre and answers, in Paul Arthur Schilpp, ed., *Sartre*, The Library of Living Philosophers (LaSalle, Ill.: Open Court, 1977).

ambitions, wishes, and hopes.‡ Every value and everything mean-ingful—as well as everything vile, offensive, or painful—comes into life through the passions. Against that familiar religious concep-tion of "happiness" and "wisdom" that would empty life of every emotion, mood, and desire in order to avoid pain and suffering, I insist that, without the passions, the very conceptions of "happi-ness," "love," "wisdom," and "joy" become unintelligible. Of the three kinds of passions, *emotions* appear to be the most sophis-ticated and complex. It is the web of our emotions that defines human subjectivity.

Moods are generalized emotions: An emotion focuses its atten-tion on more-or-less particular objects and situations, whereas a mood enlarges its grasp to attend to the world as a whole, typi-cally without focusing on any particular object or situation. Depression, for example, is aimed at the world in general, but it is constructed upon a base of particular emotions which remain at its core, visible but no longer distinctive. The emotion is the pre-cipitating particle that crystallizes the mood. The distinction is not always clear, since emotions can attend to objects of consid-erable generality. The world of a mood may also become so cramped that its focus becomes narrowed despite its universal scope. (A person can have a total view of a tiny world more easily than a broad view of a larger one. Thus, it is easier, in a depres-sion, to stay in one's room.)

To understand the nature of moods, one has to first under-stand the nature of emotions. Moods, in their indiscriminate universality, are metaphysical generalizations of the emotions. Re-ligious passion, for example, more often takes the form of mood rather than emotion. One might suggest that this is due to the in-trinsic universality of its object, but I expect that the argument ought to go the other way around; the universal nature of religious

‡ I do not intend these connections in a temporal order, as if first we perceive things, then goals, first facts, then values. This has been a common enough mistake in the history of philosophy. Rather I would want to agree with Heidegger and Max Scheler, as we argued in Chapter 2, that these are distinguished only after an extremely sophis-ticated act of reflection, that is, in the "objective viewpoint," and are not primordial distinctions of our experience.

objects is due to the fact that they are objects of a metaphysical mood. A particular emotion would inevitably shrink (and often has shrunken) the object of worship down to particular size. Not all desires are based upon emotions, of course. The most "primitive" desires of hunger and thirst, for example, precede all emotions and moods and may, in cases of extreme deprivation, give rise to appropriate emotions as desperate reactions. For a person who is well-enough fed and cared for, however, the desires that structure his or her life are not these primitive desires but rather desires built upon an emotional infrastructure, concern for personal reputations and standing among one's fellow men, desire for friendship and success, need for self-esteem, and the ultimate desire for happiness. These are not "instinctual" or "primitive" in any sense. Such desires, ambitions, wishes, and hopes are built upon the sophisticated conceptual and evaluative apparatus that is possible only in "rational" creatures who have the benefits of a complex self-referential and reflective language.* And these desires, unlike the purely biological needs for nourishment and survival, are built upon the structures provided by our emotions. Consequently, my theory of the passions will concentrate on an analysis of the emotions. (The relationship between the emotions and desires is extremely complex, and distinguishing them is not always easy.)

3. The Emotions Objectively Viewed: The Psychologist's Puzzle

An emotion is defined as a pattern of organic response. This formula is useful in the laboratory despite the fact that no one has shown how an emotional pattern can be distinguished from one which is nonemotional. A second definition has affirmed that

---

* This hierarchy of needs and the uniqueness of passions and their more complex derivative motives in man is developed in far more detail by A. Maslow, supported by R. Leeper, "A Motivational Theory of the Emotions," in Magda Arnold, ed., *The Nature of Emotion* (London: Penguin, 1962), p. 242, and in Pradines, *Traite de Psychologie*, p. 718.

emotion is a disturbance (disruption, upset) revealed by diffuse, excessive, aimless behavior.

P. T. Young, address to the Midwestern
Psychological Association, 1941

"What is an emotion?" One might think that question had long been settled by the psychologists, until, that is, he reads some academic psychology.[1] Some thirty years ago, the psychologist-scholar David Rapaport did an extensive survey of the literature on the emotions, distinguishing several prominent theoretical schools but objecting that much of it turned upon the "loose usage" and "terminological carelessness" of the idea of an emotion as a "discharge process." He concluded that psychologists had "lumped together many diverse phenomena . . . which should be kept carefully apart" and that the "physiological changes occurring in emotional states have been extremely dealt with in the literature but that the problem of 'emotion felt' had been somewhat neglected."[2]

The picture has changed considerably since then, but the "emotion felt" (one is *almost* compelled to say simply, "the emotion") has continued to be neglected. Understandably so, since emotion, as a predominantly subjective phenomenon, is hardly a fit subject matter for a conscientiously (if not defensively) "objective" science. As W. A. Hunt commented years ago, the psychologists are "willing to accept and discuss the subjective aspects of emotion, but unwilling to attempt a scientific treatment of them."[3] And Magda Arnold adds that "whether we like it or not . . . if [the] *experience* is excluded, there is not much that remains to be discussed."[4] But the very nature of the psychological discipline has seemed to exclude the characterization of any such experience, in contrast to its tangible physiological behavioral correlates. And so, as Rapaport argues, "the interest has dwelt on the problems of the expressions of emotions, the physiology of emotions in general, and the localization of the nervous actions of emotions in particular."[5]

Nothing today is as absurd as the views that were brazenly held by psychologists in the heyday of positivism, when K. Dunlap could declare, in the then-definitive Wittenberg Symposium of 1928:

> we should not be satisfied with any object of experience unless it is capable of physical or chemical registration. The "emotions" of which too many psychologists and most physiologists talk are not facts of this kind. Hence, I have no interest whatever in them. The visceral occurrences are demonstrable. Hence, when I use the term emotion, I mean these things.[6]

But the obsession with the tangible, the measurable, the quantifiable, and the visible continues.†

Here lies the psychologist's puzzle: How does one examine a peculiarly subjective phenomenon using only the tools of objective experimentation and research? How do you observe and measure this notoriously intangible dimension of human experience? One might argue that "objectivity" does not necessarily require "tangibility" or exclude the peculiarly "mental." Thus Wilhelm Wundt and E. B. Titchener attempted to objectively measure subjective phenomena in the early part of this century, but they still took the natural sciences (particularly physics) as their paradigm, beginning with the theory that emotions were nothing but feelings and complexes of feelings; consequently, they asked all the wrong questions and collected volumes of information of only historical interest, thus confirming the suspicions of the numerous anti-introspectionist psychologists that such experimental methods were futile. Today, it is simply *assumed* by most experimentalists that one cannot get objective results from subjective investigations. This view is probably mistaken, but I shall make no attempt to attack it here. It is enough to appreciate the puzzle it poses: Can a psychologist say anything of interest about the emotions?

† For example, look at the quick move from "emotions" to "emotional response" in H. Harlow and R. Stagner, *Psychological Review*, 1939; or, "emotions—or better—emotional behavior" in F. H. Lund, *Emotions* (New York: Ronald, 1939); or, at the extreme, E. Duffy, "An Explanation of 'Emotional' Phenomena Without the Use of the Concept of 'Emotion,'" *Journal of General Psychology*, 1941 (the title speaks for itself).

The answer, of course, ought to be yes, for it is clear that, in some sense, the phenomenon the psychologist investigates "objectively" ("What happens when a person has an emotion?") and the phenomenon that interests us subjectively ("What is it for me/us to have an emotion?") are the same. The mistake is only to think that either investigation can proceed without the other. Thus, the psychologists' inquiries are interesting—in fact, only make sense—in the context of the subjective experience of *personal* emotions. But then, too, it is clear that even subjectively my experience of my emotions cannot be severed from the "expression" of those emotions in the world, and an "objective" observer is often in a far better position to characterize and identify patterns in my expressive behavior than I may be myself. Psychologists often use the concept of "expression" to include physiological responses as well as actions, gestures, and verbal "expressions."[7] As we shall use this term, an "expression" is only one of a special kind of "objective manifestation" of an emotion, namely, that which "expresses." Thus, the psychologist's puzzle can be resolved only once he has willingly embraced the *subjective* phenomenon of emotions as the *basis* and subject matter of his inquiries, even if subjectivity is not his field of inquiry. The complementary puzzle, however, can be similarly resolved only insofar as it is accepted that subjectivity finds no clear boundaries between the emotion and its expression. Objective considerations, evidence from one's own behavior and its common syndromes ("being a case of . . ."), are among the most important tools in the reflective repertoire according to which one can understand and exercise his or her own emotions. Similarly, it will simply be assumed that every emotion has its correlate in the physiology of the central nervous system, on the good theory that "all conscious functions are dependent on their neural substrates,"‡ and that we can make use

‡ Ernst Gellhorn and G. N. Loofbourrow, *Emotions and Emotional Disorders* (New York: Harper & Row, 1963). There are problems with the notion of "correlate" here and notorious difficulties concerning the relations between the conscious and neurological "functions" in question. See Section 4 in this chapter and my "Doubts About the Correlation Thesis," *British Journal for the Philosophy of Science*, March 1975.

of such knowledge in altering—objectively—our own subjectivity. My interest lies primarily in the subjective nature of having an emotion, the "emotion felt" in Rapaport's phrase. This interest is neither incompatible with nor exclusive of the psychologist's interests, but one must beware of incorporating in a subjective account models and theories which are derivative of and appropriate only to the objective view. But I must insist that, in restricting attention to subjectivity, I am not thereby claiming that emotions *are* experiences and that the "emotion felt" is *all there is* to the emotion, the rest being various incidental effects. To insist on such a definition would only instigate further the all-too-protracted war between the one-sided biases of the experimental psychologists and the equally one-sided limitations of the "emotions-as-pure-experience" subjectivists.

If this project is complementary with the projects of psychology, one cannot simply proceed subjectively oblivious to the models and theories that have ruled psychological thought since university administrators determined that philosophy and psychology should be housed in separate departments. Objective models and theories are all too readily incorporated into subjective self-conceptions—for example, what I will call the "hydraulic model," appropriate to plumbing and engineering and perhaps to neurology but not, I shall argue, to a view of one's own emotions. Similarly, there is the more up-to-date computerese derivative of the same model, according to which people today often describe themselves in terms of "programs," "overload," and various quasi-electronic gibberish. When these models are themselves mistaken, even in the sphere of objectivity, the results can be disastrous. (It is worth stressing that the accuracy of a model is not necessarily a good indication of its subjective value. Freud's conception of "the Unconscious," for example, is a theoretically horrendous concept, but I would argue that there has been no more valuable tool in the struggle for human understanding despite its sometimes gross metaphorical deficiencies. The concept of the hypothalamus as the seat of the emotions, on the other hand, is probably a very good theory, but it has contributed very little to self-understanding, at least as yet. (See Chapter 4.)

There is a danger in the opposite direction as well, that psychologists might report as objective findings what in fact are only thinly veiled translations and extrapolations of their own subjectivity. (This is the point which, despite the nonsense which has followed it, earned J. B. Watson his place in psychology; he rightly objected to the free-wheeling and uninhibited anthropomorphism that had dominated animal psychology before him. It is ironic, therefore, that his own crude and extreme restrictions on the appropriate data and conceptions of psychology so limited the range of intelligible and interesting statements that psychologists could make about *human* behavior [except for the militant meta-psychological polemics which one has come to expect from B. F. Skinner] that they invited if not required this kind of deceit in order to give some substance to psychological inquiry.) But again, my concern is not that of the experimental psychologist but rather to clear the field of the objective infiltrations of psychological theories. Accordingly, while treatment of the last seventy years of psychology will be brief and critical, it should not be understood as a survey of psychology as such but rather an anticipatory goal response to our own primary motivation.*

4. The Hydraulic Model and Its Vicissitudes

Affects and emotions correspond with processes of discharge, the final expression of which is perceived as feeling.

Freud, "The Unconscious" (1915)

From an insider's point of view, the last seventy years of psychological theorizing in the United States would be extremely difficult to summarize, as one would expect in a field that is virtually overpopulated with original theorists and consequent ex-

---

* If this seems unfair, one need only glance at the one-sentence summaries afforded each of a half-dozen philosophers that grace the opening page or two of so many psychology books; e.g., Rapaport, *Emotion and Memory*, pp. 4–5 ("these few, necessarily historical sketches"), Arnold, *The Nature of Emotion*, p. 10 (one sentence), John Atkinson, *An Introduction to Motivation*, Introduction (New York: Van Nostrand, 1964).

change and embattlement involving any number of competing theories and models. From a philosopher's point of view, however, the last seventy years of American psychology can be easily summarized, as one would expect of a field in which the search for common presuppositions and paradigms is a professional obligation, if not a liability as well.†

From a seeming welter of theories and models, I want to single out a central theme. It has many variations, but in one form or another it has dominated the temperament if not also the content of both professional and "common sense" psychology for most of this century in both America and Europe. It is what I call the *hydraulic model*:[8]

> In certain persons, the explosive energy with which passion manifests itself on critical occasions seems correlated with the way in which they bottle it up during the intervals. . . . The sentimentalist is so constructed that "gushing" is his or her normal mode of expression. Putting a stopper on the "gush" will only to a limited extent cause more "real" activities to take its place; in the main it will simply produce listlessness. On the other hand the ponderous and bilious "slumbering volcano," let him repress the expression of his passions as he will, will find them expire if they get no vent at all. . . .
>
> William James, "What Is an Emotion?"

Forced to a quick generalization, acceptable to most psychologists as well as to critical outsiders, one might summarize recent history as the attempt to develop a "science" of psychology, which is, in a sense, to do no more than to make the relatively young discipline "respectable" next to its long-established colleagues in the natural and biological sciences. But the conception of "science" has changed radically in the past seventy years, stretched well past the limitations of the most vivid imagination by the turns in physics at the turn of the century. It was constricted almost to the point of suffocation by the positivism of the thirties and relativized in the sixties to the point where the best theoreticians of

† J. L. Austin is credited with something to the effect of, "I would say that oversimplification is a philosopher's occupational hazard, were I not also tempted to say that it is his occupation."

science had lost their grasp of any clear-cut criterion that would distinguish astronomy from astrology or electromagnetic field theory from witchcraft and ESP.[9] But psychology has had a problem in its choice of paradigms: It seems that its conception of "science" has always lagged behind, with its eye on achievements of the past rather than the conflicts of the present in other disciplines. A great many experimentalists are still implicitly committed to positivism in their conceptions of theory construction. (The same is notoriously true of current sociological research, and positivism still retains an unhealthily powerful hold in anthropology as well.[10])

At the turn of the century, when the claim that psychology could become a "science" was still something of a laughing matter, psychologists naturally turned to the most respectable paradigm of science they could find—the Newtonian model of force and attraction, quantitative calculations, and the movement of material particles. In the seventeenth century, Thomas Hobbes, Newton's near contemporary, had already attempted a crude psychological model much like Newton's theories. At the turn of the twentieth century, that was still the model in demand. And that is the basis of the hydraulic model, which is the attempt to characterize the workings of the human mind (or at least the behavior of the human body) in terms of Newtonian mechanical structures.

The history of American psychology has been defined by two giants, William James and Sigmund Freud. This inclusion of Freud may appear perverse, until one remembers that, whatever his origins, it was in America that Freud won his first unreservedly enthusiastic audiences, and it is only in America that he has maintained an uninterrupted claim as the foremost genius among psychologists.‡ Both Freud and James saw the foundation for a

‡ Though he may have lived his last years in London, his influence there has been and still is small despite the efforts of Ernest Jones and others. (I heard R. Sutherland bewail that matter in London in October 1974.) There are, of course, English authors who have been heavily influenced by Freud, for example, E. H. Gombrich in art criticism and R. Wollheim in philosophy, but by and large psychoanalysis has had far less impact on British thought than it has in America. In Germany and Austria psychoanalytic theory was disastrously curtailed by

scientific psychology in the newly developed science of neurology (and who could doubt that *it* deserved to be called a "science"?). In James the application of the new concepts of neurophysiology to the psychology of the emotions was direct and unhesitating. In his theory an emotion is nothing other than an awareness of certain changes in our physiology. This reduced to a mere "epiphenomenon"* the troublesome *feeling* of the emotion and refocused the psychologist's attention upon the indisputably scientific problem of the "localization" of the relevant physiological changes. James's theory (developed independently by the Danish psychologist C. G. Lange, and so called the "James-Lange theory") dominated psychology in both America and Europe until the second quarter of the century. But even when the theory had been discredited, the emphasis on the physiological correlates of emotion continued to take precedence over the emotion itself; more importantly, the physiological model that was appropriate to neurology continued to dominate thinking about emotion.

Freud's theory is far more complex than James's simple reductionist theory. Although James also insisted throughout his career that psychological concepts must eventually be demonstrated to have a neurological foundation, this "eventually" gave him hesitation and led him, often explicitly, to divorce at least temporarily his conception of the "psychic apparatus" from the details of neurological anatomy and physiology. The model he adopted, however, and which he continued to develop until his last writings, is based solely upon structures and terminology he had

---

the Nazis, forcing Freud and most of his followers to leave for other parts of the world (mainly America, particularly between Fifth Avenue and the East River above Forty-second Street). In France Descartes, Pascal, and Rousseau have always commanded more allegiance than either Freud or the Newtonian conception of "scientific psychology." Accordingly, although the French defended their own conception of "scientific psychology" at the turn of the century (introduced by Ribot and others at the same time that James was working in Boston and Freud in Vienna), their work has far more the earmarks of Cartesian subjectivity than the stress on experimentalism that we find in America and Germany.

* That is, roughly, an unimportant by-product.

derived as early as 1895 from his neurological studies.† It is in Freud that one finds the clearest statements of the hydraulic model; and it is Freud who must be singled out for his immensely influential "scientific" formulation of a mistaken model of the emotions that had ruled Western thought since the Greeks.

In "prescientific" psychological thinking the concepts of "force" and "energy," "animal spirits" and "bodily fluids" (bile, gall, phlegm, etc.), were permitted a holiday‡ of poetic and metaphorical explorations, consequently structuring language and thought about the passions within an unabashed and uncritical (though admittedly dramatic and often charming) hydraulic model. It quite literally views the human psyche as a caldron of pressures demanding their release in action and expression. With the advent of scientific psychology, however, the metaphor required a tangible basis, which James and Freud simultaneously located in the components of the central nervous system.* Even in 1895 there could be no doubting the thesis that the phenomena of consciousness were in every case to be referred back to the central nervous system, a system which was indisputably mechanical in its operations. Thus, James explicitly argued that emotions were nothing other than the *affects* of neurological processes, in particular, neurological disturbances demanding expression in action of some kind. Thus, Freud argued that the passions in general, which he variously designated as "affects," "impulses," "instincts," "psychic energies," "libidinal energies," and "forces," were precisely the pressures of a (yet unknown) "quantity" (which he simply designated "Q"). This quantity flowed through the newly identified tubular containers of the nervous system, the *neurones*. But even when he gave up the attempt to base his model of the psychic apparatus on straightforwardly neuroanatomical structures, the model of the psyche he proposed was always couched in the language of hydraulics ("cathexis" means filling, "catharsis"

† I have argued this thesis in detail in my "Freud's Neurological Theory of Mind," in Richard C. Wollheim, ed., *Freud* (Garden City: Doubleday Anchor, 1974), but will not repeat that argument here.

‡ In Wittgenstein's sense of "language going on holiday."

* See James, *Principles of Psychology*, Vol. 1, first several chapters, and Freud, esp., *Project for a Scientific Psychology*, in the standard edition of his works, Vol. 3.

release, and also "flow," "channeling," and the names of most of the so-called defense mechanisms). His famous conception of "psychic energy," for example, was but another "scientific" appeal to the established concepts of Newtonian physics.

Regarding the emotions in particular, Freud is much more difficult to pin down than James. He makes no clear distinction between the emotions and other "impulses" or "instincts," and his employment of the term "affect" is notoriously inconsistent. He often appears to identify "affect" and emotion, thus viewing the emotions, like James, as *results* of forces in consciousness rather than forces themselves. But he occasionally uses the terms in conjunction (as in the headnote to this section), and in the space of a short essay he will defend *both* the thesis that an affect is an instinct whose "representation" in consciousness is an "idea" and the contrasting thesis that an affect is a property (which he sometimes calls "affective tone") or an accompaniment of an idea which may be separated from it. (Thus, in the section of his essay "The Unconscious" entitled "Unconscious Emotions" he argues that an "unconscious emotion" is one whose affect has been displaced from its idea; only the idea is repressed, not the affect. But in that same section he discusses the possibility of the suppression of the affect as well, and also its possible conversion into anxiety.[11])

I believe that at least three different conceptions of the emotions can be identified in Freud's writings, each stressing one of the three features of "instinct" (the psychic forces that threaten consciousness), "idea" (the representation of an instinct in consciousness), and "affect" (the conscious *effects* of an instinct, which may or may not accompany its idea). The terminology varies, but, trying to hold these three terms in place, the three conceptions are:

1. The emotion as the "instinct" itself, the force that rages against the ego demanding expression. Thus, when talking about "instincts," Freud typically mentions emotions, particularly love, anger, hatred, jealousy, and guilt. In fact, most of the "instincts" he discusses, particularly the "ego-instincts," are emotions rather than "instincts" or mere "impulses."

2. The emotion as an instinct bound to an idea. In his middle works (1900–15) Freud often talks about an instinct "bound" to

an object through the "cathexis" of an idea in what he calls the "secondary process." In this view, the emotion is not merely the instinct alone, which need have no particular object, but a particular attitude toward a particular person or event.

3. The emotion as affect. Freud, like James, often talks as if an emotion were nothing other than an epiphenomenal effect in consciousness of the dynamic interchanges of forces, appearing as *anxiety*. (It is worth noting that Freud's classification of the various "instincts" varies systematically with the view of emotions he holds.)

Whichever conception is given preference (and all occupy significant portions of Freud's discussions), here is the hydraulic model in its clearest form: Pressures from the unconscious threaten to enter consciousness in their demands for "discharge." On any of the three conceptions, an emotion is not our doing but something that happens to us. On the first and second conceptions, it is a force that threatens us; on the third, it is the effect of a force that threatens us. Whatever happens in consciousness, it is but the resultant of a dynamic system of forces operating outside of and independently of consciousness.

The hydraulic model need not be based upon physiology. (In fact, the hydraulic model preceded any suggestion of the influence of the nervous system on psychology by many centuries.) Nor does it require anything like Freud's conception of an "unconscious." It requires only the category of *passivity* regarding consciousness—the idea that the emotions (and the passions in general) are inflicted upon us or caused in us by psychic or bodily or environmental forces beyond our control. They demand "discharge" in action, whether direct (for example, punching one's boss, who has just made him furious), symbolic (kicking one's desk, because the boss has just made him furious), or aimless and diffuse (jumping up and down, screaming, and tearing one's hair, because his boss has just made him furious). The key to the hydraulic model is the idea that emotions and other passions (or their determinants) exist wholly independently of consciousness, effecting (or "affecting") consciousness and often forcing us to behave in certain discernible ways.

The net result of the contribution of both James and Freud and the hydraulic model in general is to minimize the importance of consciousness.† There is no need, on this model, to speak of a conscious *agency* at all; consciousness is an "epiphenomenon," in James's phrase. There are forces pressing for discharge in behavior, which have effects in consciousness. From here, it is but a small step to the suggestion that consciousness can be *ignored* in the study of behavior, and an even smaller step, though replete with metaphysical atrocities, to the thesis that there is no need to talk about "consciousness" in psychology at all.‡

In other words, "behaviorism"* is in fact a purified and streamlined version of the hydraulic model, focusing its attention exclusively on the variables determining behavior and their observable effects without bothering with the "mental way station" (in Skinner's phrase) of consciousness. It is the completion of that model, perhaps overdoing it by a step or two, and underscores the great *un*importance of consciousness in psychology by failing to reckon with it altogether.

Of course, it is not the case that all of psychology of the past

† One is reminded of an observation by Nietzsche (himself very much a hydraulic "energy" theorist) that we do not begin to appreciate consciousness until we realize just how dispensable it is (*Gay Science*).

‡ When Watson made this final move in 1924, in his *Behaviorism*, the previous steps had been firmly established for thirty years. Like most "revolutions," the behaviorist turn in American psychology had been virtually completed before the revolution. Watson may have stormed the Bastille, but only after James and Freud had emptied it of its inmates and convened the convention already signifying without yet celebrating the fall of the old order. If Freud in particular is curiously neglected in contemporary academic psychology, one need only be reminded that he was in fact responsible for the shift away from the mandatory introspective discursions of consciousness to the emphasis on third-person observation, behavioral analysis, and hypothetical inference that define twentieth-century psychology.

* By "behaviorism," I do not mean that "black box" variety that rigorously insists upon an absolute void of content: no hypotheses of inner working, no inferences to unseen structures, forces, instincts, or mechanisms; just independent and dependent variables with nothing in between. This is not a version of the hydraulic model. It is not a model!

forty years is behavioristic; but it must be admitted that even those who staunchly opposed behaviorism were intimidated by the well-established arguments against the primacy of consciousness. Nor am I suggesting that every psychological theory of the emotions since James and Freud fits the hydraulic model; there are exceptions, particularly recently, to which I will refer in subsequent discussion. But the hydraulic model has certainly been the dominant if not definitive structural theory of the psychology of the emotions,[12] and not surprisingly, considering that the same model has been almost exclusive in our prescientific thinking for over two thousand years.

Psychological theories of emotion have tended to focus selectively on either the physiological correlates of emotion, the "emotion felt" or "feeling" of emotion, or the effects of the various emotions on behavior.[13] The attempt to *define* an emotion in terms of its physiological correlates has been generally conceded to be a hopeless enterprise (since W. B. Cannon's rebuttal of the James-Lange theory in the 1930s; see the following chapter). Yet an extraordinary amount of research has been devoted to distinguishing and, where possible, localizing these various neurological and visceral correlates. At least one prominent theorist has recently attempted to revive the equation of emotions and their physiology; D. O. Hebb has defended the James-Lange theory and proposed the strictly physiological thesis that "the word 'emotion' can be useful to refer to the neural processes that produce emotional behavior."[14]

Focusing rather on the experiential component of James's theory, a great many theorists—and most nonpsychologists—have held to the traditional mentalistic interpretation of an emotion as a species of feeling or "affect"—a sense of flushing and pulsing, anxiety and nervous tension, a feeling of slight breathlessness and a combination of weakness and preparedness. For each emotion, it was supposed that there would be a distinct set of vague yet identifiable feelings and sensations. The idea that "emotions are feelings" strikes most people as a trivial truth, not as a psychological theory at all. Yet it was the attempt to translate this common-sense view into a scientifically respectable theory that brought about the introduction of the "experimental method" in psychology.[15] However, whatever its common-sense support and its seeming triviality, this "feeling" view of emotions does violence to our concept of the emotions, whether or not it is coupled with the hydraulic model as such. (Usually it is; the feelings are taken to be the epiphenomenal "affects" of psychic or physiological hydraulic pressures. [See Chapter 7, Section 2.])

The hydraulic theory as such has remained the model of most followers of Freud, retaining the quasi-Newtonian concepts of "energy" and "force."[16] The concept of "psychic energy" has long been central to psychoanalytic theory, in Freud's own late theories,[17] in more recent work by Morton Prince,[18] and in Kenneth Colby.[19] Such energy theories, however, predate Freud's "scientific" version. For example, in Spinoza's *Ethics* we find, "By emotion [*affectus*] I understand the modification of energy of the body by which the power of action is aided or restrained." C. G. Jung's theory is also based almost entirely upon the hydraulic model (combined as in Freud with an instinct theory plus his own contribution, a theory of archetypal symbolism): "Emotions are not 'made' or willfully produced, in and by consciousness. . . . They appear suddenly, leaping up from an unconscious region."[20] To Freud's more Newtonian theory, Jung adds a dramatic personification: "An emotion *is* the intrusion of an unconscious personality. . . . To the primitive mind, a man who is seized by strong emotion is possessed by a devil or a spirit; and our language still expresses the same idea, at least metaphorically. There is much to be said for this point of view."[21] It is this passivity of the hydraulic theory that is basic to the Myth of the Passions, whether or not it includes a conception of the emotions as feelings or "affects," and whether it takes the physicalistic form of Freud's theory or Jung's more mythological archetypes. Any theory that views the emotions as forces, effects, or intrusions which are anything other than our own activities must be subjectively rejected.

Most of the theories that have dominated psychology in America and England have been neither purely physiological nor simple-mindedly mentalistic nor straightforwardly hydraulic as such. William McDougall, for example, borrowed a single strain of Freudian theory and identified an emotion as "a specific quality that is the affective aspect of the operation of an *instinct*,"[22] a "mode of experience incidental to the striving activities of the organism."[23] This instinct theory of the emotions borrows from the respectability of biology in much the same fashion that the straightforward hydraulic theory borrowed from physics. It has enjoyed continuing popularity in the now widely known experiments of Konrad Lorenz[24] and Nikolaas Tinbergen,[25] dubiously extended to human behavior by Lorenz[26] and Desmond Morris.[27] The instinct theory has even been resurrected within the professional confines of behaviorism.[28] But whatever its popularity, the instinct theory, related in temperament if not always in form to the hydraulic model, emerges as a hollow technical pretense which again attempts to reduce our emotions to something less than wholly human and distinctly beyond the range of our own responsibilities. However appropriate such a theory might be in the demonstrably unlearned, inherited, stereotyped, and unadaptable behavior of the courting patterns of a certain kind of fighting fish, human behavior and emotion can never be so characterized. Every time one adopts such a viewpoint (for example, "It's only human nature"), he or she is guilty of precisely this self-serving and irresponsible self-deception.

Closer to my own thesis is a number of theories which have emerged in recent years—those which interpret emotions as a species of *motives*[29] (although then it becomes a question of whether motives are to be considered as our own doings or not) and those which call themselves "cognitive" and "appraisal" theories.[30] This last set of theories already anticipates my own theory of the emotions as evaluative *judgments*, not the blind or stupid forces that one finds in all hydraulic and instinct theories. In European, particularly French, psychology, this "cognitive" view of the emotions has long been preferred to the more mechanical models of hydraulics. Pascal,[31] for example, insisted that the emotions gave us a special kind of "insight," and in this century Henri Bergson[32] has defended a similar notion of "intuition" regarding the emotions. In Germany Leibniz once argued that the emotions were a "confused" intelligence, and more recently the psychologist Johann Friedrich Herbart and the phenomenologist Max Scheler[33] have developed such theories of the emotions in some detail. And in England a number of recent philosophical and psychological works have stressed the close *logical* relationships between emotion and cognition in general.[34]

There have been many other theories, of course, most of them variations on one or another version of hydraulic, motivational, or instinct theories,[35] given the distinct behavioristic preferences of most recent authors. There are also variations on the common-sense "feeling" theory.[36] These particular variations are of no special concern. The thesis I am challenging is quite general, cutting through the often hair-breadth distinctions between one psychological school and another. *Are our emotions beyond our control?* Jung has said that "there are things in the psyche which I produce and those which I do not, but which produce themselves and have their own life."[37] Jung has argued, along with virtually every psychological theorist of this century and before, that emotions are of the latter variety. I shall argue that they are rather of the former.

CHAPTER 4: PHYSIOLOGY, FEELINGS, AND BEHAVIOR

1. Physiological Complications

> . . . our feeling of [bodily] changes as they occur *is* the emotion.
>
> William James, "What Is an Emotion?" (1884)
>
> . . . these [visceral] disturbances cannot serve as a means for discriminating between . . . emotions.
>
> W. B. Cannon, "The James-Lange Theory of Emotion" (1927)

Of course, it is true that every emotion has its distinguishable neurological correlates.* Or at least there is utterly no reason to believe that it is not true, at least in some sense.† But what does

---

* See, for example, Ernst Gellhorn and G. N. Loofbourrow, *Emotions and Emotional Disorders* (New York: Harper & Row, 1963); and M. Arnold, *The Nature of Emotion*, essays nos. 23 and 27, and, by the same author, *Emotion and Personality* (New York: Columbia University Press, 1960); D. G. Glass, *Neurophysiology and Emotion* (Sage Foundation, Rockefeller University Press, 1967); and West and Greenblatt, *Explorations in the Physiology of Emotions* (APA Report 12, 1960).

† There are serious but often unappreciated problems concerning what is to be correlated with what. The old "phrenological" assumption of a one-to-one correlation between a mental process and a brain process has been repudiated by most neurologists. The workings of the "higher" centers of the brain are simply not that simple. (See my "Doubts About the Correlation Thesis," *British Journal for the Philosophy of Science*, March 1975.) But the thesis can surely be restated in some such way that the ever-increasing fund of "correlations" and "localizations" can be given some indisputable role in a psychophysical theory.

that have to do with *my* having an emotion? Most philosophers would be a little too quick to say "nothing," assuming that our concept of an "emotion" included only those properties which are commonly recognized by virtually all speakers of the language. It is easy enough to show that our everyday concept of "emotion" has no *logical* connections with neurology. For example, Aristotle could identify his emotions perfectly well without knowing the first thing about neurophysiology; he thought their physiological source was the heart, not the brain. The "man on the street" probably knows less about the workings of his brain than Descartes did three hundred years ago; yet he has an adequate conceptual grasp of the language of emotions. But this facile argument is worth far less than many philosophers have thought. It may be a "knock-down" argument where "ordinary" language is concerned, but it arbitrarily excludes the idea of *embellishment* of our present-day conception (something short of a *change* of concepts) by physiological knowledge, an embellishment that has proceeded rapidly in the past decade but which was beginning even with Aristotle. We all know that certain chemicals—alcohol, Dexedrine, barbiturates, hashish, and mescaline—alter our states of consciousness considerably, and we have an idea of how they do this: They affect certain centers in the brain, speed them up, slow them down, open them up. As this admittedly crude knowledge of neurology progresses, there is no reason to doubt that, several generations from now, the man on the street will have a language of emotions heavily embedded in neurological jargon.‡ There is only a difference in the precision of the knowledge now increasingly embellishing our conception of emotions and the knowledge that will embellish the conceptions held by our grandchildren. And the difference between our knowledge and that of Aristotle is a matter of precision, not ignorance versus knowledge. I do not wish to make it sound as if the very recent science of psychoneurology is doing no more than mopping up details, that,

‡ The extremes of this thesis—the idea that such neurological understanding could *replace* our mentalistic language of the emotions— has been persuasively argued in a now-classic paper by R. Rorty, in S. Hampshire, ed., *The Philosophy of Mind* (New York: Harper & Row, 1966).

from within the scope of that science, there are no "qualitative" leaps in our knowledge—almost yearly. My point is only that the situation is not as if we now have *no* knowledge which affects our conception of our emotions; even Aristotle knew that heavy drink made a man insensitive and potentially brutal, and his thesis that the emotions are "more primitive" than the clarity of reason surely included this essential correlation between drunkenness and the emotions. Similarly, we also know that our emotional lives become much richer with certain drugs, much more "open" with others, and are virtually paralyzed with yet others. It is this knowledge that provides the basis for much of our thinking about the emotions, particularly what we have called the hydraulic theory. These are also precisely the considerations that led James and Lange to their now famous theory of the emotions—to the effect that an emotion is *nothing but* our awareness of these chemical and physiological changes in our bodies. (Lange, in particular, stresses these arguments.) Our problem, therefore, is to understand the role of this "objective" knowledge in the subjective conception of ourselves.

The most tempting thesis, and a most disastrous one, is simply to accept the "objective" findings of neurology as the exclusive truth and to incorporate these findings into one's self-conception, relegating his "feelings" and the subjective components of emotion to the role of "illusions" or "epiphenomenal affects." This was the thesis argued by James and Lange,[1] and it dominated psychological thinking for thirty years. That thesis is, in its most basic form, that the physiology of emotion is primary, the "emotion felt" a secondary consequence; it is, in James's words, "the priority of the bodily symptoms to the felt emotion":

> Our natural way of thinking about these standard emotions is that the mental perception of some fact excites the mental affection called the emotion, and that this latter state of mind gives rise to the bodily expression. My thesis on the contrary is that the bodily changes follow directly the PERCEPTION of the exciting fact, and that our feeling of the same changes as they occur *is* the emotion.
>
> William James, "What Is an Emotion?"

The James-Lange thesis was proven to be incorrect on physiological grounds, primarily by W. B. Cannon,[2] who argued conclusively that the same visceral and neurological changes accompanied very different emotional states and that artificial induction of these changes did not produce the appropriate emotions:

> Since visceral processes are fortunately not a considerable source of sensation, since even extreme disturbances in them yield no noteworthy emotional experience, we can further understand now why these disturbances cannot serve as a means for discriminating between such profound emotions as fear and rage, why chilliness, asphyxia, hyperglycemia and fever, though attended by these disturbances, are not attended by emotion. . . .
>
> W. B. Cannon, "The James-Lange
> Theory of Emotion"

Related experiments have often been repeated since,[3] each time with a sense of "break-through," so entrenched is the *kind* of thinking that the James-Lange thesis represents in contemporary psychology. That thinking is fundamentally to pay close attention to the tangible and mechanical; and to neglect or ignore, what is glibly and conciliatorily designated as "the emotion felt." It should not come as a surprise that the refutation of the James-Lange thesis almost exactly coincided with the upsurge of behaviorism in America;* having lost the warrant to identify the emotions with physiological processes, psychologists turned to the equally tangible equation of the emotions and their behavioral expressions. If decidedly different emotions could not be distinguished on the basis of their physiological correlates, perhaps one could do so on the basis of their behavioral expression, still without entering the forbidden realm of subjectivity (see Chapter 6, Section 2, but cf. the Young quote, pp. 134–35).

Since Cannon's discrediting of the James-Lange theory, the particular error of identifying the emotions with the epiphenomenal affects of physiological changes in the body has not been a problem. But the danger of the James-Lange thesis was not dependent

---

* In Germany it gave way to the more subjective movement of the Gestaltists. See, for example, A. Lehman's early critique of James and Lange, in M. Arnold, *The Nature of Emotion*, pp. 37–42.

on its particular claims so much as its over-all tendency to incorporate into our conception of ourselves and into our own emotions concepts which were wholly neglectful of subjectivity.† The opposing position, far more popular among philosophers than psychologists, is not better—that the "emotion felt" *is* the emotion, as if neurology had *nothing* to do with it.

This is why I began by warning that our everyday emotional conceptions are not exclusive of quasi-neurological knowledge and influence. So long as we focus on the technical disputes between those who believe that emotional reactions are centered in the hypothalamus and those who more conservatively defend the role of the thalamus, the relevance of neurology to our conceptions of our own emotions will be negligible. But turn instead to our everyday experiences with neurology, leaving the "localization" and the neural and endocrine mechanisms of these processes for the experts, and the problem is much more interesting. At the present time, narrowly neurological conceptions have virtually no role in our subjectivity, excepting a small number of professional neurologists and hypochondriacs.

Consider: This morning I drank three cups of coffee. (My "limit" is one cup.) I was "wired" and irritable; I growled at my students and bitched to the personnel office; I almost got into a fight with another driver and sent my lunch at Gino's back to the "kitchen" with an angry complaint. My students were innocent; the matter at the personnel office was the usual red tape which I wade through unthinkingly every morning; it was I and not the other driver who had been inconsiderate; and the lunch at Gino's was just another lunch at Gino's. Yet I was angry in each case—or had some related emotion (I was *impatient* with my students but indignant with the personnel office). Now, the philosopher's argument that the charging up of my limbic system is irrelevant to my anger is no doubt correct. But what of these cases? My coffee drinking quite obviously *caused* my anger in each case. The general relationship between my drinking too much coffee and my being "irritable" is well known to me. And afterward, at least with my students, I will surely apologize and dismiss my irritation with

† "Emotion felt" was merely a concession to Cartesian dualism.

them as "just the coffee" or "just irritation," not anger *with them* at all. Was this, because of the cause, not "really" anger at all? What does my knowledge of the *cause* have to do with my conception of my anger? The answers to these questions can only be anticipated, since I have yet to provide a general account of the nature of an emotion in which the concept of "cause" can be given its place. But the following can be said: *Whatever* the cause, my emotion itself is "real"—I should say "surreal." That is, I am angry with my students *because* of my having had too much coffee, but I am angry nonetheless. My after-the-fact apology is surely justified, but my denial that "I was 'really angry' " or that "I was angry *at them*" is not. That is my *excuse*—my attempt to blame the coffee (or possibly to accept the blame for having let myself be given the second and third cups). I was really angry, but unjustifiably so. It is the *unjustifiability* of my anger that requires the apology. The coffee, the cause, has nothing to do with it. If this were not the case, then one could plead innocence to all his emotions! We all accept, in some form or another, the neurologist's claim that all of our emotions have their neurological causes. And even though we don't have the foggiest notion what such causes might be, we accept the claim that *every* emotion has its sufficient neurological cause, thus allowing us to excuse ourselves from "really" having that emotion in every case. But this is absurd. Whether I am angry or not, in love or not, jealous or not, has nothing to do with whether or not my anger, my love, or my jealousy has been caused. We may presume, in every case, that it has. But my emotion has nothing to do with the fact that it is caused. (With even this simple understanding of this "excuse" system, one can see why the hydraulic model, which is nothing other than a system of providing, in every case, some such causal excuse, will be so well worth our constant opposition.)

To say that physiological cause has nothing to do with emotion or that *the fact that* an emotion is caused by some physiological alteration has nothing to do with the (sur)"reality" of the emotion is not yet to say that my *knowledge* of such causes and facts has nothing to do with the emotion. In retrospect, I remembered the fact that I had drunk three cups of coffee, and knowing the effect coffee always has on my temperament, I then understood *why* I had gotten so unusually irritated that day. But suppose that

I had come to that realization during, not after, the period of my anger. What would have happened then? I would have stood in my class, fidgety and cranky, but fully aware that I was likely to find fault where there was none. I would have become impatient when there was no reason for it, and I would accordingly *cancel* all such emotions as they appeared (perhaps warning my students as well). My knowledge of the cause *undermines* my emotion. I am still irritable, but I do not allow myself to be irritable *about* anything or *at* anyone. I am simply irritable. In retrospect, I cannot cancel the "aboutness" of my irritability and deny my anger; but in the process of becoming angry I surely can do so. And so, coupled with the thesis that the cause of my emotion has nothing to do with the emotion, there is a second thesis, superficially contrasted with it: My knowledge of the cause of my emotion tends to undermine the emotion. This is a partial explanation of the fact that apparently any crackpot psychotherapy, no matter how absurd its theories or ludicrous (or lucrative) its practices, tends to have a calming effect on the emotions. It is the attribution of a cause, *any* cause, that does it.

One of the best known psychophysiological experiments concerning the emotions performed in recent years was that carried out by S. Schachter and J. E. Singer. They injected their subjects with epinephrine—the adrenal secretion that is responsible for the most marked sensations of emotions (flushing, pulsating, anxiousness)—and then provided different subjects with different social situations. What was "discovered" was that the physiological changes and their accompanying sensations had nothing to do with the differentiation of the emotion, a conclusion reached by Cannon thirty years before. In fearful circumstances, the injected subject reported feeling fear; in offensive circumstances, he reported feeling anger. For those who continue to cling to the art of experimentation as the only source of truth, here is an empirical foundation for the claims that I shall be making "subjectively," that the chemistry of the body and the sensations caused by that chemistry have in themselves nothing to do with the emotions.‡

‡ It is not unusual for the National Science Foundation to provide elaborate funds and equipment for the empirical substantiation of what any philosopher worth his salt could prove to be a logical truth in a matter of an hour or so. And philosophers are much less expensive as well.

But it is also worth heeding the warnings of equally experimentally oriented critics of that experiment, who rightly comment that the "injection procedure limits the conclusions that can be drawn about emotion in the normal life situation."[4] To put it mildly. Apart from the students' minor trauma of injection and the artificial sterility of the laboratory, there is a logical thesis that is relevant here; namely, the *knowledge* that their emotions have been caused by the injection is already sufficient to undermine the emotions themselves.

There are other causes of emotion besides physiological causes, and an adequate defense of the two theses above should wait for a more general account. (See Chapter 8, Section 2.) My purpose here has been only to show the simple-mindedness of the two usual methods of dealing with the relationship between emotions and physiology—reducing the former to the consciousness manifestations of the latter or denying the relevance of the latter to the former altogether. Matters are not so simple. We are not simply hydraulic mechanisms, voltage cells, or boilers, who happen to have this curious attachment, consciousness—like a galvanometer attached to the cell or a valve on the boiler—that passively registers the pressures within. But neither are we Cartesian spirits, attached to our pumping and pulsing bodies through a thin passage in a minor gland at the base of our brains, for whom the workings of the physical world are a matter of interest but, so far as our passions are concerned, of no relevance. What we know partially determines what we "feel," and this is as true of the workings of our brains as it is of our circumstances.

2. Emotions as Feelings and Sensations

With or without the hydraulic model, the most common and even unquestionable thesis among nonpsychologists is that emotions are *feelings* of a special kind, typically conjoined with certain specific and readily identifiable *sensations*.* Even our lan-

* The concept of "feeling" has many different uses, ranging from the "feeling" (i.e., sensation) of cold water running down one's leg to the "feeling" of satisfaction one gains after winning a difficult tennis match, to "feelings" of anxiety and depression and "feeling like" leav-

guage embodies this identity: We "feel" angry or jealous; love and hate are our "feelings" for other people; disappointments and insults "hurt our feelings." But this linguistic phenomenon is only the result, not the origin, of this familiar and trivially obvious equation. Whatever the hidden "dynamics" of the emotions, their essential manifestation is thought to be *in consciousness* as *feelings*. (Thus, Freud constantly complained that his view of "the Unconscious" flew in the face of common sense and the usual "way of talking" (*façon de parler*).

It is obvious that "being in a passion" and "becoming emotional" are regularly associated with certain feelings and sensations, the flushing and pulsing and tightness of the throat, tension in our arms and legs and mild cramping in the stomach, slight breathlessness and nausea, an over-all feeling of readiness and excitement. But it does not follow from this regular association that these feelings and sensations *are* the emotion. Thus, in the last chapter I noted that Freud and a great many other psychologists augment the Jamesian claim that an emotion is simply an affect (that is, simply a feeling) with some version of the hydraulic theory that would allow that an emotion also has a role in the dynamics of the personality (for example, as energy or instinct, as motive or cognitive appraisal). However predictable the association of feelings and emotion, the feelings no more constitute or define the emotion than an army of fleas constitutes a homeless dog. They are always there, take the shape of the emotion, but just as easily move from one emotion to another (love to hate, fear to anger, jealousy to resentment). Feeling is the ornamentation of emotion, not its essence.

It is easy to appreciate this in a simple "introspective" way (although it has been given more objective experimental support in the Schachter-Singer experiment discussed in the previous section). What is the difference in feeling between a common pair of emotions—for example, embarrassment and shame? People are

---

ing town. And, of course, there is the central synonymy between feelings and emotions (love, hate, jealousy, etc.). As I am employing the term here, a feeling is but a nonlocalizable sensation, as, for example, "feeling nauseous." I will define the term more distinctly in the discussion on "intentionality" (Chapter 8, Section 1), distinguishing it sharply from "emotion."

rarely, if ever, confused about which emotion they "have," but, when asked to differentiate between them, they find themselves speechless. Of course, one might say that differences in feelings and sensations are typically difficult to articulate, like the slight difference in taste between two bottles of wine that are so easily distinguishable but about which one has no vocabulary to express the difference. But this is not the problem; emotions are not distinguished by discriminating one set of feelings and sensations from another. In fact, the feelings and sensations associated with the one emotion may be and usually are no different from those associated with the other. But now imagine two situations: In the first, you are standing in line to board a bus when a crowd behind you pushes you abruptly and you fall, unable to catch yourself, into an elderly woman, knocking her into the rain-soaked gutter. In the second, obeying a malicious whim, you push her—with the same result. Following both incidents, you find yourself confronting an irate elderly woman and suffering from an intense feeling of . . . of what? In the first case, obviously embarrassment, in the second, shame. But how can we even guess what we would *feel* in some hypothetical example? How can we be so sure which is which? Because the feelings and sensations involved in the two emotions are of little relevance to discriminating between emotions. What allows us to do so is what I shall call the "logic" of the situation. Briefly, the first case is one of embarrassment because it is a situation in which, though we find ourselves in an awkward situation, we see no need to take responsibility for that situation. In the second case, we recognize our own action— however "spontaneous" and unthinking—as the cause of the situation: We are responsible. Of course, there are feelings in both cases; they might even, upon close inspection, have some differences between them. (Perhaps shame involves more constriction of the throat, and embarrassment includes more flushing. Physiologists, for example, have separated two distinct adrenal secretions, one more prevalent in "fight" reactions and the other more prevalent in "flight" reactions; presumably there would be some differences in feeling as well.) But the emotions are not merely the feelings, and the feelings are not what distinguishes one emotion from another. (The same sort of argument applies to any number of other emotion pairs—for example, love and hate, anger and indignation, resentment and envy, sadness and remorse, guilt and despair.)

A second objection to this familiar equation between emotions and feelings consists of the simple fact that we often have an emotion without experiencing any particular feeling. Anger or envy may be sufficiently subdued, perhaps with the long discipline of suppression, perhaps simply because it is long-established and familiar—still as powerful as it was in the beginning, but no longer given to "outbursts" of intensity and feeling. In fact, we sometimes find that our passion is so intense that we can feel absolutely nothing. In the most extreme indignation, one finds oneself completely numb. In panic, running from fear, one might find that one feels nothing. Or, more positively, there are those tender moments of love after "making love" when all the feeling has been drained from us, but the emotion is at its peak. Emotions may typically involve feelings. They may even essentially involve feelings. But feelings are never sufficient to identify or to differentiate emotions, and an emotion is never simply a feeling. One can have an emotion without feeling anything, and one can feel anything (including all of the "symptoms" of emotionality, for example, flushing, pulsing) without having any emotion whatever.

The close association of emotions and feelings is symptomatic of a dangerous misrepresentation of the emotions that I attacked in Chapter 5. There are, of course, those impassioned or emotional states of crisis and urgency, in which emotional *feeling* is at its height as a consequence of the preparatory posture we assume, for example, immediately before we allow months of "pent-up" anger to "explode." Such crises are apparent as one approaches an object of fear, ready for the decisive battle, or as I confess an obsessive love to the person I once thought I knew, but who now stands before me in ominous and foreign silence. But having an emotion is not limited to these moments of crisis. A person might be angry for years about some betrayal in youth, for decades at parental offenses in childhood scarcely remembered, for months about a friend's careless insult now stale (but still true). Surely through that duration there are no characteristic and continuous feelings; in fact, one might well feel nothing at all during that entire period and face no situation which would bring matters to a head and force the confrontation within which such feelings typically appear. Anger may "erupt" only in certain isolated moments, but the anger may exist for years, unexpressed and even unrecognized, as one of the defining structures of our existence. Resentment may on occasion manifest itself in the venom of public persecutions and temporary moments of viciousness, but most of the time it hides unobtrusively at the very foundation of our world, giving that all-too-familiar defensive posture and bitter taste to every act and statement. A romance which attempts to maintain itself on the peaks of crises of uncertainty and doubt is not the prototype of love despite its frequency in "romantic" novels and in our more adolescent adventures. Of course, love at its best does not remain unperturbed and without feeling, but surely it is a serious if not neurotic misunderstanding to think that love is "true" only when it is in a state of crisis. To the contrary, love, like anger and resentment, is most "true" precisely in those moments of calm and continuity, when it is not called upon to defend itself or prove its existence. An emotion is not a crisis; that is as if one said, continuing our quasi-architectural metaphor, a structure has strength only in those moments when it is threatened with collapse. That indeed may provide the *test* of the structure, but not the structure itself.

Philosophers commonly distinguish between "episodic" and "dispositional" mental concepts, the former designating episodes or occurrences, the latter not designating but rather acting as "inference tickets" to various possible episodes.[4] (For example, the breaking of a glass is an episode, but the brittleness that makes possible the breaking of the glass is a disposition.) But this very influential distinction already contains within it the misunderstanding described above: the idea that an emotion is *either* an "episode" or occurrence *or* a disposition for those episodes or occurrences. To argue that an emotion is an occurrence is surely a misunderstanding of emotions (my anger is not simply my "getting angry"), but so is the idea that an emotion is a disposition to have certain feelings. My emotion is a structure of my world, which may at times manifest itself in certain specific displays of feeling or behavior. But my emotion *is* neither such displays nor the disposition to such displays.

It is worth noting, by way of a clue rather than a full-blown argument, that we often say of our emotions that they are "reasonable" and "unreasonable," "warranted" and "unwarranted," "justifiable" and "unjustifiable," "legitimate" and "illegitimate," "sensible" and "foolish," "self-demeaning" and "enhancing," and even "right" and "wrong." Yet no such evaluations are appropriate in the realm of headaches and bellyaches, warm flushes and nausea. Headaches are neither reasonable nor unreasonable; there is no such thing as a "sensible" flush; it is never right or wrong to be nauseous. Yet we say without hesitation that "you were wrong to be angry at him," that "he was unjustified in being jealous," that "loving her was the wrong thing to do." And although one wants to be careful about taking ordinary attitudes toward emotions as a philosophical argument (considering how often we are "ordinarily" wrong about the emotions in other ways), these sorts of evaluations should give us a further reason to reject the seemingly indisputable thesis that emotions are mere feelings, occurrences that happen to us beyond our own control. Feelings and occurrences are not "reasonable" or "unreasonable." They simply *are*. Only what we *do* can be so assessed.

A further argument against the identity of emotions and feelings is this: It is obvious that we are frequently mistaken about our emotions. We deny that we are angry when there is every reason to suppose that we are; we laugh at the idea that we are in love when even the laughter itself, hysterical and defensive, is further proof of our affections. We feign anger and fool even ourselves, realize after years of apparent tenderness that what seemed to be love was not love, believe that we are self-righteously indignant when we find that we are envious or resentful. We sometimes think ourselves depressed when we are really angry, sympathetic when we are being vicious, loving when we are jealous and possessive, merely sad when in fact we are guilty or depressed. We think ourselves, perhaps, angry at the cat when we are angry with the policeman who has just given us a stiff speeding ticket; we think we love a wife when (if Freud is right) we really love only our mothers. Such complex and common mistakes would be difficult to understand if they were simply misinterpretations of various feelings or complexes of feelings. One is rarely mistaken about his having a headache or a toothache, about a feeling of queasiness or nausea, the dullness that comes with a hangover, or the giddiness that follows the inhalation of hashish. Of course, there may be mistakes here as well, due to inexperience or a confusion of sensations. But mistakes are neither so common nor so complex as in the case of emotions. This is a phenomenon that will be understood only when we have said something more about the structure of emotions. But as a piece of evidence, it should already give another clue to the conclusion that emotions are something far more sophisticated than mere feelings.

3. Emotions and Behavior

> We feel sorry because we cry, angry because we strike, fearful because we tremble. . . ."
>
> William James, "What Is an Emotion?"
>
> To say that he did something from that [emotion] . . . is to say, "he *would* do that."
>
> Gilbert Ryle, *The Concept of Mind*

A familiar move in the analysis of emotions, following the discovery that emotions are not feelings or sensations, is the suggestion that emotions are patterns of behavior, or, in the psychologist's hydraulic terms, a "drive" or "tendency" toward a certain behavioral response. Of course, to have an emotion, such as anger, is not to perform any *particular* actions, for example, stamping one's feet or screaming, punching, kicking, writing an "angry" letter, or whatever. To be angry is to be "disposed" to enter into any one or more of an indefinitely large number of patterns of "anger-behaving," depending upon the particular circumstances.

In behavioral psychology, of course, such an analysis is adopted as a matter of methodological principle (for example, R. Plutchik:[5] "An emotion is to be defined primarily in terms of behavioral data [or, to use Tolman's phrase, in terms of 'response as affecting stimulus']"). Considered solely as a methodological thesis, the reduction of the emotions to their behavioral manifestations is not my concern. It is only when behaviorism indulges itself in philosophical and metaphysical polemics that it enters into combat with common sense and philosophy. Then behaviorism becomes the thesis that an emotion *is* nothing other than its behavior manifestations. In response, common sense wants to say, "Nonsense! Emotions are feelings. Their expression in behavior is altogether another matter." But I have already argued that emotions are not feelings. And is it the case that the behavioral expression of emotions is "altogether another matter"?

Behaviorism (that is, philosophical behaviorism, as opposed to the merely methodological behaviorism of psychology) begins with an indisputable empirical observation and then attempts to turn it into a logical thesis, typically under the direction of some antimentalistic philosophical principle. The indisputable observation is the regular connection between our emotions and certain characteristic behavior patterns. As James says: "Can one fancy the state of rage and picture no ebullition of it in the chest, no flushing of the face, no dilation of the nostrils, no clenching of the teeth, no impulse to vigorous action . . . ? The present writer, for one, cannot."[6]

The demand that we "picture" the state of rage is already a covert insistence upon its outward manifestations, but the point is surely well taken; we cannot imagine someone in an intense emotional state who is not driven to "vigorous action" of one kind or another. But the *identification* of the emotion and the behavior is yet another matter. In an emotion of considerable duration, it is quite possible that one will only rarely indulge in characteristic behavioral expressions.†

† This point is well covered by Gilbert Ryle's now famous dispositional analysis: The emotion does not consist of any particular behavioral episodes but of an indefinitely complex "multi-tracked" disposition to behave. However, Ryle also argues that the behavior that constitutes the emotion is as much a matter of "agitation" and breakdown in normal behavior as any particular and distinctive pattern of behavior as such. (*Concept of Mind*, Chapter 4.) It must also be noted, however, that Ryle, unlike the more ruthless psychological behaviorists, does not deny "the mental realm" entirely; he retains various "itches, twitches, and feelings" that no true behaviorist would accept. He claims to attack "the myth of the ghost in the machine" (Chapter 1) but succeeds only in emasculating the ghost.

If I am angry because of the governor's new tax laws, and I am in the opposition party, I will make a public speech. If I am not in a position of power, I will write an angry letter to the newspapers. If I work for the government, I may just bitch to my wife, or punch the sofa, or tear apart the evening newspaper. This "disposition" is "indefinitely complex": Under different conditions, my behavior will be different as well. In a discussion among my friends over the tax program, I may well express my anger by spitting, by drinking too much, by refusing to participate. There are certain behaviors that are characteristic of anger—raising one's fist, making threats, stomping one's foot—but under any number of ingeniously formulated circumstances, a person might do virtually *anything* to express his emotion.

The thesis that emotions are dispositions to behave has a plausible ring to it, particularly considering the convincing arguments against the traditional identification of emotions and feelings. But consider the case in which two emotions exist simultaneously, for example, love and hatred toward the same person, the former emotion much weaker and less confident than the other. In such a case, the one emotion will never manifest itself in behavior, leaving the behaviorist with an endless set of counterfactual conditionals. But how, then, can it be the case that the person who has that emotion so easily recognizes its presence? Or consider the many instances in which we pretend to have emotions which in fact we do not have; in other words, we *act as if* we had the emotion. But if the concept of "pretending" is to have any significance at all, there must be some logical gap between the emotion and its behavioral expression. Similarly, we must be able to account for the fact that we recognize, not only in ourselves but in other people (particularly if they are very "close" to us or in very similar circumstances) emotions which are not manifested in any expression whatsoever. ("I know how he must feel.")[7] And then there is that "defense mechanism" that Freud entitled "reaction-formation" which we can now recognize in our own and other people's behavior as a matter of daily routine: A person expresses his emotion by behaving in *exactly the opposite* way than he would normally be expected to behave (rewarding someone at whom he is furious, treating someone he loves in a brazenly cruel or callous way, praising someone he hates). All of these concerns chop away at the allegedly logical connection between emotions and behavior. But the final severing blow is a general realization that, once we attempt to grasp the various "patterns of characteristic behavior" that are supposed to constitute the emotion, they are potentially infinite in number. The "suitable" expression of an emotion in "particular circumstances" by a particular person is as varied as the mathematical product of persons and circumstances. The key to the expression of the emotion in behavior is a matter of *intention*. Why is this person expressing his anger this way rather than that way? *Why* is he pretending to be angry when he is not? *Why* is he not now expressing his anger? *Why* is he treating the person with whom he is so furious with such extravagant kindness and concern? But once we have entered the realm of intentions, we have moved back into the realm of subjectivity. Intentions, unlike the behaviors they intend, are not behaviorally observable. Neither, therefore, are the emotions. And so the logical behaviorist thesis falls back to the obvious but probably still contingent thesis that "having an emotion makes one likely to behave in certain ways in certain circumstances."‡ Of course! But what is it then "to have an emotion"?

If further argument against the behavioral analysis of emotions is deemed necessary,* one can profitably return to the insistence that emotions are essentially *subjective* phenomena, items in my world to which I have "privileged" (but surely not "incorrigible") access. If emotions were but patterns of behavior, surely my recognition of my own emotions would be a peculiar process. I should have to watch myself behave, notice that I behave angrily in certain circumstances and not in others. Now *sometimes* this is indeed the case, particularly in those troublesome cases of self-deception in which my own view of myself is clouded over or blocked by certain concerns and emotions: The central thrust of all psychotherapy—in whatever version—is the need to provide

‡ An excellent and detailed argument against behaviorism in general can be found in Charles Taylor's study *The Explanation of Behaviour* (London: Routledge and Kegan Paul, 1964).

* Frithjof Bergmann has written (quoting Hegel on Christianity) that behaviorism cannot be usefully attacked because "no matter which version of it one assails, someone will always say at the end, that is not what he means by it."

just such a *reflection* of myself through which the clouds and blocks can be penetrated. But these are special cases, and even here, it is not my behavior viewed "from the outside" that provides the insight into my emotional structures, but a straightforward "seeing" which may be triggered by such a view. In short, I do not recognize my own emotions by observing my behavior, even if that is the way (perhaps the only way, short of being told firsthand) that I recognize the emotional states of other persons. My emotions are *essentially* and structurally part of my experience, of which my behavior is at best a criterion for other people and, occasionally, for myself. Yet the behavioral analysis does underscore a point which one must never forget: that emotions are never simply introspectable feelings or sensations and that, no matter how careful we are, our own reflective inventory of our emotions might always be upset by conscientious attention to our behavior and the ways we appear to other people.

Perhaps one could reply to behaviorism in a rather mild manner; an emotion is a disposition to behave *plus* a disposition to have certain feelings, attitudes, and intentions. Or combining those two dispositions, in a sophisticated "hypothetical construct" view,† an emotion is a postulate which explains and unifies a variety of behavioral and phenomenological manifestations. Unlike behaviorism, this view might even be applied to "one's own case," since it would be the phenomenological manifestations that would provide the "privileged" access which would only be available to the person who has that emotion.[8] On the face of it, this view seems reasonable enough; but something has been left out, and that "something" seems to be the emotion itself. The problem here is a Kantian problem of synthesis: *How* does a hypothetical construct or complex dispositional view sort out those "manifestations" which belong to one emotion from those which belong to another? What could "manifestation" mean here? "Manifestations" of what? Again, one cannot deny that an emotion has its characteristic feelings and expressions, but it is a mis-

† See, for example, R. Brandt and J. Kim, "Wants as Explanations of Actions," *Journal of Philosophy*, 1963, for an account of this sort of regarding motives in general. I argued a similar thesis with a certain misplaced confidence in my *Unconscious Motivation* (1967).

take to suppose that the emotion is but a disposition or set of dispositions to have those feelings and expressions. It is *because* one has a certain emotion that one ascribes those dispositions to oneself, and to understand why such ascriptions are valid we must *first* understand what the emotion is. A hypothetical construct or dispositional analysis, even in its nonbehavioristic form, captures only the surface of the emotion, not its essence. But again, it is worth noting the *form* of all such analyses—they are paradigmatically hydraulic and antiexistential. An emotion is, according to them, a complex resultant of affects (feelings) and behavior. Not surprisingly, both Freud and James can be easily included with the proponents of such views.

Before the behaviorist analysis is weakened too much, however, it is important to keep in mind a vital but often forgotten truth of behaviorism. That truth has best been expressed by James (although for somewhat obscure reasons). It is indisputably true that each emotion has its predictable and characteristic expressions in behavior, but this is not to be viewed, as it so often is, as a *causal* claim. Given, on his theory, that an emotion is nothing other than "the feeling of its bodily manifestations,"

a necessary corollary ought to be that any voluntary arousal of the so-called manifestations of a special emotion ought to give us the emotion itself. . . . Everyone knows how panic is increased by flight, and how the giving way to the symptoms of grief or anger increases those passions themselves. Each fit of sobbing makes sorrow more acute, and calls forth another fit stronger still, until at last repose ensues only with lassitude and with the apparent exhaustion of the machinery. In rage, it is notorious how we "work ourselves up" to a climax by repeated outbreaks of expression. Refuse to express an emotion and it dies. Count ten before venting your anger, and its occasion seems ridiculous. Whistling to keep up courage is no mere figure of speech. On the other hand, sit all day in a moping posture, sigh, and reply to everything with a dismal voice, and your melancholy lingers. There is no more valuable precept in moral education than this, as all who have experience know: If we wish to conquer undesirable emotional tendencies in ourselves, we must assiduously and in the first instance cold-bloodedly go through the *outward motions* of those contrary dispositions we prefer to cultivate. . . . Soothe

the brow, brighten the eye . . . pass the genial compliment, and your heart must be frigid indeed if it does not gradually thaw![9]

It is curious that James constructs this oft-confirmed thesis on the basis of his epiphenomenalistic and hydraulic model of the emotions. In fact, this is the heart of just that theory that I shall argue against James and the hydraulic model. If emotions are not merely "affects," however, but *judgments* that we ourselves *make*, then a voluntary change in our outward behavior will have unavoidable implications for certain related and equally voluntary aspects of our inward behavior, namely our emotions. This is the truth of behaviorism that is rarely accounted for in the usual "feeling theories" of the emotions. Curiously, it is also equally ignored by the behaviorists themselves, who, though stressing the primacy of behavior, attempt to shun the notion of the "voluntary" as itself covertly subjectivistic (which, of course, it is, since it presupposes the concept of "intentions"). If the emotions cannot be convincingly argued to be *nothing but* their behavioral expressions, one shouldn't fall into the opposite analysis, either, that these behavioral expressions are altogether something other than the emotion. If emotions are judgments, their behavioral expression is very much a part of them. In fact, the intention to behave is indistinguishable from the emotion itself, and consequently one can agree with James and the behaviorists, but in very different terms, that an emotion without "an impulse to vigorous action" (or at least behavior of some sort, even sulking) is unthinkable.

Against these well-established models, I want to argue that emotions are not disruptions or irrational or occurrences, not forces or feelings or mere tendencies to behave. I will analyze the emotions as constitutive structures of our world. Through our passions, we constitute our (subjective) world, render it meaningful and with it our lives and our Selves. The passions are not occurrences but activities; they are not "inside" our minds but rather the structures we place *in our world*. My anger—even that simmering suppressed anger that is allowed no expression—is my projection into the world, my silent indictment of someone who has wronged me, my judgment of the offensive state of the world. My control of my anger is not (as the very concepts of "suppression" and "repression" suggest) the containment of an invading force from the mysterious depths "within" me. The anger is my own as well as the control; the "suppression" is but part of the structure which I am imposing upon the world through my anger. To think otherwise is to view my anger as *not mine*, not my responsibility, allowing me to abuse other people and self-righteously condemn them (whether silently or publicly) without ever taking responsibility for my own judgment. Accordingly, we can appreciate the tremendous appeal behind the traditional analyses; how much we would like to view our embarrassments and cruelties as not our own! But we will not even be in a position to understand much less to change ourselves until we have learned to accept this responsibility, to view the passions as our own and our doing, and to ask, not "What *causes* me to feel this?" but always "What *reason* do I have for *doing* this?"

CHAPTER 5: A SUBJECTIVE THEORY OF THE PASSIONS

> Like Leporello, learned literary men keep a list, but the point is what they lack; while Don Juan seduces girls and enjoys himself— Leporello notes down the time, the place and a description of the girl.
>
> Kierkegaard, *Journals*

Like Leporello, psychologists . . . But the point is what they lack. A description of someone else's emotion is one thing; understanding one's own is something else. And our problem is to understand, *for me* (*us*), subjectively, what it is *to have* an emotion.

1. Intentionality

> All consciousness is consciousness of something.
>
> Edmund Husserl

Emotions are not feelings, yet feelings are typically if not almost always associated with our emotions. And yet neither are emotions *merely* their objective manifestations in neurology or behavior, although we may agree that such manifestations might always be found. But this hardly constitutes a "theory of the emotions." The most prominent feature of our emotions has yet to be introduced—that which distinguishes them from mere feelings and that which firmly ties them to behavior and our world.

Emotions are *about* something. One is never simply angry; he/she is angry *at* someone *for* something. Even an "angry young man" is angry about something (namely, everything). It is impossible to fall in love without falling in love *with someone*, whether or not he or she is largely a fabrication of the romantic imagination, whether or not he or she represents a "stand-in" for someone else, a mother, a dead brother, or an old and not-forgotten lover. One is not simply afraid, but afraid of something, even if the object of fear is something unknown. There are emotions which seem virtually always about something specific, for example, sadness; there are emotions that are typically general, for example, despair, resentment, and guilt. In these emotions, a particular incident seems to act as a catalyst, crystallizing out the ornate precipitate that soon becomes supersaturated consciousness.

There are passions which need not even begin with a particular incident or object, which need not be *about* anything in particular; these are *moods*. The difference between an emotion and a mood is the difference in what they are *about*. Emotions are about particulars, or particulars generalized; moods are about nothing in particular, or sometimes they are about our world as a whole. Euphoria, melancholy, and depression are not about anything in particular (though some particular incident might well set them off); they are about the whole of our world, or indiscriminately about anything that comes our way, casting happy glows or somber shadows on every object and incident of our experience. It is with particular reference to moods that Heidegger suggests the notion of "being tuned" to the world. I again insist that this distinction between emotions and moods is not a sharp distinction, and that the relationship between emotions and moods is one of mutual support and even identity. Every emotion, no matter how specific, structures our world and has definitive influences on the whole of our experience. And every mood, no matter how apparently metaphysical, can usually be found to have a number of nodal points, around which the rest of the structure is shaped.

Following recent phenomenological tradition, this feature of emotions can be called their *intentionality*; that is, all emotions are *about* something. That which the emotion is about is called its *intentional object*, or simply its object. As a matter of logic, every emotion has its particular object. Furthermore, it is this particular object which constitutes the emotion. To understand an emotion, therefore, it is necessary to understand its "object." This raises difficulties, however, which are among the most stubborn problems of contemporary philosophy.

The following two sections may seem formidable to the nonprofessional reader. They are necessary to my thesis, however, although I have simplified them as much as possible (so much so, I am afraid, that my colleagues will find mammoth gaps at several turns; these can be substantiated in appropriate journals). I ask the reader to bear with me in what follows. The thrust of my argument should become evident soon enough.

The peculiarity of the intentional object becomes evident when cases are considered in which this object does not exist (if, that is, the "object" is a person or a thing), or in which the object is not true (if the "object" is a proposition or claim of some kind), or is not the case or has not occurred (if the "object" is a "fact" or incident or state of affairs). I may be afraid of Communists under the bed, although there are no such Communists; I may be angry with John for stealing my car when in fact he did not. For most transitive verbs, "P verbs Q" may be analyzed as a relationship between P and Q (e.g., "John kicks Fred"). Since there are no Communists, however, my fear cannot be analyzed as a relationship between me and the Communists, and the object of my fear cannot be "the Communists." Since John has not in fact stolen my car, my anger cannot be a relationship between me and the fact that John has stolen my car. There is no such fact. But, then, what am I angry about? Surely not my *belief* that John has stolen my car. (Why should I be angry at my belief and blame it on John?) I am angry *that John stole my car*.

Because the object of an emotion need not exist in order for it to be such an object, it has been often suggested that this "object" is a peculiar sort of "nonexistent" (or "subsistent" or "irreal") object. At the turn of this century, logicians populated fantastic universes with such nonexistent and even self-contradictory "objects" in order to account for those cases of emotions (and beliefs, assertions, dreams, and illusions) in which the intentional objects were not "real." But now consider the case in which I am rightfully afraid or justifiably angry, such that there really is a cell of Marxist-Leninist guerrillas hiding under my bed or John really has stolen my car. Are the intentional objects of these emotions the Communists and the facts themselves, or are they intentional objects of some mysterious sort (as in the former cases) which stand "in front of" or "beside" the real objects? Either way, the result gives rise to intolerable confusions and paradoxes. If one argues that the intentional object is an object, person, incident, or fact in the real world, then it appears that a great many emotions are not intentional after all. On the other hand, if it is argued that the intentional object is a special kind of object, not a real object (a real person or incident or fact), then the account of cases in which there are bona fide objects is absurdly complicated. On the one hand, we want to say that all emotions and their objects are "in the world," not simply "in our minds." On the other hand, we must take account of the fact that many if not all emotions have objects which are not wholly real, which are in part imagined, in part distorted, and which are peculiar to the emotion in question.

In the past seventy years, logicians have often followed the German genius Gottlob Frege in distinguishing certain linguistic contexts which he called "indirect" and which are now usually called "opaque." An opaque context, for example, "John believes that . . ." or "Fred is angry at . . ." is distinguished by the fact that only certain descriptions can be used to complete the sentence without changing its meaning and its truth. For example, it might be true that "John believes that Stendhal wrote *The Red and the Black.*" As a matter of fact, Stendhal was the pen name of Henri Beyle. Yet although it is true that "Beyle wrote *The Red and the Black,*" it is not true that "John believes that Beyle wrote *The Red and the Black,*" since John does not know this identity. Similarly, it is true that John loves Mary. It is also true that Mary was a prostitute in St. Louis for five years before meeting John, a fact she has never told him. Consequently, it would not be true to describe Mary *qua* John's lover as an "ex-prostitute," even though the woman he loves is in fact an ex-prostitute. The significance of calling these contexts "opaque" is that the descriptions of the "objects" of belief or emotion must be geared to the mode of conceiving of them by the person who has them, not upon the "facts." A man may be afraid of his own shadow; but we can be sure that the object of his fear is not his own shadow, but rather something else which he sees *through* his shadow. The notion of "opacity" is an attempt to get around the problem of mysterious and unreal "intentional objects" in favor of an analysis of the linguistic apparatus we use to describe certain "acts" or "attitudes." Given the confusion and absurdities that have been generated by the notion of intentionality, we can easily understand the motivation of this move. However, it is clear that what I am afraid of or angry *about* is not simply a certain kind of sentence. It is an object (or person, incident, state of affairs), which may or may not "really" exist or be the case. What are we to say of such objects? How are we to account for the "opacity" of their descriptions?

Underlying the various dilemmas the notion of "intentionality" has produced, there is an insidious dualism which I have already rejected. In general, it is the "mental-physical" dualism so celebrated by Descartes. With particular respect to the emotions, this dualistic analysis, which has been actively promoted by philosophers on both sides of the English Channel, distinguishes two "components" of an emotion: (1) having the emotion, a feeling, an act or "attitude," and (2) the object of the emotion: a thing or person or incident or state of affairs or "fact" (see, for example, D. F. Pears).[1] The first is mental or subjective, and the second is "in the world" and objective. But as soon as this distinction is introduced, the status of such "objects" becomes impossibly problematic. How can an object be "in the world" but not exist? Or if one says that such objects need not exist, then how can they be "in the world"? What of those cases in which the object of the emotion is indisputably real, "in the world"? And how, then, is the emotion *logically* connected to its object?

It is this set of paradoxes that lay behind my theory of "subjectivity" in Part I. Emotions are subjective; their objects are not simply objects of the world, not "facts," not part of an anonymous and scientifically ascertainable Reality. The objects of the emotions are objects of *our* world, the world as we experience it. (In the case of moods, the object is our world as a whole.) Once again, this is not to defend an absurd "two-worlds" view, a "private" world within which we enact our emotional dramas and a public world of "the facts." There are rather two standpoints, one detached and one personally involved. All objects of our emotions are in surreality: Reality is irrelevant except on reflection. It is always open to question whether or to what extent those objects are also in *the* world and publicly verifiable. There are cases, for example, in the extremes of paranoia, panic, or romantic raptures, in which the object of emotion may have no status in Reality at all; it may be "just a matter of self-delusion." On the other hand, there are many cases in which the object of the emotion has an indisputable position in Reality: when I am angry at what in fact is the case, when I hate someone who is very much flesh-and-blood. But the objects of emotions are rarely Real or unreal;* they virtually always have *some* basis in Reality (the most extreme paranoid does not *make up* the objects of his fear), and no object of an emotion is simply what it is "in Reality." The objects of an emotion are objects of great personal importance to us; Reality knows nothing of "personal importance." I am indignant about the Strangelove tactics employed by my government in instigating a revolution in Chile; in Reality, that is "just the way things are." For me (and hopefully, for all of us), those tactics are a matter of great concern. But that concern, unlike "the facts," is not part of the Reality in question, except *for us*. Thus, the object of an emotion, in this sense, is *never* simply an object (person, incident, fact) in *the* world, in Reality. It's an object—an object of considerable importance—in *our* world, in our surreality. The objects of emotions are the objects of the world experienced through our concerns and values. Even where the object has no status in Reality, it is based upon the world as we experience it, interpreted and hypostatized, projected into the world by our concerns and values. No matter how much a lover is the fabrication of our own fantasies, the basis of the fabrication and the evidence for his or her existence must be the "facts" or the "real" world. This is true not only in those familiar cases in which we glamourize and glorify our lovers with attributes they possess only to a very limited extent (lauding intelligence as "genius," reasonable looks as "beauty," adequate sex as "voluptuousness"), but even in extreme fantasies, the wandering knight in the medieval morality play who falls in love with a few golden locks or possibly a shoe or two strewn strategically around a cave or a castle. There must be at least a lock or a shoe, or at any rate a reputation or rumor.

The intentional object of an emotion is not a peculiar kind of object that is common to both those emotions which also have a "real" object as well as to those which do not.[2] An intentional object is nothing other than an object, as subjectively experienced,

---

* A distinction some German philosophers attempt to squeeze between with a concept of *irreal*.

whatever its status or basis in the "real" world. Even in cases of delusion and fantasy, the intentional object is experienced as "in the world," that is, in *our* world. Its status as an intentional object (of emotion) need have nothing to do with its status in Reality; but neither, then, does it make sense to speak of intentional objects as either real or not real, *qua intentional objects*. The conception of such objects is applicable only within the subjective point of view. As soon as one attempts to extend it to the sphere of objectivity, the result will be instant paradox and confusion.

Returning again to the discussion of subjectivity, it is clear what is so seriously wrong with the analysis of emotions into "components": An emotion is not distinct or separable from its object; the object as an object of this emotion has no existence apart from the emotion. The object of my being angry with John for stealing my car is not the alleged fact that John stole my car (for he may not have), nor is it simply John. The object is irreducibly *that-John-stole-my-car*. But even this is an incomplete description. Having long wanted to get rid of my car, I may also be *relieved* that John stole my car. Of course, the fact which stands at the base of my anger is identical to the fact which stands at the base of my relief. But my anger and my relief are not separate feelings or acts or attitudes which are directed toward one and the same object. The object of my anger is an offense; the object of my relief is a boon. Thus the object of my anger is not the same as the object of my relief. The distinction between the emotion and its object begins to collapse. The emotion is determined by its object just as it is the emotion that constitutes its object (which is not to say, except in extreme cases, that it creates its own "facts"). There are not two components, my anger and the object of my anger. Borrowing a clumsy but effective device from the translators of more difficult German philosophical concatenations, we might say that every emotion has the unitary form of "my-emoting-about . . . ," "my-being-angry-about . . . ," "my-loving. . . ." I will not attempt to maintain this typesetter's nightmare in the text, but it must be kept in mind when attempting to understand the intentionality of the emotions; there are no ultimately intelligible distinctions between the emotion and its object. The emotion is distinguished by its object; there is nothing to it besides its object. But neither is there any such object at all without the emotion.

This technical point can support and be supported by an immensely practical consideration. A change in beliefs typically inspires a change in emotions. How can this be? If an emotion were a feeling, the explanation would be a still tentative hypothesis about psychosomatic disorders—like losing one's headache five minutes after one's mother-in-law has left the house. Most feelings are absolutely indifferent to what we believe. But my being angry at John for stealing my car changes radically upon being told that my car has not left the garage all evening. Believing this, my anger vanishes in an instant, not as a matter of cause-and-effect, but rather as a matter of logic. I *can't* be angry at John for something I believe he did not do. Similarly, my evaluation of a situation has everything to do with my emotions of embarrassment and pride, not merely as cause but as their structure. I cannot be embarrassed if I do not believe my situation to be awkward; I cannot be proud if I do not believe myself to have accomplished something or to have been bestowed with some honor. The relationship between beliefs and opinions on the one hand and emotions on the other is not a matter of causation or coincidence but a matter of logic. The emotion is logically indistinguishable from its object: Once its object has been rejected there can be no more emotion. A headache hangs on with a momentum of its own for minutes or perhaps hours after its instigating cause has ceased, but my anger vanishes immediately upon the refutation of the "fact" I was angry about.

Now we can understand, too, why it is so important to insist not only that an emotion is not identical to a feeling but that a feeling is not even a component of emotion. Of course, emotions may typically involve feelings; they may even always involve feelings. But feelings are neither necessary nor sufficient to differentiate emotions. An emotion is never simply a feeling, even a feeling plus anything. One can be angry without ever feeling angry—for days or weeks or years. Moreover, it makes no sense to say that someone feels angry unless he *is* angry. On the traditional view of emotions as feelings, of course, this claim would seem strange indeed; how could one not feel whatever one feels in anger without being angry? But one could have those same feelings after drinking three cups of coffee or swallowing some amphetamine; what one feels is not anger or angry but simply flushed, excited, irritable, etc. When I do have those feelings when I am angry, the feelings are at most an accompaniment to the anger, like the excitable fans following an athletic team. I am angry at John for stealing; now I find out he did not steal. My anger vanishes instantly, but the feeling—that is, the pulsing and flushing—remains for a moment. Even though those feelings were induced by my anger and are now the same feelings I had when I was angry a moment ago, they are no longer feelings of anger. They are just feelings. One cannot feel angry without being angry.

To say that emotions are *intentional* is to say that they *essentially* have logical connections with the objects of our world. This is why I found it necessary to spend so much time introducing our notion of subjectivity in Part I. Emotions are not "mental" states or events or acts, if by that one means that they are "in our minds" rather than in our world. An emotion is not something locked "inside," even in those cases in which it is brutally suppressed and kept from expression. An emotion is a structure linking ourselves and the objects of our world which provides the structures of our world. We have yet to understand the nature of these structures and their immense importance to us. In breaking down the old Cartesian picture of the emotions, however, as feelings and sensations in our minds that have at most contingent (if not downright mysterious) connections to our world and its objects, a major step has been made in laying the groundwork for a new subjective theory.

2. Emotions, Objects, and Causes

> She's so in love with me she doesn't know anything.
> That's why she's in love with me.
>
> Marx (G.), A *Day at the Races*

The intentionality and nature of an emotion have nothing to do with its *causes*. This point was made briefly before when I insisted that my anger, even if caused by a drug I had taken, is still anger, and nothing else. What I am angry about is not the drug or my having taken the drug. (In fact, I may have forgotten, or may never have known, that I had taken any such drug.) Similarly, I may be particularly prone to romantic fantasies and "falling in love" because of protracted sexual deprivation; but even if the cause of my consequent love is sexual deprivation, the object of my love is not my sexual deprivation or someone to cure my sexual deprivation. Whether or not my love survives the cure of its cause, the cause is no part of the love itself.

This technical distinction between the causes and the objects of emotions is absolutely vital considering the all-too-frequent dismissal of emotions on the basis of the knowledge of their causes. For example, under the dramatic influence of lysergic acid, one's view of the world may become one of universal affection and enthusiasm, one's relationships with others "clarified" in such a way that intimacy becomes possible where it had not been before. Drug-induced expression of long-suppressed anger, envy, and hatred may display the emotional structure of our everyday world as a purple dye might render visible the otherwise invisible membranes of a tiny piece of tissue. The cause of this clarity, and perhaps even the cause of the emotions themselves, is the drug. Yet the emotions are nothing other than what they are. They are no less "real" (surreal) because their chemical causes are in this case known with certainty. (Our everyday emotional life is similarly chemically dependent; that does not make our everyday emotions any less "real" [surreal] either.) The distinction between "real" (surreal) and "false" emotions has nothing to do with their causes. An emotion is distinguished by its object, not by its causes, and the "surreality" of an emotion depends only upon its role in our subjective lives, however it may have originally been instigated.

There are several very different categories of causes of emotions. The easiest to distinguish from the emotion and its objects are those physiological and chemical causes already discussed. A convincing case can be made for any number of causal laws concerning the effect of certain neurological changes and emotions, despite the fact that a subject need never know anything about them. (In fact, very few people know even the most elementary of these laws, and no one, as yet, knows very many of them.) Slightly more complicated are such factors as inherited temperaments, which may similarly lie beyond any conceivable knowledge of the subject and can no doubt be traced to some complex series of genetically regulated physiochemical processes. The same might be hypothesized about human instincts, if there are any (aggression? territorial imperatives? motherly love?), but it is preferable to suppose—at least as a matter of practical principle if not as a theoretical necessity—that what in any case is called an "instinct" is in fact a motive, a *psychological* factor, whatever its physiological substrate.

The distinction between *cause* and *object* of emotion becomes difficult with the introduction of *psychological* causes. Learned emotional reactions, for example (which probably includes all of them), might be causally explained in terms of emotional traits and habits (for example, having "a bad temper," being "a Romantic at heart," having "a streak of jealousy" or "a morose personality"); or in terms of past experiences or training (for example, "He was brought up cruelly and without love," or "His first girl friend crushed him when she left," or "He saw his parents having intercourse when he was three and ever since . . ." or "Well, he was brought up by *those* people"). The complication arises because, in every case, the cause of the emotion might be argued to be necessarily *experienced*. In some cases, this raises no special problems: For example, whether or not one recognizes himself as "bad-tempered" or as "an incurable Romantic," such causal factors do no more than describe a *pattern* of emotional reactions into which any particular emotional reaction finds a suitable place. But consider the kind of case which is so crucial to Freud's early clinical experiences: An ongoing set of emotions is causally attributed to a childhood trauma in which, for example, a young boy was sexually assaulted by his aunt. (Complicating the case, of course, may be the idea that the trauma has been repressed, but, for my purposes here, let's suppose that the subject ["patient"] has already accepted this causal hypothesis after some time in therapy, and he now attempts to understand its effects upon him.) What is the object of an emotion with such an experience as its cause? A first guess would be: the sexual assault. Notice, however, that the fact of the assault is not sufficient to play this causal role: Unlike the causal theories linking physiology and emotion, this hypothesis requires the connection of the *fact experienced* and the emotion. But even this is not nearly sufficient.

Early in his career, Freud commented that if the "memories" of his patients were true, the perverseness of the private life of the outwardly staid bourgeois Viennese was no less than shocking, to put it mildly. He soon came to the conclusion, however, that most of the traumas he investigated were based upon fantasies, not facts; fabrications, and not memories. Accordingly, so far as the cause of the emotion is concerned, the facts need have nothing to do with the case; it is simply the experience that is at stake. Insofar as the emotions are subjective phenomena, the distinction between Reality and surreality cannot be drawn; what is essential is only that the incident occurred in one's surreality. (This raises grave problems for those psychologists who would make any attempt to identify the "stimulus" of behavior in an objectively designated set of circumstances [so many days without food, such and such an incident before the subject's eyes]. Even a rat has a surreality, and so never merely responds to a "stimulus."[3])

Even this is not sufficient; if the cause of the emotion is the experience, is it not identical with the object of that experience? It is not. First of all, the object of an emotion is not an experience, but the object of experience; it is not the experience toward which I feel anger or guilt or shame or fear, but toward my aunt and what she (supposedly) did to me. Moreover, the experience that is the cause of the emotion is a past experience, but the object of our emotion must be in our present experience, even if the object itself refers to a past experience.† (Of course, the object of the present experience will very probably be, as Freud so richly illustrated, considerably edited and embellished due to subsequent experiences and associations.) The cause is the original experience in the sense that, as in Freud's theoretical papers, a certain kind of experience is linked in a causal lawlike generalization to certain kinds of subsequent emotions and fixations in adults. The cause is past, and it does not matter whether I am now aware of it; the object, on the other hand, must be the object of my *present*

---

† Lévi-Strauss, for example, argues that all "recollected experience" must be treated as "contemporaneous experience" (*Le Temps Retrouve*, p. 62).

experience (even if it is a past event). The cause and the object are thus different, even if they should refer to "the same fact."

Even more complicated still are those causes of an emotion which are both present and related to the object of the emotion. For example, one says that he became angry because he saw a certain item in the newspaper; it was the spying of the item that caused him to be angry, but what he was angry about was presumably what the newspaper item was *about*, or something of which it reminded him. Or one falls in love because the other just happens to say something precisely right at the right time; but one does not fall in love with the comment, which only acts as a catalyst for an emotion directed toward the whole person. Similarly, sex might easily act as such a cause for falling in love, but we must not confuse the cause for the emotion, which is always directed at the person and never at the sexual activity (no matter how central to the relationship).

The distinction between object and cause is most confused because of the kind of case in which the object seems to *be* the cause. For example, I might be made (that is, caused to be) angry by John's stealing my car. In this case, we are tempted to say that the cause of my anger and its object are the same—John's stealing my car. But what if it is the case that John did not steal my car? The object would still be *his stealing my car*; the cause would not be his stealing my car but only my believing that he did. And so the two are not the same, not only in those cases in which what I am angry about is not the case but also in those cases in which what I am angry about is the case. The object of an emotion is *never* identical to its cause. The object is always *subjective*, a part of the world as one sees it, whether or not it is in fact the case or not. The cause is always *objective*; it must be the case if it is to be the cause. (It makes no sense to say that A caused B if A never occurred.) Moreover, the cause must not be a cause *for me*, but, in line with the objective or scientific method in general, it must be demonstrable *for anyone* that it is the cause. A cause plays a role in a lawlike generalization which can be proven only through comparison and extrapolation with other more or less similar cases. The cause of my anger can be shown to be my having taken amphetamines because there is a lawlike generalization which has been well confirmed in a great many cases to the effect that amphetamines make a person irritable and therefore tend to make him angry at the least disturbance or apparent offense. The object of my anger, on the other hand, requires no such lawlike generalization or confirmation. As far as the object of my anger is concerned, I can consider it one of a kind. This is not to say that the objects of my anger may not fall into a neat and discernible, even familiar, pattern. Nor is it to deny that I may be unaware of the objects of my anger. It is only to say that the objects of anger (and all emotions) are strictly subjective, dependent only upon the person who "has" them. The causes of an emotion, however, have nothing to do with subjectivity and individual experience. The cause of my anger can be John's stealing my car only insofar as there is some demonstrable evidence that the knowledge of such thefts typically bring about such reactions. If, for instance, John has often taken my car without my permission (but with my knowledge) but I have never before gotten angry, then clearly it is not simply his having stolen my car that has caused me to be angry this time. Nevertheless, I may indeed be angry that he has stolen my car.

Psychology and physiology are typically concerned with the objective (that is, scientific) aspects of the emotions. Accordingly, they are primarily interested in their causes—in lawlike generalizations between certain stimulations or circumstances and typical emotional reactions. But if what characterizes an emotion is its object—as distinguished from its cause—we can appreciate how far short of a comprehensive understanding of the emotions any psychological or physiological theory must fall. To balance this account (and it need not condemn the "objective" approach by any means) my analysis will remain wholly within the subjective standpoint. I will make no attempts to theorize about the particular causes of emotions (what Freud would call their "aetiology"). *To me*, my passion is my way of seeing and structuring my world, whatever might be going on in the synapses of my brain, whatever long-forgotten childhood traumas may have set up this or that "complex" of reactions, and whatever chemicals might be peddling their unseen influence in my experiences. Of course, a change in such causes will manifest itself as a dramatic change in our emotional lives as well. What makes the causes of our emotions so insidious—whether they are "complexes" set up by our peers and parents in childhood or chemicals wittingly or unwittingly ingested—is precisely the fact that they have no place in our experience at all. The causal instruments which may cause such changes in experience are not the sphere of the philosopher but rather the neurologist, the developmental psychologist, and the pharmacologist. One might say that their interest, not ours, is the "technology of the experience," the discovery of techniques and instruments to alter our consciousness "from the outside." As a philosopher, however, I am only interested in what R. D. Laing has called the "politics of experience," changing oneself from within. The strategies of politics are ideology and persuasion, changing the object of passion rather than the cause. And however we might change other people by any number of causal techniques, it is only self-overcoming that interests me here. If we adapt Lévi-Strauss's well-known declaration about society for philosophical purposes: "Our own society is the only one which we can transform and not destroy, since the changes which we should introduce would come from within" (*Tristes Tropiques*). To change someone else, whether for "better" or for "worse," is, in a sense, to "destroy" him. But to change oneself is to *grow*.

3. Emotions as Judgments

> It is judgment that makes it possible, in fact indispensable, to think teleology as well as mechanical necessity in nature.
>
> Kant, *Critique of Judgment*

What is an emotion? An emotion is a *judgment* (or a set of judgments),‡ something we *do*. An emotion is a (set of) judg-

‡ It is a matter of indifference whether one says that an emotion is a judgment or a set of judgments. If one circumscribes a single judgment by a simple declarative sentence ("*a is b*"), then every emotion is a complex of judgments. But this criterion is surely arbitrary; how many judgments is "Fred is a repulsive and lecherous bore"? One? Two? Or three? All emotions are constituted by complex judgments with a number of dimensions, but the question of individuation may be ignored.

ment(s) which constitute our world, our surreality, and its "intentional objects." An emotion is a basic judgment about our Selves and our place in our world, the projection of the values and ideals, structures and mythologies, according to which we live and through which we experience our lives.

This is why our emotions are so dependent upon our opinions and beliefs. A change in my beliefs (for example, the refutation of my belief that John stole my car) entails (not causes) a change in my emotion (my being angry that John stole my car). I cannot be angry if I do not believe that someone has wronged or offended me. Accordingly, we might say that anger involves a *moral* judgment as well, an appeal to moral standards and not merely personal evaluations.* My anger *is* that set of judgments. Similarly, my embarrassment *is* my judgment to the effect that I am in an exceedingly awkward situation. My shame *is* my judgment to the effect that I am responsible for an untoward situation or incident. My sadness, my sorrow, and my grief *are* judgments of various severity to the effect that I have suffered a loss. An emotion is an evaluative (or a "normative") judgment, a judgment about my situation and about myself and/or about all other people.

Needless to say, this is not the usual portrait of the emotions. The emotions are usually thought to be *consequent* to judgments, perhaps a slightly delayed reaction to their import, but not the judgments themselves. Or, even more usually, the notion of judgment is omitted altogether, and the emotion is said to follow—again as a "reaction" to—some incident before us. (Thus, James's theory, as well as the theories of McDougall and most motivational theorists, holds that the emotion is the feeling that follows a perception of some disturbance in the "external world," and most behaviorists, insofar as they recognize the category of emotions at all, hold that the emotion is nothing but a preparatory or avoidance reaction to a disturbing "stimulus.") But an incident or a perception of an incident alone is never sufficient for emotion, which always involves a *personal evaluation* of the *significance* of that incident.[4] How else could we account for the fact that

---

* It is not always clear that anger involves such standards. Sometimes it surely does. John Rawls, in A *Theory of Justice* (Cambridge, Mass.: Harvard University Press, 1971), Sec. 73, suggests that it does not, contrasting anger with indignation. See my Chapter 11.

different persons have very different "emotional reactions" to the same incidents? Of course, it can be correlated with and attributed to differences in background and "conditioning," but that explains only the genesis of the differences, not their nature. Those differences can be easily accounted for once we have given up the influential model of the emotions as passive "reactions." They are not reactions but interpretations. They are not responses to what happens but evaluations of what happens. And they are not responses to those evaluative judgments but rather they *are* those judgments. Of course, we might still say that an emotion is a "reaction," namely, a conscious judgmental reaction to what happens before us and involving us. But there is nothing passive about that reaction (except, of course, that it presupposes something happening, which may or may not be the person's own doing, to which he reacts). There is no *given* in the emotions, except of course the "facts" of the case. But they are no more than an author's research notes, from which he has yet to choose his leading heroes and villains, themes and plots, digressions and climaxes.

Not all evaluative judgments are emotions. Legislating a dispute between two of my friends, I disinterestedly judge in favor of one against the other. At the supermarket, I casually judge one cantaloupe better than the other. Walking out of a Bogart double feature, I calmly argue the superiority of *Casablanca* over *To Have and Have Not*. Of course I could become "emotional" about any one of these issues, if I owe a heavy allegiance to one friend rather than the other, if I am a finicky and no doubt neurotic connoisseur of cantaloupe, if I feel a strong romantic preference for Ingrid Bergman rather than Lauren Bacall; in short, depending on what we have called my personal "investments." But it is clear that most such judgments are not "emotional" and are not emotions. The key to the difference is the adverbs, "disinterestedly," "casually," and "calmly." Emotions are self-involved and relatively *intense* evaluative judgments. They are always, whether implicitly or explicitly, judgments involving oneself as well as whatever else —disputes, cantaloupes, movies, other people or situations. The judgments and objects that constitute our emotions are those which are especially important to us, meaningful to us, concerning matters in which we have invested our Selves. Not surprisingly, most of our emotions involve other people, not only as their objects but also intersubjectively, in our concerns for our relationships, trust and intimacy, suspicion and betrayal, what others think of us as well as, insofar as we identify with them, what we think of them.

There are no a priori limits on the scope and objects of the emotions. One might have invested himself in anything and thus be emotionally committed to just about anything—pets and gardens, collections of model ships or medieval coins—with a passion that is more usually reserved for lovers and children. But what distinguishes the emotions is not *what* they value but *that* they value, that they endow our lives with meaning. A man whose life is meaningless is a man who is not emotionally committed, or whose commitments are not at all what they seem. *There* is the content of Camus's sense of "the Absurd"—not a sense of "confrontation" but a sense of emptiness, not the ruthless conclusion of Reason but the hollow logic of a reasoning that has no passionate base to which to anchor itself.

Emotions are self-involved not only in the sense that they are important to us; they are also *about* us, about our Selves, whether explicitly or not. Every emotion, as a uniquely subjective judgment, involves a judgment of both one's Self and his surreality. It is through our emotions that we constitute ourselves. In many emotions, this self-involvement is explicit and obvious, as in pride and shame, self-love and guilt. Many emotions, particularly those which tie us closest to other people, are what I shall call "bipolar," neither solely about oneself nor solely about another person and not a conjunction of the two but rather about the *relationship*, as in love and hate, anger and jealousy. Many emotions, however, leave the judgment of Self implicit or in the shadows, in admiration and worship, indignation and envy, for example. Anger, which always involves a judgment that one's Self has been offended or violated, may nonetheless focus its fervor strictly outward toward the other person. Resentment, although clearly self-involved and based upon a personal stance of defensiveness, protects its Self with a projected armor of objectivity, focusing all of its attention on its alleged oppressors. But in every case, explicitly or not, the Self is an essential pole of emotional judgment, the standpoint from which our judgments of our world and of other people begin.

The ultimate object of our emotional judgments is always our own sense of personal dignity and self-esteem. Whatever its particular object and strategy, whether it is committed to collecting butterflies or to ruling Asia, an emotion is ultimately concerned with personal status, self-respect, and one's place in his or her world. Insofar as an emotion is "about" another person, as in love or hate, anger or pity, it is the constitution of an intersubjective identity, a relationship of one sort or another, perhaps competition or comparison, within which one attempts to elevate his self-esteem. Sometimes, as in love and mutual respect or admiration, the strategy is to work together and jointly increase self-esteem, through mutual identification (in hate as well as in love) and through "self-expansion" (including another as part of one's Self). In anger, however, the strategy may be rather to boost oneself up with the leverage of accusation, casting oneself in the role of martyr or "defender of the right." In pity, one might boost his self-esteem through contrast with another person, much like himself, whose fortunes are considerably less fortunate. Even those emotions which ostensibly are not about our Selves at all, envy and resentment, faith and worship, are judgments whose ultimate object is our own self-esteem. This is not to say, however, that they always succeed in attaining this object. It will be my task in Part III to show just how, despite the common goals of our emotions, some emotions are eminently more successful than others.

Emotions are not only judgments about our present situations. Emotions are also judgments about our past, editing and organizing the countless incidents and acts of our previous years into coherent and meaningful heritages, depending upon our judgment of the present circumstances. (In love, for example, one tends to view his or her entire life as "preparing for this." But in anger at the same person, history shifts quite quickly to a history of offenses and betrayals.) Most importantly, emotions include intentions for the future, *to act*, to change the world and change our Selves, to revenge ourselves in anger, to punish ourselves in guilt, to redeem ourselves in shame, to restore our dignity in embarrassment, to help another person in pity, to caress and care for another in love, to destroy—but at a safe distance—an oppressor in resentment. In the next chapter, I will call this future-oriented aspect the "ideology" of the emotions. It, too, is an intrinsic part of our emotional judgments, even those that ostensibly focus themselves exclusively on the past, for example, remorse, sadness, and grief.

It is important to stress continually the difference between the emotion itself as a judgment and our reflective judgments about our emotions (judgments about our judgments). My being angry is my making a judgment; my recognition that I am angry is a reflective judgment about my anger (as is my judgment that my anger is justified, that, on reflection, the other person deserves [or doesn't deserve] my wrath, etc.). The self-involvement of anger, however, is not limited to the judgment of the anger alone; it may be shared by my reflective judgments which may also be aimed at the maximization of self-esteem. Reflective judgments are often straightforwardly objective; "I see myself as if I were someone else." And they always appear to be so. But there is a tangle of logical and pragmatic relationships between my judgments (my emotions) and my reflective judgments about my judgments such that it is impossible to separate them entirely. If I judge *that* I am angry, that judgment lends vital support to my being angry. (We often make ourselves angry precisely by reflecting on the idea that we are or ought to be angry.) Similarly, the denial that I am angry (when I am) surely affects the anger. It may not rid us of it, of course, or even diminish it. (In fact, traditional theory, particularly Freud's theory, would tell us that such anger denied is always intensified by the denial.) But the denial of a judgment of anger, like a lie regarding one's beliefs (see Chapter 13), has inevitable complications in the formation of other judgments and conceptions of our Selves. In the various versions of the Myth of the Passions, anger was thought to be an atomic force or feeling that remained pretty much the same whether reflectively recognized ("conscious") or not. But in this theory, the anger has a position in a network of emotional judgments which includes the reflective judgments about our emotions. Accordingly, anger acknowledged and anger denied are not the same anger at all; they are constitutive of very different emotional surrealities.

If emotions are judgments, why should it seem as if they "happen" to us? Why do we not remember making them?—as we might remember choosing between two automobiles at the car lot? How can we do something without knowing it? Not all judgments are reflective or deliberate; and not all judgments are articulated as such. Our prototype of a "judgment" is that explicitly rational, publicly expressed, deliberated decision that one finds in a courtroom or an assessor's office. But not all emotions are explicit; we make thousands of judgments every day—reaching for the light switch, glancing at the clock, turning off the fire under the scalding cappuccino—perceptual judgments, aesthetic judgments, even moral judgments, that are never articulated, deliberated, or "thought about." Emotions are such judgments, undeliberated, unarticulated, and unreflective (except on rare occasions: "Should I be angry or not?" "Should I allow myself to continue to love her or not?"). Emotions can become deliberate without lessening their intensity (though this flies in the face of one of the most established doctrines of the traditional "reason vs. the passions" dispute). They can of course become articulate (whenever we verbally express them, for example) and we are all familiar with the fact that our emotions often become more intense *as* we express them. (This, too, must be explained, since Freudian theory and most psychological theories since seem to think that emotions are "ventilated" through expression and are intensified through suppression.) And emotions *can* become reflective, aware of themselves, their purposes, and their objects. It is clear that not all emotions can stand the scrutiny of reflection, and most of us have experienced the wilting of unreasonable anger in the light of reflection. But, again, the fact that some emotions are so affected does not imply that all are.

It is because our judgments have already been made when we normally come to reflect on them that we are able to view them as "not ours" at all. By focusing on the feelings and flushings that typically accompany our emotional upheavals in times of crisis, it may well seem as if the emotion—mistakenly identified with the feeling that accompanies it—is involuntary and an unrequested result of the secretions of the autonomic nervous system. But this strategic confusion of cause and effect is only a vehicle of irresponsibility, a way of absolving oneself from blame for those fits of sensitivity and foolishness that constitute the most important moments of our lives.† It is the emotion that causes the feeling, our judgment that spurs the adrenal glands into actions, not the secretions that cause the emotion. The Myth of the Passions has so thoroughly indoctrinated us with its notion of passivity that we are no longer capable of seeing what we ourselves are doing. Once the Myth is exploded, however, it is obvious that we make ourselves angry, make ourselves depressed, make ourselves fall in love. We are like infants who for months watch our legs bobble before us, and then one day we discover that we ourselves are doing the bobbling. Once discovered, it is not a lesson unlearned. Once we have accepted responsibility for our emotions we will not ever allow them to slip away from us again.‡

4. A Note on Morality and Aesthetics

"Stealing money is wrong" expresses no proposition that can be either true or false. It is as if I had written "Stealing money!!"— where the shape and thickness of the exclamation marks show that a special sort of moral disapproval is the feeling which is being expressed.

A. J. Ayer, Language, Truth and Logic

It is only the expression of sentiment that gives the arts their meaning.

Leo Tolstoy, "What Is Art?"

The idea that an emotion is an evaluative judgment wreaks

† One of the few places in which we must side with traditional Christianity against the rapacious thrusts of Nietzsche is on the matter of the voluntariness of the emotions. Nietzsche objects to the biblical teaching that a man is responsible not only for what he does but for what he "feels" as well. Nietzsche argues that this thesis is unintelligible; but here, for once, we must violently disagree with him and defend an insight of Christian psychology that has too long been lost under the metaphysics of its theology. But see, too, Nietzsche's discussion of "the four errors," in which such strategic confusion of cause and effect plays a central role (Gay Science).

‡ Perhaps we should make the distinction between getting into emotional states (making an initial judgment) and simply being in

havoc with several long-cherished theories of morality and aesthetics. On the one hand, there is a long tradition of moralists who have argued that morality is a matter of reason, of principle, of duty, in which the passions must be allowed to play either no part whatever or, at best, a secondary and supportive role (in guilt and remorse, for example). Kant, for example, wholly excluded the passions from his conception of "moral worth," and he once called them "pathological" where duty is concerned.* On the other hand, there is an equally long tradition according to which all values, including moral values, are matters of emotion, of "sentiment" rather than reason and judgment. Hume's often-quoted phrase "Reason is, and ought to be, the slave of the passions" is the hallmark of one such theory and is still accepted by a great many British and American philosophers as the cornerstone of any adequate moral philosophy. But if in fact every "sentiment" is already a matter of judgment by its very nature, then the alleged distinction which lies at the base of this long-standing dispute between rationalists and "cognitivists" on the one hand and teleologists and "emotivists" on the other has no comprehensible interpretation. An ethics of principle differs from an ethics of sentiment only in the fact that the judgments of the latter remain unreflective and unchallenged whereas those of the former are tediously rationalized and canonized. The one is an ethics of prejudice, whereas the other is typically an ethics of dogma.

A similar set of considerations applies to the long-standing dispute over various "expression" theories of art—all of which embody the popular idea that art and its objects appeal directly to our emotions as expressions, in some (usually mysterious) sense, of the artist's emotions. Hydraulic models are often invoked in this context (as if a poem or a painting were the "outpouring" of

---

one (that is, getting angry vs. being angry). But nothing turns on this distinction. Being in an emotional state as well as getting into one, like God's maintenance of the universe as well as his creation of it, requires continuous and devoted activity. We are responsible, in other words, for being in an emotional state just as much as we are for getting into one.

* A milder version of this position is currently maintained by Rawls, op. cit., esp. Sec. 3.

its creator's "bursting" sensitivities), and the theory is in virtually every case a *causal* one, the idea that the *affect* of the viewer (or reader, listener, etc.) is *induced* by the work, which is in turn the *effect* of the artist's own sensibilities. Thus, it is suggested that the most appropriate viewing (reading, hearing) is also the most naïve, the least mediated or interfered with by critical judgment (thus, the general disdain of critics, who are thought to be unduly judgmental and ruinously critical in a realm that is supposed to give free and unhampered flow to the passions alone). But if it is true that art appeals to and expresses our emotions (and this surely is at least part of the aesthetic story), then aesthetic appreciation is already riddled with judgments, including judgments about the medium, about the subject matter, about the artist, and about the art *as* art. Accordingly, the traditional versions of the "expression" theory—and the objections to it—require some serious reconstruction.†

5. Emotional Constitution: *"the way the world is"*

> There are no facts, only interpretations.
>
> Nietzsche, *The Will to Power*

> There is no way the world is.
>
> Nelson Goodman, "The Way the World Is"

Emotions are *constitutional* judgments. They do not just *find* interpretations and evaluations of our world, identifying objects of fear and loathing, for spite and loving, intimately binding us to this person but repulsively separating us from that one, giving us a sense of superiority concerning him, a sense of inferiority regard-

† Kant's notion of "feeling," which he used like our "emotion" and contrasted with mere sensation in his third critique, might be used as a historical prototype for such reconstruction. His notion allowed him to squeeze in between his usual dichotomy of "subjective-objective" to include a form of "intersubjective" validity that is clearly appropriate in these contexts. (We might lament the fact that he did not consider similar applications in the realm of moral judgments.)

ing her. They constitute them. They do not merely *apply* standards of interpretation and evaluation to our experience but in an important sense *supply* them. This is not to say that, through our emotions, we create *de novo* the ideals and values of our world. None of us is that original. Nor is it to say that our emotions constitute "the facts" of the world. Objectively, we need not hesitate in admitting the independence of Reality from our passionate tamperings within it. But the Way the world is for us is never simply the way the world is. We do not live in Reality but in surreality, a world that is populated with objects of value and objects of fear, gains and losses, honors and injustices, intimacies and inequalities. It is our passions—and our emotions in particular—that *set up* this world, *constitute* the framework within which our knowledge of the facts has some meaning, some "relevance" to us. This is why I insist that the emotions are constitutive judgments; they do not find but "set up" our surreality. They do not apply but supply the framework of values which give our experience some meaning.

Consider the difference between a magistrate's declaration, "The defendant is guilty," and the similar statement by a court reporter telephoning his editor after the hearing. There is a sense in which they have both "said the same thing," namely that the defendant is guilty. But there is a vital difference. The magistrate, by virtue of his position, *makes* the defendant guilty by declaring that he is. The reporter only reports that he is. Regarding our own emotions, we are always in the position of the magistrate (although in uncritical reflection we may act as reporter as well). Our emotions are self-confirming judgments about our world and about our Selves. We might say that the emotions are preverbal analogues of what J. L. Austin called "performatives"—judgments that *do* something rather than simply describe or evaluate a state of affairs.[5] In anger, we judge that a friend's casual comment is offensive; but the anger is not merely a report or a "reaction" to an offense; it *declares* that the comment is offensive precisely in the same way that the magistrate declares that the defendant is guilty. One does not become angry because the comment *is* offensive: the comment is offensive by virtue of its being an object for anger. A megalomaniacal artist may become angry at the compliment that his use of color is as good as that of Pierre Bonnard (he thinks it is *better* than Bonnard). The comment is itself not offensive, but it is so constituted in the artist's anger. The emotions, like magistrates, do not find but rather are responsible for the objects of their judgment. Of course, a single judgment can be overruled. The magistrate's verdict can be reversed by an appellate court; an emotion may seem unwarranted or absurd in the court of reflection. But it is important to stress that neither can be shown to be "incorrect" or "wrong," for such terms apply only to descriptive judgments, which claim to "correspond to the facts," not to constitutive judgments, which do not "correspond" to anything. Consider a simple Austinian example: "I christen this ship the S.S. *Albanie*"; the name might well be ridiculous, or politically inappropriate, or not what was intended. But the christening cannot be wrong about the name of the vessel, for the vessel has no name before it is christened. (Austin calls these "infelicities," as opposed to "mistakes.") The magistrate's declaration may be ill considered, unjustified, irresponsible, or absurd. It may even be "unconstitutional," in which case it may be shown to be beyond the bounds of his jurisdiction. Such constraints, however, only point to the constitutional limitations of the individual magistrate: They do not deny his magisterial or constitutional powers. It is through the legal system and by virtue of his position *within* it that he is empowered to declare guilt and innocence. But then we might say it is the legal *system*, acting through its representative, that constitutes the defendant as guilty through its choice of laws and interpretations.‡ The same can be said for the emotions: One's anger may be unjustified (the allegedly offensive comment may have been an obvious compliment—that is, obvious to everyone else); it may be unwarranted (the comment may have been misunderstood or heard inaccurately). It may be overly harsh (the

‡ The fact that the court "finds" the defendant guilty is a verbal symptom of absolutist pretensions. The court makes, not finds, guilt. One is reminded of De Sade's perverse legal relativism, "a man is hanged in Istanbul for an act for which he would be handsomely rewarded in London." The notion of guilt (or innocence) makes no sense outside a constitutional system of laws. (Thus, the tired but clever quip that one could eliminate crime altogether by simply eliminating the criminal statutes that constitute certain acts as crimes.)

intensity of the anger may be out of proportion to the seriousness of the offense) or it may simply be absurd (since the person did not say anything at all). On reflection, the anger may indeed be recognized to be unreasonable, inappropriate, unfair, or foolish. But for the anger itself, its object is no less offensive (and the anger no less "real") than anger that is fully reasonable, appropriate, and fair. As a constitutive judgment, anger is never simply "incorrect" or "wrong." Its object is as it is constituted.

A single emotion may be but a near-repetition of any number of others (a "pet peeve," for example, or Don Juan serial romanticism), rigidly following its predecessors and a set of standards that have become virtually stagnant and dogmatically unquestionable ("instinctive"). A single emotion, viewed in isolation from the rest, may appear to be following rather than constituting the guidelines and structures of our surreality and our personality. But together, our emotions form an organic system of projected rules and standards within which any particular emotion takes its place, borrowing from but also contributing to that system in much the same way that a magistrate both borrows from the law and contributes to a common-law and "constitutional" legal system. Every emotion is a judgment that presupposes the entire body of previous emotional judgments to supply its context and its history as well as "paradigm cases" for it to consider if not follow. But every emotion is also an individual bit of legislation, whether striking out on its own and shifting the weight of precedent, attempting to establish itself as a new paradigm case, or merely reinforcing the biases of our already established emotional constitution. No two cases and no two emotions are precisely the same, even if they should differ only in the fact that one has come before the other. (Our emotions, unlike the law, make a great deal of this particular and objectively trivial difference: Some repetitions are celebrated as rituals—for example, making love with the same lover or making sacrifices to an object of worship. Others are damned as tedious and offensive: For example, one word of advice can be gladly accepted as an indication of well-meaning concern, whereas the second or third "word" of identical advice becomes offensive, intrusive nagging or lack of respect in one's intelligence.)

We do not create but are taught the forms of interpretation

and standards of evaluation which we employ in our emotional judgments, by our parents and our peers, by instruction and by example. Our problem, in this society at least, is that there are virtually always alternative sets of such forms and standards, providing competing laws and loyalties at war with each other. Our parents typically disagree with our peers, and what we learn through instruction is often at odds with what we learn from examples. We are taught both selfishness and selflessness, aggression and meekness, ambition and resignation, competition and compromise, the need to belong and the ideal of autonomy. We are proven superior in one world and inferior in another, all of which is confused by the persuasive ideology which teaches us that all of us are "equal" in some ill-defined sense. We are taught to stand up and fight by the same culture that teaches us to "turn the other cheek," and we are taught the power of possessions by many of the same people who advise us of the evils of greed and covetousness. And the upshot is that we must always choose among alternatives. Our emotions are always legislative decisions. Our pettiest anger and our most casual romances are existential commitments to a system of constitution, a decision about the way our world will be.

Even where there is but a single set of criteria (for example, in those small timeless societies that anthropologists paternalistically call "primitive") every application of a rule is in fact legislation regarding the existing system. Philosophers and jurists have long been concerned with the fact that, no matter how precise the law, there is never a unique and indisputable application to any particular incident.* Regarding the emotions, this becomes important every time we must decide whether two cases are "the same," and every such decision establishes or reinforces a certain precedent for future decisions. For instance, it may be clear that verbal insults are appropriate objects for anger and indignation, but it remains an open question which comments in which contexts are to be interpreted as insults. Adolescents, for example, have a practice of filling their jibing with comments of the form "your mother . . ." and "you couldn't even . . ." which in any other so-

* This problem of application greatly exercised Kant, for example (*Metaphysics of Morals*).

cial circle would appear to have all the earmarks of brutal offensiveness. Yet, in that context, an angry response is considered inappropriate and even despicable. We often find people like our megalomaniacal artist becoming offended and angry at compliments, and it is not unknown for persons to become grateful for the most cruel mockeries. And all of this is to say that there are no fixed standards of interpretation or evaluation for any emotion, and so *every* emotion must be viewed as constitutional, as an existential decision concerning the way one is to view his world.

The constitutional character of the emotions is a partial account—and a partial vindication—of the often alleged "dogmatism" and "blindness" of the emotions. When we are emotional—it is always objected—we do not have an "open mind"; we have already determined what we shall see and what we shall not. This is true. But the role of the emotions in our lives is not the same as that of those "objective" judgments in which we seek and compare, observe and experiment, test and confirm. An emotion is not a hypothesis, following certain rules of inquiry and aspiring to truth and accuracy. An emotion is an evaluative framework, which sets up, not follows, a set of rules and guidelines for itself. A child's fear of dogs, for example, is never a hypothesis or mere belief—subject to confirmation or refutation—about dogs. The fear is a predetermined framework within which dogs are *presumed* to be dangerous. Of course, such fears may well be "irrational," based upon some latent symbolic role of dogs whose manifest content is clearly unjustifiable. But such "phobias," as Freud described them, are no different in their structure than the legitimate fear of a child who has actually been attacked and bitten by several dogs before. The origin of the fear is different, and the warrant of the fear—as seen in reflection and therapy—differs accordingly. But every emotion, whatever its origins and whatever its warrant, is a before-the-fact constitutive judgment, a predisposition to react in certain ways. Compared with "open-minded" and disinterested curiosity, such predetermination will indeed seem dogmatic. But we do not *live* with open minds and curiosity, accepting whatever comes our way. We survive on our predeterminations and expectations, on our resolute decision to treat cruelty as wrong, not as a fact of life, to be grateful for kindnesses rather than take them for granted, to esteem the respect of other people, and to take every opportunity to act according to our predetermined ideals. The "dogmatism" of the emotions ought rather to be viewed as something of a virtue, one always to be coupled with objective open-mindedness perhaps, but one whose closed-mindedness, or *resoluteness* (to use Heidegger's more flattering term), is a presupposition of any meaningful or moral view of the world. Where the constitution of meaning and the establishment of standards is concerned, "open-mindedness" is no more than another name for wishy-washy indecision.

Consider what it means to "fall in love": To begin with, it is not a matter of "falling" at all, but of choice, a matter of constitution. But what does this mean? Our language of love is typically passive, from its poetic metaphors to its quasi-religious aetiology ("We were made for each other"). It is surely true that love often begins with an apparently spontaneous "attraction" or "chemistry," that we sometimes have the sense of someone as exactly the "right" person, as if the categories of companionship have been set up for us in advance. In fact, they *have* been "set up in advance"—not for us but *by* us. Our love is not a conclusion, a well-confirmed judgment of praise based upon intensive research into the virtues and vices, talents and failures, of this particular person, as if we were personnel officers interviewing for an open post. Love is a set of constitutive judgments to the effect that we *will* see in this person every possible virtue, ignore or overlook every possible vice, celebrating faults as well as charms in the context of his or her total personality.

We constitute, not find, the charms and virtues of the person whom we *choose* to love. In desperation and loneliness, we loosen our ideals to fit a broader class of people. At the extremes of desperation, we might reduce our criteria to the minimal requirement that the other person need only love us (or seem to love us) in return, no matter *who* he or she is. But even this open commitment, indiscriminate as it is, is a commitment, and a basis for the shared experiences and mutually reinforcing opinions that soon provide "something to love" in anyone. Then there are those cases in which we "fall in love at first sight," often with someone who bears little or no resemblance to the prototypes one has envisioned and adopted in the past. But even here, it is not a matter of "finding" a set of virtues which "cause" one to "fall," but rather it is a matter of discovering (or rediscovering) a set of attributes that have long been circumscribed by emotional legislation that has been developing for a lifetime, perhaps unheeded or ignored because of the more superficial and misleading demands of peer group pressures, self-imposed false images, or a certain (also self-imposed) blindness to one's own needs and circumstances.

Stendhal's famed notion of "crystallization" is part of the same phenomenon, a consequent commitment rather than mere "discovery." It might be said that the lover "creates," not finds, the virtues he continually discovers. "The facts," perhaps, are there to be found. But it is not "the facts" one discovers but newly imposed interpretations. There is no blemish that cannot be viewed as a beauty mark, no moral failing that cannot be viewed as a "wicked" charm of some peculiar but enticing variety. Similarly, André Gide's parasitic concept of "decrystallization" is not a matter of a lover's losing virtues or our discovering new vices and flaws but rather a matter of reconstituting our attitudes toward the other with diminished resolve and commitment, an attempt to break down the sense of shared identity and re-establish ourselves as *separate* individuals. And, at the extreme, there is the pathetic man or woman who guards his or her individuality so vigorously that he or she finds everyone flawed and "unworthy" of his or her intimacy. Of course, he or she always finds convincing reasons for rejecting this or that person (and aren't there always such reasons?).

The parameters of love are a set of ideals and standards which one legislates for oneself. They may be so narrow that they include one and only one person, or so stringent that they in fact (but not, of course, in intention) include no one. They may be so broad as to include any of an indefinitely large class of people, or they may be so indiscriminate and promiscuous as to include virtually anyone. But in any case, love is not so much "attraction" as it is resolution, a commitment to trust and share, to mutually praise and encourage, to mutually identify and esteem.

What we have just said about love is true of all emotions; every emotion establishes a framework within which we commit ourselves—or refuse to commit ourselves—to our world and to other people. Every emotion lays down a set of standards, to which the world, other people, and, most importantly, our Selves are expected to comply. Of course, there are emotions and emotional systems that resemble the self-indulgent and less than honest rules of a rainy-day children's game, reinvented from moment to moment and momentarily absolute—until the slightest change of fortune dictates a self-serving change. At a party, we find ourselves outraged at the "obnoxiousness" of one character, disdainful of the timidity of another. On reflection, we come to see that each of these emotions was but a self-indulgent attempt to defend ourselves against a growing sense of insecurity and self-imposed isolation. Accordingly, we determined in advance to find some sufficient fault with each of the people whom we viewed as our antagonists, thus constituting the party as a whole as an alien and repulsive landscape within which we were glad to feel excluded and delighted to leave. Without reflection and occasionally "catching ourselves," such constitutional abuses might be continued indefinitely, choosing criteria inconsistently and arbitrarily for the defensive convenience of the moment. "Incapacity to love" is typically the result of such adjustable criteria, not simply a matter of "not finding the right person" but a matter of rigorously excluding every candidate for affection with some made-for-the-occasion criticism. ("He's too short" but "He's too tall"; "She's too intellectual" but "She's not smart enough.")

It is such inconsistency and arbitrariness that give the emotions a bad name. But, rendered reflective and maintained consistently, it is this same predetermined and "before the fact" resoluteness that stands at the foundation of all love and respect, all ideals and values, all relationships and senses of community. The way we are, and the way our world is, is the collective and systematic resultant of all of our various judgments—from person to person and from time to time—our judgments of value and our judgments of status, our judgments of power and our judgments of responsibility, our judgments of trust and judgments of intimacy. If we may adapt another line from Shelley, we might say that the emotions are "the unacknowledged legislators of [our] world."

6. The Mythology of the Passions

. . . we are no less guilty of anthropomorphizing than the most unregenerate savages. Of this same fallacy we are guilty every time we think of anything whatsoever with the least warmth—we are endowing it with human attributes.

B. Berenson, *Italian Painters of the Renaissance*

The systematic unity of the judgments of the emotions corresponds to a systematic unity of the objects of the emotions. What we have been calling the "object" of an emotion is in fact only its focus, circumscribing an incident or singling out a person or an action for particular consideration. The status of an object as an object of fear or reverence, love or anger, hatred or envy, depends upon its role and its relations in surreality as a whole. Thus, the object as well as the emotion that constitutes it belongs to an extensive system of such objects. At its extreme, for example, in moods or in a very prominent emotion (a romance or rage that virtually defines a person's life), the systematic connections of an emotional object may extend to the whole of our surreality. In rare cases, an emotion may be sufficiently "out of character" or a situation may be sufficiently unusual such that its connections to other objects is minimal. But most often, the object of any single emotion belongs to an extensive drama which permeates a certain realm of our experience. To underscore the dramatic nature of these systematic connections—as well as to underscore their often fantastic imagery and dependence upon the imagination—I want to call these extended objects of our emotions. "*mythologies*."

Our emotions subjectively reorder our world, casting minor characters from the rambling plot of Reality as epic heroes and protagonists in its own intensive theatrics. We ourselves, our friends and enemies, become the focus of our world, which itself becomes a stage for the personal Thespianism of everyday life. For the emotions, the Realities of power and politics provide only the skeleton of plot, the bare bones of characterization that are listed in the cast of *dramatis personae*, introducing but not determining the surreality that is constructed around them. The emotions create their own hierarchies of status and importance, their own sense of power, often in the face of objective impotence. The emotions have their own surreal politics, sometimes in spite of the fact that their struggles for status and power are purely subjective and often without any result more manifest than the smug expression of "psychological" satisfaction.

By "mythology," I do not mean, according to the usual cynical, self-righteous definition, *somebody else's* foolish and primitive theory, a fantastic but erroneous account of a phenomenon that we can explain "correctly."† Nor is a mythology merely "idle play or coarse speculation" (Lévi-Strauss). Neither is it true that the purpose of mythology is to make the world "intelligible." According to this familiar account, a myth is an alternative to (or a species of) scientific explanation, and scientific explanation (or our more "advanced" form of scientific explanation) is naturally preferable. The purpose of mythology is rather to make the world *meaningful* (which must, of course, include or presuppose an account which makes it intelligible, but these are not the same). The Greeks distinguished sharply between *logos* and *mythos;* the first was concerned with truth, the second with imagination and meaningfulness.

> To the Hellenic mind *logos* and *mythos,* "reasoning" and "myth," are two antithetic modes of thought. The former includes everything that can be stated in rational terms, all that attains to objective truth, and appears the same to all minds. The latter includes all that cannot be subject to verification, but contains its truth in itself or, and this amounts to the same thing, in powers of persuasion arising out of its own beauty.
>
> P. Grimal, *Larousse World Mythology*

Unlike our Christian conceptions of faith (which, needless to say, are not "mythologies" at all, but rather the "gospel truth"‡), the

† Our use of "myth" in our discussion of the Myth of the Passions and the Myth of Innocence, for example, had this particular significance.

‡ Cf. Ernest Renan, who in 1855 distinguished the "Semites" from the other peoples of the ancient world because they "never had a mythology," rather a "clear and simple conception of God." Thus, we so often find that "myth" is a category reserved for other people's mythologies. Because, for example, Egyptian allegories are so filled with animal spirits and Greek stories so filled with anthropomorphic gods, these become characteristic of myth, but the tales of miracles and divine vengeance which populate the New and Old Testaments are not thought of as "myths" at all, despite the fact that they are usually as fantastic as anything that one could find in either Egyptian or Hellenic fables.

Greek mythologies were never accepted as the "truth" at all, but only as allegories of the imagination that portrayed the world in fanciful and dramatic garb.*

If a mythology is not literally "true," neither is it "false," for it is not an attempt at explanation (whatever its objective underpinning) but interpretation. It is not merely a story but neither is it a quasi-scientific or objective account of our world.† A mythology is a subjective interpretation of our world, one which may require an objective basis, but which may also allow itself the luxury of a lifetime of allegories and fantasies in its constitution of its world. No mythology may controvert "the facts," but no mythology is limited to "the facts." The mythology of emotion interprets those facts in a dramatic setting, invoking its most powerful and familiar images to do so. It does not surprise us, having been raised in a society dominated by sexual and Christian mythology, that our emotional expressions are typically cast in sexual and Christian terms—for example, "Screw you" and "Damn you" or "Go to hell" and "Bugger yourself." Good love affairs are "made in heaven," and lovers are often credited with possession of a spark of the Divine. In a society that has more concern for and spends more time with

* For example, see P. Grimal, *Larousse World Mythology* (Paris: Larousse, 1968). I am grateful to my brother, Jon D. Solomon, for some exciting discussions on this topic.

† The now popular thesis that science itself is but contemporary mythology has admirable reason behind it—the insistence that we do not use our science with a superior air to ridicule and dismiss vital mythologies which are more primitive (i.e., less scientific) and magic-oriented (i.e., concerned more with teleological explanations and questionable causal principles than the mechanical canons of Newtonian physics). But the thesis thus stated yields only confusion, since the very virtue of a myth, unlike science, is that it does not endeavor to be unbiased and anonymous, to account for the world in unreligious terms. Contemporary science is not itself a myth, although one can persuasively argue that it has usurped just that position in our lives which myths once held, leaving nothing (except for the passing enthusiasm of "scientific curiosity") in its place. (See, for example, Nietzsche on myth in *Gay Science*, in which, seventy years ago, he warned of the despair and cults of power that would soon replace the collapse of the very human if also all-too-human and brutal myths that had always structured and given significance to men's lives.)

animals and agriculture, the expressions and the mythologies behind them are more likely to contain a zoological and botanical vocabulary, tracing human events to biological ancestors and casting all forces in animal forms. There are remnants of this in our expressions (for example, "you dirty rat" and "you pig") and our frequent treatment of friends, lovers, and enemies in terms most appropriate to pet cats and dogs (occasionally to caged birds and fish, "chicks," insects and worms). It is only to be expected that our highly urbanized lives would be more impoverished in these comparisons than the farming societies of ancient Egypt and Babylon. (Once again, the anthropomorphism that is often used to characterize a more "primitive" society is only a matter of a difference in experience and allegories; is our mythical condemnation of an antagonist to hell any less primitive than the Egyptian recognition of the divine indifference of a spoiled cat?)

The basic categories (or what Jung called archetypes) are status and power, and it matters little whether these categories are expressed in biological or theological or even "scientific" terminology.‡ Nor does it matter, for the purposes of the emotion or the mythology, whether its terms are to be taken literally or not.

‡ Cross-mythological identities in structure, of course, have been the central concern of Claude Lévi-Strauss and the anthropological movement that has loosely been identified with him, appropriately called *structuralism*. Although we are not concerned here with the range of myths in various societies or with the defense of the "fundamental properties" of the human mind that Lévi-Strauss claims the structures of myth display, no employment of any theory of myth today can proceed without taking account of the vital claims of this movement. On the one hand, "structuralism" can be easily enough criticized as a new quasi-empirical version of the age-old Cartesian French fetish for universal rational structures. But the field in which Lévi-Strauss has forced this once introspective and restrictively European and bourgeois probe is dramatically new, for it no longer forces "primitive" people into the netherworld of nonrationality but recognizes them (in the style of Rousseau) as "reduced models" of the rational structures in all of us. I shall not be defending any such universal claim here, but the claim I am making, that myths are rational structures, whatever their literary or allegorical embellishments, is one which is deeply rooted in structuralist claims. See, importantly, *Tristes Tropiques, Pensée Sauvage,* and *Mythologique,* Vol. I.

Of course, one does not believe for a second, when James Cagney accuses his antagonist of being a "dirty rat," that he has made a zoological discovery. But this categorization structures the role of the antagonist in Cagney's world and prescribes the treatment he is to receive. Only a few of us literally believe that we are giving directions when we angrily tell someone to "go to hell," but the phrase is an apt indication of our attitude. We would very much like the offensive Other to spend some time in the flames, though it would not be merely our decision (and therefore not our responsibility) for sending him there. Or again, when one finds him or herself uttering a religious appeal in the throes of extreme pain or sexual pleasure, it is of no importance whether the theology invoked is literally believed or not; it is sufficient that it is such an appeal, an attitude of awesome helplessness and giving oneself over.

The categories of mythology and emotion are often hidden by the rich imaginative tapestries of the fables and fantasies expressing them. But the essence of every mythology and every emotion is a set of the most powerful values in our lives, our sense of power and impotence, our sense of uniqueness and identity, our sense of belonging and exclusion, our sense of status and interpersonal roles. In metaphorical terms, these concerns easily translate into images of activity and passivity, genetic identity through myths of genesis and reincarnation, allegories of up and down, heaven and hell, in and out (whether sexual or digestive [eating and excreting], a structure from which Lévi-Strauss gets considerable mileage, and which Freud used similarly in his notion of "identification"). The basic ingredients in myth, as Lévi-Strauss has pointed out, are typically concerned with kinship and status, including the apparently autonomous but demonstrably common rituals and experiences of eating and sexuality, terror and horror, power and impotence, identity (eating or being eaten) and exclusion (being exiled) and the rites of sacrifice and magic, murder and worship. We *live* these categories, whether literally embellished in allegory or not, and it is only the blindness of a restrictedly "scientific" fetishism that refuses to see the indisputable surrealities that underlie the admittedly fantastic and unreal stories of mythology. Far from pure fantasy, and far from the exclusive distinction between *logos* and *mythos* of the Greeks, every mythology has its demonstrable logic. Thus, every emotion has its logic as well, and, in another chapter, in which we shall discuss in detail this "logic of the emotions," we might well call that structural analysis "mythologic" as well, the logic of mytho-logy, though without thus confusing the logic of mythologies with the logic of objective thinking. The two are, in some features, very different indeed.

The mythology of emotion is the construction of surreality in dramatic form. It always, therefore, includes anthropomorphism, whether the casting of animals, plants, and idols with human attributes or the elevation of human forms to godlike status. (There is little difference between the elevation of the human to the divine, and the secularization of the divine in human terms.) The scope of such anthropomorphism varies, of course; some peoples, with a preference for teleological explanation, will allow themselves to use it anywhere. For others, notably ourselves, who insist that objective explanations must be as causal as possible, saving teleological accounts as a desperate explanatory measure,[6] the scope of anthropomorphism must be extremely restricted indeed, limited only to other people (since the treatment of them, at least, certain behaviorists and radical reductionists aside, may be "anthropomorphic" without the threat of protest). This is part of the reason (though the explanatory arrow might well turn the other way) that our emotions are primarily intersubjective, taking other people as their objects. When we do allow ourselves to get angry at the weather or fall in love with plants or automobiles, such emotions are necessarily accompanied by a peculiar anthropomorphization that may well strike us, in our more objective moments, as childish, foolish, or amusing. But it is the nature of emotion that it constitutes our world in mythological and meaningful terms, and that means *human* terms. And it is here that our emotions and mythologies so often run counter to our science; our science stresses the impersonal, the inhuman, the mechanical, forces of nature, whereas our emotions and our mythologies stress the personal, the human, the purposes and wills of our animated world. In a society with a conception of science which lies closer to mythology, it is only to be expected that men will have a rapport with nature that we typically lack. In our society, we allow ourselves the luxuries of teleological explanation only in the realm of interpersonal relations (and perhaps with a pet or two). Accordingly, our world of meaning is limited to the social world, while the natural world, the world of nature, is ever more closed off to us the better we understand it. And perhaps, when one day the physiologists have given us an adequate causal account of human behavior . . .

The danger is always the confusion of our mythology with science; the Greeks were always careful to keep these apart. But with the recent relativization of science and rediscovery of the importance of mythology, the line between them is increasingly blurred, elevating once clearly mythological disciplines to the status of candidates as scientific theories, and inversely, relegating the claims of established science to the role of alternative mythologies. It is easy to see how this has happened; as scientists became increasingly aware of the *constructive* nature of the "theoretical" or "hypothetical" entities they invoked in their explanations, the emphasis moved from the *truth* of their accounts to their coherence and adequacy, their "elegance" and their explanatory richness. But with this shift, once discarded theoretical constructions reappeared with new claims for recognition, and confirmed scientific theories found themselves humbly unable to demand exclusive recognition. By mixing the verificationist demands of science with the dramatic demands of mythology, the lines between the two have all but disappeared. For example, science will tell us authoritatively that the movement of the stars and planets depends solely on the laws of gravity and so on. But what a lifeless view! And what, then, should the stars and the heavens *mean* to us? An occasional topic of "wonder"? Suppose instead that we supposed, on the basis of precisely the same facts plus a few other questionable correlations, that the movements of the heavens were not distant clockwork but rather direct influences on our own lives, dispositions, fortunes, and abilities? How much more "meaningful" the stars would become in that case. Objectively, the defense of these additional correlations and postulated "influences" may be exceedingly difficult. But subjectively it is not the objective defensibility that is at stake; it is meaningfulness. And, short of an actual breach in the objective correlations (and they are intentionally imprecise to preclude any such breach), the objective view cannot refute the subjective view, and the subjective view has an appeal that the objective view cannot have. It is exciting; it is dramatic; it portrays our lives as pawns in the distant arms of cosmic forces. The fact that it *may* be false, or at least without specificable content, is of little subjective interest.

The line between subjectivity and objectivity, mythology and "the facts," may be difficult to discern in emotion, but the distinction can in most cases be clarified.* Of course, there will always be legions of the soft-headed who will believe in any subjective substitutions for objective and well-confirmed scientific theories just because they are more exciting (if only because they are very new or very old). Just as often there will always be those "hard-headed realists" who will not accept any belief which is not based on the cold-blooded confirmations of science. But there is enough room and need in our lives for mythology that we do not have to usurp the established claims of science. For example, the woman I love is scientifically but a few dollars' worth of chemicals, or a textbook illustration of cardiac type A, or an exemplary sociological specimen of the female *Bourgeois americanus*, subspecies *Rebellious bohemius*. To me, however, she is an answer to a prayer (whatever my religion), an incarnation of ideals and hopes. Her skin is hardly an epidermis populated by freckles, warts, hairs, sebaceous glands, and scar tissues; my love makes that view impossible (even were I an overzealous medical student or dermatologist), and I cannot help but describe her complexion (with varying degrees of clumsiness) in poetic metaphors. You may accuse me of being "unscientific," if you like, but I will hardly take that as a term of abuse. Similarly, I glorify if not exaggerate her intelligence and her beauty, her talents and her sensuosity, not by way of falsification—I do not deny a single "fact" about her—but by way of celebration, as a religious community might celebrate and even worship the attributes of its spiritual leader, whatever they might be. You might complain that no emotion is "objective," but an emotion, like a Greek allegory, is not intended to be objective or merely "true." Its purpose is to lend our surreality and our lives some significance. Love need not be blind; and an objective recog-

* This, again, is Sartre's dilemma in *Being and Nothingness*, Pt. I, Chap. 2, Sec. iii.

nition of "the facts" about our lovers and ourselves is not the least bit incompatible with our love.

As in our general discussion of subjectivity (Chapters 2 and 3) we must again warn that there is no easy criterion, from the first-person or subjective viewpoint, to distinguish Reality from subjective falsification. In the world of the paranoid schizophrenic, the world of hallucinatory wish fulfillment, the world of fictional literature and film, and in the world of unbridled emotion, the mythologies of the emotions may well give themselves to imaginative abandon, express themselves in the degenerate forms of histrionics and adventurism, or quash all fine distinctions in Manichean divisions of good and evil which have little correlation with the subtleties of our knowledge of Reality. But mythology and Reality are no more at war than subjectivity and objectivity in general; the one supports the other. Reality provides mythology with its problems and parameters, its factual ingredients and its chronological sequence. Mythology interprets and selects, edits and personifies, aggrandizes and dramatizes, our Reality and gives it meaning. In Reality, we are all recruits standing in line at preparing to be classified by an impersonal doctor according to our warts and bare qualifications. It is only with mythology that we come to see ourselves and other people as fellow strugglers in a common quest. There is no Reality so degrading that a man cannot mythologize himself as a martyr, someone else as an oppressor from whom he shall liberate himself or against whom he shall avenge himself. There is no loss that cannot be used as a cause for mourning, a celebration of the transience of happiness, no error that cannot become a Christian morality play of guilt and redemption, and no person whom we cannot love, with whom we could not share a piece of our world, no matter how small. It is by mythologizing the world (in which boredom is an essential but hopefully not dominant aspect) of our everyday lives, that we create the sense of drama. It is something less than a creative enterprise as such, but its imaginative and constitutive character leaves open room for creativity that few people ever attempt to use, except in the wholly unreflective desperation of an untoward passion that requires the misuse of the imagination to rationalize its already unintelligible scenario into some coherent mythology. Our emotions are our personal projections onto our own world.

The fact that our emotional surrealities are so tediously similar
and often degrading and our projections so uniformly defensive
speaks to the fact that we have, because of the reflective myths
(in the derogatory sense) in which our emotions have been
couched, taken poor advantage of our most powerful and most
personal instruments for making our lives meaningful—our emotions.

CHAPTER 6: "WHAT IS TO BE DONE?"

An emotion is a transformation of the world.

Sartre, *The Emotions*

1. *Personal Ideologies: "How the World Ought to Be"*

A tablet of the good hangs over every people. Behold, it is the tablet of their overcomings. Behold, it is the voice of their will to power.

Nietzsche, *Thus Spake Zarathustra*

Through our emotions we constitute and mythologize our world, projecting our values and passing judgments on ourselves and other people, our situations and the various "intentional objects" in which we have invested our interests. But our emotions are more than this, more than detached and critical appraisals of a static and "external" world. This is *our* world. A historian reviewing Wellington's strategy at Waterloo is only a judge; he does not alter his subject matter. We, however, live our surreality. We are always in the midst of the battle rather than safely reflecting upon it in calm and comfortable retrospect. Our emotions are not only projections; they are our *projects*. They are not only directed toward intentional objects; they are laden with *intentions to act*. Emotions are concerned not only with "the way the world is" but with the way the world *ought* to be. Every emotion, in other words, is also a personal ideology, a projection into the future, and a system of hopes and desires, expectations and commitments, intentions and strategies for changing our world.

It is often suggested (for example, by Ryle and a great many psychologists) that our emotions interfere with purposive action, that they are disruptive and disorienting, mere "agitations" or "affects." But nothing could be further from the truth; every emotion, even those that are ostensibly backward-looking (for example, sadness and shame) thrust themselves into the future ("What will I do now?"). Usually the connections between the emotion and its various desires and hopes are obvious—for example, the desire of anger to punish, of hatred to hurt, of love to share, to be with, and to caress, of jealousy to take away, of sadness to restore, of shame to redeem, of embarrassment to hide or excuse oneself, of gratitude to thank, of spite to destroy. Thus, James told us that he found it "unthinkable" that there could be rage without a "tendency to vigorous action." One can be more specific; that "vigorous action" (even if it be no more "vigorous" than pulling a trigger or writing a damning letter) is an act of punishment, and the connection between the emotion of anger and that act of punishment is *logical*. There can be no anger (or outrage, fury, indignation, etc.) without the desire to punish. Anger is essentially a judgment of condemnation, setting up a judicial mythology in which one is both judge and jury. The punitive sentence follows upon the indictment and the verdict just as assuredly as it does in a real-life courtroom. Of course, it is not always the judge who carries out the actual punishment, and thus it need not always be the angry person who actually performs the punishing act. But the demand for punishment is as much a part of the anger as the judgment itself. Anger is not only a constitutive judgment of accusation and guilt; it is also an ideology which demands rectification and the balance of justice in the world.*

The same is true of love and hatred. To love someone is not merely to praise him or her from a distance, or to abstractly constitute a relationship of trust and intersubjectivity. To love someone is to desire to be together, to wish and work for the best for each other, to desire to touch and to be touched, to adopt as one's own the desires of the other. The ideology of love is an ideology that would focus the universe on the happiness of one's lover and provide the cosmic cement that would hold the two together. ("We were made for each other.") Conversely, the ideology of

* Christian ethics, in speaking of anger, insists upon "forgiving and forgetting." Why mention both? The first is aimed at the indicting judgment and the second at the punitive judgment (which will be carried out by other Hands anyway).

hate is an ideology of hurt, not necessarily punishment so much as the destruction of evil, as if the enemy were, by his or her very existence, a blight in the world, a monstrous dragon or troll who must be destroyed. Not surprisingly, the mythologies of love and hate more often than not resemble medieval morality plays. Their ideologies are charged with conceptions of guilt and innocence, absolute good and evil, and the Romantic conceptions of heroism and chivalry.

Not all ideologies involve desires and intentions as such. Many emotions involve situations which are beyond us, and the ideology is consequently one of hope and expectation rather than desire and intentions. For example, envy hopes for the worst (for someone else), whereas faith hopes for the best—and expects it, regardless of one's own actions. Respect for another person includes a huge number of expectations regarding his or her behavior but no desires which one can do anything about. (In fact, the mark of respect of another is precisely the lack of any sense of need to interfere and control the other's behavior.) In many cases, the ideology of an emotion may involve impossible counterfactuals; for example, grief and sorrow wish for—but could not possibly expect—the restoration of an irrestorable loss. Guilt, to take a very different example, craves nothing more than its own redemption, a redemption which, by its very nature, it knows to be impossible. Here is where guilt differs most dramatically from shame, which always allows itself the possibility of redemption. It is worth noting that the most spectacular ideology of guilt—the guilt of "Original Sin," which has dominated so much of Christian thought for so many centuries—is an apt metaphysical expression of precisely this sense of impotence in the face of guilt. One cannot, by the very nature of this emotion, redeem himself. However degrading and nonsensical this religious doctrine might sometimes appear to us, it is impossible to feel guilty and not appreciate the profound insight of that still dominating mythology and the very short step between the smallest irredeemable slip (or "Sin") and the cosmic self-indictment that is characteristic of "Original" (inescapable) Sin.

There are emotions whose desires and intentions carry such moral weight that one is justified in calling them commitments. For example, indignation, unlike simple anger, seems to call for a moral commitment to rectify a wrongdoing, not simply as a matter of personal desire (as in petty anger against an uncalled-for insult, for example), but as a matter of moral principle. The same is true of rage and, regarding one's own offenses, shame. A strong case can be made that such ideologies of commitment apply as well in love and hate, despite the fact that the desires included there need not involve any moral principle. In love, notably, it seems that a certain commitment to one's lover is essential to the emotion. The commitment is a very general one—namely, to make the other's welfare one's own, although the specifics of that commitment (sexual fidelity, financial assistance, "till death do us part" attachment, varieties of obedience and servitude) may vary dramatically from instance to instance. Similarly, hatred, unlike simple anger or a large number of other "negative" attitudes toward another (contempt, spite, envy, loathing, disdain), seems to involve a strong commitment to the destruction of the enemy.

There are also emotions whose desires and intentions are precisely *not* to act, but rather to accept the world "as it is." This, too, of course, is an ideology (just as a conservative or a reactionary political position is an ideology). In resignation, for example, we accept, though unhappily, a state of affairs that is unsatisfactory to us. In contentment, we happily accept a state of affairs as satisfactory. To loathe someone is inactive in this sense also; these emotions, unlike hatred, are willing to tolerate (and may even celebrate) the existence of the object of their disdain without taking any action toward it (him or her). Similarly, there is that familiar emotion of indifference (which, on closer view, is anything but indifferent) whose most visible characteristic is its unwillingness to take any action—even the barest act of recognition—toward its object.

In general, every emotion, in its constitution of our world, establishes an ideology—a set of desires, hopes, demands, expectations—which it seeks to satisfy. To say that an emotion constitutes our world according to our values is *not* to say that we create the world as we would like it to be. The constitution of our world through our emotions is one thing, but the satisfaction of our emotional ideologies is quite another. In indignation, for example, we constitute someone's behavior as cruelty and vigorously condemn it. But condemnation is not yet rectification. Satisfaction, in many cases, requires effective action. Sometimes, it requires outside help or just "good luck." In those emotions whose desires are impossible (for example, grief and guilt), there can be no satisfaction. But even in those emotions in which the desires are obviously straightforward and satisfaction is clearly possible, there are complications. Not only is it the case that many desires are not easily or even possibly satisfied, but, many times, the satisfaction of our desires dissatisfies *us*. And here is where the ideologies of emotions (like political ideologies) become involved in a complex dialectic of changing desires and over-all strategies.

The first complication in a great many of our emotions, to state the obvious, is that we are not omnipotent. We become angry at a powerful figure, but find ourselves incapable of effectively punishing him. We love someone who is out of reach, beyond our hearing and beyond our help. We envy a hero or a celebrity who lives in a different world than we do; we regret a previous offense or feel sorrow at a loss without any possibility whatever of erasing the former or restoring the latter. Such emotions remain unsatisfied. A satisfied emotion, like a satisfied desire, ceases to have any role in our subjectivity. An unsatisfied emotion, however, sits and smarts, not as a thorn, but as a seed of discontent, which grows in importance and becomes increasingly dominant in our outlook on the world, sprouting other emotions in its own image and possibly coming to dominate the whole of our lives.

It is often said that an emotion "expressed" is an emotion gotten rid of. Where expression leads to satisfaction, we can see that this is true. But not all expression leads to satisfaction, and many emotions (for example, faith and hope) can be satisfied without being expressed at all. Moreover, "expression" has come to mean many different things regarding our emotions. An "expression" may be an action seeking to satisfy the emotion, or it may simply be some behavior (a grimace or gesture) which is symptomatic of the emotion. Many expressions are indirect and can be linked to the emotion only through the circuitous chain of reasoning of a possibly complex emotional strategy, and some expressions are only "symbolic," not leading to satisfaction at all. And some "expressions," for example, James's increased pulse and flushed face, are not expressions at all. In the following sections, I shall pursue these complications in some detail.

The impotence of an emotion need not be its *inability* to satisfy itself so much as our *unwillingness* to satisfy it. One source of such unwillingness is the presence of intolerable consequences of expression. Upon becoming angry—even furious—at the six-foot-seven goon in the local bar, my ideology and surely my mythology includes the David and Goliath fantasy of my laying him low with a single well-placed blow. But I'm not that stupid. I know full well the probable outcome of the slightest gesture of intended violence on my part. Of course I could also inflict enough damage and embarrassment to satisfy my anger, but it just isn't worth it. Better to leave my anger unsatisfied, or to satisfy it in some other, less direct and less dangerous way.

Another source of impotence in our emotional ideologies is a conflict of emotions. My anger may well conflict with my pride, or my love, or my contempt. If I conceive of myself as an unflappable paragon of fair play and calm negotiations, my anger in any form of expression is unacceptable to me. No matter how easily the anger might be satisfied, *I* would be less satisfied, because of my pride. Similarly, when I become angry—no matter how rightly so—at someone I love, the anger conflicts with the love. The first involves an ideology of punishment and hurt; the second includes an ideology of concern, forgiveness, and help. However essential or inevitable anger might be in any love relationship, it must be recognized that there is always an initial contradiction. In contempt, our anger conflicts with a more powerful sense of avoidance: The anger insists on confrontation and concern; the contempt demands distance and indifference. Thus, many emotions may be insatiable because they conflict with other more powerful emotions. (Similarly, an act of seeming political urgency may well be suppressed for the sake of longer term and more general ideological considerations.)

A far more interesting complication emerges from the role of emotion in our lives, whatever the consequences, whatever the ease of satisfaction, and without any conflict whatever with other emotions and desires. To satisfy an emotion or a desire is to "be rid of it." But our emotions are not merely intrusive needs, to be satisfied and thus eliminated as quickly as possible, like bursting bladders in a business meeting. Our emotions give meaning to our lives. Thus the total satisfaction of all our emotions (which is different from having an emotion of satisfaction) would be, in effect, to leave life utterly without meaning (that dubious "peace" or "Nirvana" that is so closely linked with death in both Freud and Buddhism). It is often the case that the emotion or the desire itself is more desirable than its satisfaction. To choose a simple example, the long build-up of a craving for sex or a sweet may turn out to be far more enjoyable than a too-quick moment of satisfaction. An ambition satisfied is an ambition no more, and it is not uncommon for such "satisfaction" to be greeted with an overwhelming sense of depression or meaninglessness. The playwright Schiller, for example, complained that the most despairing moments of his life were those immediately following the completion and performance, no matter how successful, of one of his works. Similarly his good friend Goethe complained that "from desire I rush to satisfaction; and from satisfaction I rush to desire" (*Faust*).

Our emotional ideologies are not just sets of desires and demands for satisfaction; they play a vital and definitive role in endowing our lives with meaning, and it is the *dis*satisfaction of our emotions that allows them to be durable structures in our lives. Anger and indignation provide us with a certain sense of judicious self-righteousness, and the sense that self-righteousness may well be more desirable than the satisfaction of the desire for punishment that is part of the emotion itself. And we all know that unfortunate loss of passion and meaningfulness that may come with the realization that the person whom we so desperately desire desires us even more desperately in return. There is a moment of elated satisfaction, and then a seemingly inexplicable letdown. ("Why should I feel so unsatisfied, when I finally have exactly what I wanted?") Stendhal, in his brilliant novels of Romantic gamesmanship, insists that "love requires uncertainty" (*D'Amour*), a continuous shift in demands and their satisfaction such that the love is kept alive. The love is more important than the satisfaction of its demands. (A little chastity, for example, may be a far better incitement of love at certain times than continued repetition of satisfying love-making.)

Similarly, nothing leaves us more lost than the successful vanquishing of a hated enemy. (What did St. George do *after* he slayed the dragon?) The quest itself gives purpose to our lives; its satisfaction robs us of that purpose, even while it satisfies the emotion. In general, our emotions and the meanings of our lives depend upon these gaps between emotions and their satisfaction, between "the way the world is" and "the way it ought to be." In frustration, we often think that what we would really like is to have all of our desires and emotions satisfied. We daydream cosmic fantasies in which the universe as a whole is aimed at nothing other than our emotional satisfaction (the daydream of Camus, whose disappointment led him directly to its antithesis—"the Absurd," the *indifference* of the universe). Because the meaning of our lives depends on the continuity of our emotions rather than their satisfaction, we so often put ourselves into emotional attitudes which cannot possibly be satisfied. "Of course," we can agree with those wise men whose idea of wisdom is to eliminate life, "our lives would be easier, even more rational, if we would not make such demands upon ourselves." But no understanding of the passions is possible until we come to appreciate this all-important and perhaps surprising feature; that their unsatisfied existence is, in general, often more important to us than their successful expression and satisfaction.

The various ideologies of our emotions have a common goal—personal dignity and self-esteem, the ultimate goal of all subjectivity. The particular demands of our emotions, however, are often objective—that is, they demand a change in *the* world as well as in *our* world. In anger, for example, it is not enough to believe that one has been vindicated; anger demands that one be vindicated *in fact*. In love, it is not enough to think that one's lover is well-off; love demands the *real* welfare of the lover. But the fact that the satisfaction of the particular demands of our emotions is often a matter of *the* world while the ultimate goal of our emotions is subjective, introduces a fascinating complication into our emotional lives. The satisfaction of an emotion may require a change in the world, but *our* satisfaction—that is, the maximization of our self-esteem—may turn precisely on the dissatisfaction of the emotion. Thus, ultimately, it is our *over-all* surreality that is at stake, not the real satisfaction of any particular demand or desire. Self-esteem may be maximized with a minimum change in the world; for example, the frustration of desire, which initially tends to lower self-esteem, may be more than compensated for by a stoical attitude, "It's all for the best," or by the conversion of frustrated desire into self-aggrandizing paranoia ("Everyone's trying to keep it from me") or protective envy, resentment, or spite ("They don't deserve it"), which look past our own frustration to the Sins of the World, portraying ourselves as self-righteous victims of oppression.

Mythologies become ideologies when we play a role in them, live in them, take action and take sides. But the roles are varied, from hero to pariah, from saint to buffoon, from martyr to nebbish. The consequences range from guaranteed success to certain disaster, and our own abilities to act vary from omnipotence to impotence. Accordingly, the ideologies of our emotions may manifest themselves in direct action, or, like their political counterparts, they may develop a complex and sophisticated quasi-historical manifesto, recasting the past as a documentary and predicting the future in terms of inevitable outcomes which may or may not require (or even permit) direct action. In moral indignation, for example, an ideology of injustice and abuse requires some attempt at personal vindication and retribution. In envy and resentment, however, our ideologies are such that our own impotence is built into their very conceptions. The familiar ideologies of evangelical Christianity and Marxism are but canonized and "objectified" examples of the subjective demands and hopeful expectations and fears of these powerful emotions.

Our emotional ideologies involve a delicate balance between demands for action and purely subjective reconstitutions of our world. An emotion is never an isolated impulse, and a person who simply "acts on his feelings" is probably a person whose "feelings" —that is, whose emotions, mythologies, and ideologies—are seriously impoverished. Demands for action are in fact only a small component of our emotional ideologies spurred by hopeful expectations and anticipated consequences, inhibited by conflicts and by alternative demands. Yet an emotion without action is often self-defeating, a fortress of defensiveness which, in return for security, locks us away from other people and denies itself any opportunity to change the world as our emotion demands. Accordingly, the *expression* of our emotions is a complex matter, sometimes involving direct and effective action, but more often than not involving a complex and circuitous strategy as well as "symbolic," and even "magical," gestures and silent incantations with no apparent effect whatever. It is to these various "vicissitudes" of expression to which I now turn.

2. Emotions and Their Expression

> I was angry with my friend:
> I told my wrath, my wrath did end.
> I was angry with my foe:
> I told it not, my wrath did grow.

William Blake, *Songs of Experience*

"S'press yourself!"—so goes one of the more contemporary contractions of a new virtue. It is believed, and sometimes rightly so, that an unexpressed emotion tends to "poison" the personality somewhat like urea poisons the blood when it is denied its normal excretory exits. The comparison is not gratuitous, for the usual model of emotional expression—the hydraulic model—envisions "pent-up" and "repressed" emotions as just such poison, filling the psyche, crippling the personality, and interfering with our "normal" mental functioning. The key to Freud's therapeutic theory, for example, was the thesis that the poisonous emotion could be weakened and controlled just by "discharging it" through "catharsis." Similar hydraulic pronouncements may be found in the tenets of virtually every therapeutic theory, from primal screaming to encounter grouping and Gestaltist "hot-seating." The ability to express one's emotions has long been accepted as the hallmark of mental health; their suppression or repression is known to be the cause if not the criterion of most common neuroses.

What is "expression" of emotion, and why is it so necessary? The very word gives us a clue, that is, a false one, "ex-press," from the Latin, *ex* + *primere* (to "force out").† The implicit metaphor is already known to us, the hydraulic metaphor of emotions as forces and pressures, filling up the psyche like blood boiling in a

† See Richard Wollheim, "An expression is the secretion of an inner state," *Art and Its Objects* (New York: Harper & Row, 1968), p. 27.

roasting pig, kept from bursting only by the thin membranes of the terrified ego. With luck and a great deal of effort, the forces can be contained completely and denied expression; otherwise, they may be channeled, dispersed, or redirected as harmlessly as possible, possibly in art or sports, or perhaps in the high-priced privacy of an analyst's office.

According to the hydraulic model, the need for expression is easily explained by this tangible and familiar picture of pressure and containment, "discharge" and retention. Psychology becomes a version of urology, less tangible but equally mechanical. We cannot help our need to express our emotions any more than we can help our need to excrete. We can be held responsible for the precise timing and character of our expression, of course, but even this responsibility may be waived in cases of overwhelming pressures. (We excuse even a murderer if he is sufficiently "hot-blooded"; and who among us has not appealed for clemency on the appeal that he was "under great pressure" or "great strain"?) In most cases, we are not expected to "give in" to our emotions, at least not without a struggle. But the very notion of "giving in" already affirms the wholesale acceptance of the hydraulic model, as if the emotions themselves and their demands for expression were wholly beyond our grasp. All we can do, according to this model, is suppress or channel such forces and needs into as "non-disruptive," as unembarrassing, and as "sublime" an expression as possible. The highest accolades of our society are reserved for those who practice total "self-control," remaining cool in the face of not only fearful opposition but of love, respect, and affection as well.

As always, the hydraulic model is the metaphorical and pseudoscientific structure of the Myth of the Passions; its purpose, to free us of responsibility. Once it was the case that we could excuse only our more violent expressions by appeal to the overwhelming force of our passions. But today, with the new post-Freudian fetishism for "openness" and expression and the neo-Romantic counterattack on inhibition and "up-tightness," the hydraulic model provides us with an always acceptable excuse to say nasty and destructive things to each other—and even to act them out in limited ways—by appeal to our "mental health." ("I'm just telling you how I feel, so you have no right to be angry with me.") Not all emotional expression is a matter of "discharge" and "release," however. Even limiting our attention to straightforward expressive actions, it is clear that they often have both the intention and the effect of *intensifying*, not eliminating, the emotion. Brooding anger and resentment, for example, do not attempt to satisfy themselves so much as to provoke further the very conditions which have prompted them. Lovers intentionally "work themselves up" to heights of passion, creating epic traumas on the basis of faint nagging doubts just in order to intensify their mutual feelings. Mourning is not a means of forgetting but rather a way of remembering and increasing one's grief.

Love and respect are not emotions from which we desire "release." Nor is pride. Even the painful emotions of shame and remorse do not desire "catharsis," but rather forgiveness and redemption. Anger does not want "discharge" but satisfaction. So long as we focus our attention on those few instances of emotion which fit Freud's quasi-urological model, the variety and "vicissitudes" of emotional expression will remain a total mystery to us (or else we will be tempted, like Freud, to reduce all emotions to that simple class of pressures that he so glibly identified as "libidinal energy." As if the physiological pressures of male sexuality could serve as a paradigm for virtually any emotion!).

The concept of emotional expression is complicated by the fact that it is so often used to refer to many different manifestations of emotion. There are "facial expressions"—for example, frowns and grimaces, smiles and looks of terror. But it is not always clear that such "expressions" are expressions at all; sometimes they are *symptoms* or *signs* of emotion. William James includes quickening of the pulse and flushing as "expressions" of emotion, and many psychologists would include *any* publicly observable manifestation of an emotion, even neurological changes, as its expression.

The hydraulic metaphor and strict etymology would lead one to look for emotional expression or "forcing out" in terms of an emission, a psychical excretion of some sort. Accordingly, screams and shrieks and other barely intelligible and seemingly squeezed-out violent utterances have often been chosen as the paradigm of emotional expression. (The inarticulate "primal scream," for example, has recently been given the leading role in one of the simplest as well as most expensive therapies since medieval exorcism.)

It is true that screams and shrieks and also more articulate verbal expressions form a solid core of our expressive repertoire (as Darwin argued nearly a century ago). But if we are to single out a paradigm of emotional expression, it would surely have to be *action*, and namely that direct action which is demanded by an emotional ideology. This includes verbal action, of course, and a few well-chosen words may often prove far more direct and effective than a brutal punch or a swift kick. But then even a dirty look or a smile, in the appropriate circumstances, may provide wholly satisfactory expression for our emotions. As a general rule, we may say that an emotional expression is action demanded by the logic and ideology of the emotion and particular circumstances. Accordingly, facial expressions may sometimes be true expressions—that is, when they tend to serve the ideology of the emotion, but other times they may be mere habits, symptoms, and signs, not expressions at all. Physiological responses, flushing and pulsing, on this account, are not expressions at all.

Regarding verbal expressions, one must be cautious of a certain ambiguity between "expression" as acting out, which is my concern here, and "expression" as articulation (as in "verbal expression" in general, "expressing a thought," for example). The caution is required because verbal expression of an emotion is no different in form, but very different in its function, from *verbal description* of an emotion, as in reflection. "I am angry" and "I love you," for example, may serve as apt emotional expressions; but they may also be passionless self-descriptions which have no expressive function whatever. In fact, a verbal expression may well be *false* as a description, when the distraught lover screams "I hate you" as an unmistakable expression of love. Verbal expression *uses* words to effect its demands; description is concerned with the truth and falsity of its claims. To honestly describe one's emotion is not yet to express it, and the sense of candor and forthrightness that accompanies the former must not be confused with the satisfaction that is achieved by the latter. The relation between these two is often complex, needless to say, and a single verbal utterance may serve both functions simultaneously. (For example, I am about to say, "I am sorry," but "I am angry" slips out in conversation. This would seem to constitute both recognition of my anger and an expression of it.)

In general, an emotional expression is an action which functions to realize the demands of our emotional ideology. Thus the "natural" expression of anger is punitive action, as direct and as effective as possible under the circumstances. However, this is not always possible, and when it is not, the vicissitudes of expression become far more complex.

Even more complicated, however, are those many expressions of emotion which are ostensibly neither directly nor indirectly effective. After the state trooper has given me a speeding ticket, I violently kick the steering column of the car. The employee who has been chastised by his superior returns to his desk muttering curses and giving angry looks to his wastebasket. Not yet confident enough to express my love openly to the woman across the room, I caress the arms of my chair. In resentment and envy, we gnash our teeth, swallow hard, and shove our fists into our pockets. All of this is expression, too, not merely symptomatic of emotion (like a flush or a quickened pulse), but not evidently intended to realize the demands of our emotional ideology. Accordingly, these are often called "compensatory" or "symbolic" expressions, not effective in fact but rather abbreviated versions of expressions which would be effective. The muttered curse spoken to the wastebasket is spoken *as if* it were intended for the superior; the kick to the steering column is given *as if* it were intended for the shins of the trooper. But the logic of this "*as if*" is peculiar. I shall discuss it specifically in the next section.

I spoke a moment ago of the "natural" expression of an emotion, namely, the direct and most effective means for satisfying its ideological demands. This is not, of course, the usual denotation of that phrase. Again, according to the hydraulic model, the "natural" outlet of an emotion is that which is predetermined by "nature," as if our emotional expressions were stereotyped and uniform gestures and behaviors, something like the mating rituals of a squirrel fish. But in this sense, there are no "natural" expressions of emotion. In anger, the nature of the offense and the vulnerability of the offender determine the particular form of punishment that will be required. For a small child, a dirty look may be more than sufficient; for a friend, a few words of abuse will suffice; for a fiend, nothing short of crippling physical harm or death may seem sufficient. In love, the "natural" expression surely depends upon the nature of one's affection and the sensitivity and desires of one's lover. Wanting to touch (or to be touched) may be the norm, but it need not be "natural," at least not in the sense that it is built into the ideology of love. (Consider, for example, a nun's love of Christ; why should one call that "a different kind of love" just because the satisfaction of its ideology does not include the need to touch or to be touched?) In short, the "natural expression of emotion" can mean only that open-ended class of direct and effective actions that will satisfy our ideology—hurting in hatred, depriving in envy and in spite, praising in admiration, and showing off in vanity. But no specific action is dictated by any of the above. The "natural expression of emotion," in other words, has nothing to do with nature.

The logic of the emotion dictates the logic of the expression. Anger demands an angry expression; love requires a loving expression. Even where direct and effective action is not possible, the logic is intact, adding to its parameters its own inability or unwillingness to act directly and effectively. In desperation, we mask our impotent resentment under a smile of superiority and a mask of arrogance. But even in pretense it is the logic of the emotions that determines the expression, which presupposes but abuses this logic much as a clever but unscrupulous lawyer or politician might presuppose and abuse (even as he adamantly defends) the legal system which he twists to his own advantage.

On the hydraulic model, the connection between emotions and particular expressions has always been something of a mystery. Why should a certain pressure "inside of us" require a particular outlet, often a very subtle and sophisticated bit of behavior? Is it because the psyche, like the bladder, has certain prearranged routes of excretion? (Thus the age-old fetish for "maps" of consciousness, from the millennia-old plumbing charts of the ancient Hindus to the modern "topographical" charts of flushing Freudian hydraulics.) Why are not all of our "pent-up" emotions released by a single primal scream, a bout of boxing or aggressive sexuality, a few drinks or tranquilizers? How is it possible, on the hydraulic model, to "talk out" as well as "act out" an emotion? (And why should it matter *what* we talk *about*, or *whom* we are talking *to*?)

In my theory, the connection between the emotion and its particular expression, particularly when that expression is a direct action, can be easily accounted for. The ideology of the emotion, coupled with our judgments of the circumstances, dictates, usually quite clearly, the appropriate expression. Quite the contrary of a Newtonian interplay of compressed forces, the emotion is related to its expression through the "logic" of an Aristotelian "practical syllogism": "Offenders ought to be punished; Socrates is offensive; Socrates can best be punished by writing a sarcastic play about him; therefore . . ." The expression of an emotion is not its "forcing out" at all, but rather its realization. The expression is an attempt, no matter how feeble, to *make* the world the way our emotion judges that it *ought* to be.

According to the hydraulic model, there is a logical gap between an emotion and its expression. The connection between the two is a matter of contingency, perhaps of arbitrarily developed habits or inexplicable "instincts." This gives rise to a curious problem, which I call the "Problem of Contingency." In an abstract form it has dominated Anglo-American and European philosophy for most of this century under the title the "Problem of Other Minds." It has, however, a more familiar and everyday manifestation: in the skepticism that has become a healthy rule of thumb in a society in which plastic smiles so often mask manipulation and rage; at the jagged end of a long and intimate love affair when there is the crushing doubt that "she/he never loved me; it was pretense all the time"; in those everyday paranoid fantasies in which we wonder whether we can really trust any of the people who surround us. The "Problem of Contingency" is the suspicion that we cannot ever really know the emotions of another person. At most we can take a person's behavior and what he tells us, his facial expressions, and his gestures as a clue. But since there is no logical connection between the emotion "inside him" and the public expressions we observe, we can never know for certain. At best, we can *assume* that people are not "putting us on." But why should we trust them, since we have no evidence for that either? We know how people sometimes feign emotions, in various rituals (funerals, weddings, and public meetings), as a matter of mock pretense (on the stage or in a game), and as a matter of manipulation and deceit. Could it be that this is *always* the case?

Such might be our fears regarding other people, but in our own case, subjectively, we know otherwise; we know how difficult it is to feign sincerity and sympathy toward a person we despise, how impossible it is to pretend indifference toward one we love. If our emotions and our behavior were but contingently related, it should be an easy matter to train ourselves in any behavioral repertoire we choose, suffering our feelings as they come but always acting in our own best interests. But how obviously false are those smiles without friendliness, how hollow that phony indignation. We know the difficulty of prying open the slightest logical gap between our emotions and our expressions. We try to act as though we were not depressed, but what emerges is forced laughter and gallows-style wisecracks; we try to act friendly to someone we despise but find ourselves unctuous and unwittingly biting even in our faked compliments. We try to pretend confidence and charm, and our behavior becomes frozen and rigid ("plastic" is an apt contemporary characterization), as the only way to maintain false postures over any period of time.

In *The Counterfeiters*, André Gide argued that the connection between feigning an emotion and really having it is far more intimate than is usually expected. We know that intimacy. In order to be congenial with a group of new-found friends, we feign indignation along with them—and soon we find ourselves genuinely indignant. We know how easily feigned envy and resentment, feigned infatuation and love, turn into "the real thing." But on our model of emotions, this should not surprise us. To have an emotion is to adopt a system of judgments, a mythology and an ideology, demanding that the world be a certain way. To feign an emotion is to step into that logical and ideological system, to act in such a way as to change the world as that emotion demands. To feign an emotion (for more than a few minutes, anyway) is not merely to indulge in one or two isolated bits of behavior; it is to adopt a living role and an outlook on the world. Not surprisingly, if the pretense is to be successful at all, one must already share many of the judgments and presuppositions of that outlook. And since the emotions are, by their very nature, our most self-involved and important judgments, the basic structures of our world, to feign an emotion is to dangerously toy with our most persuasive and self-interested concerns. To feign an emotion we must ultimately live *against* our own Selves and deny our own world. Accordingly, it is never in our interest to protractedly feign our emotions.

There are limits to pretense, which is effective only because it presupposes and only occasionally abuses the logic of emotion. There may always be those clever people whose convoluted logic of expression will more often allow them to "con" us to their own advantage. But even there, it is not the Problem of Contingency that allows us to be misled, but only our own self-deceptions and our own lack of insight, our unreflected needs to believe in a sham which, just because it is a sham, will always lapse into moments of authenticity and betray itself. Against the Problem of Contingency, therefore, I argue that the connection between an emotion and its expression is always logical and not contingent, no matter how convoluted that logic may become in any particular case. *Emotions will out.* As projects and projections into our world, they cannot separate themselves, except for an occasional moment, from their own expressions.

Discussions of the "Problem of Other Minds" usually turn on the least interesting and least expressive "expressions," such as facial expressions. It is, for example, pointed out that the Chinese open their eyes to express anger, whereas we narrow them. Edgar Rice Burroughs once envisioned a people whose emotional expressions were the "opposite" of ours, crying to express happiness and laughing to express sorrow. But this contingent relativism is plausible only so long as we remain on the most superficial planes of description, restricting our attention to the most minimal and least effective expressions—if they are expressions at all. What will not differ from society to society or from person to person is the ultimate *significance* of those expressions, however foreign and different the conventions, values, and strategies that constitute the logic of their emotions.

The expression of an emotion is, in general, those actions, gestures, utterances, and postures that will satisfy the demands of our emotional ideologies—directly if possible and indirectly, through varied and possibly devious strategies, if necessary. Yet there are those expressions which are clearly not effective in satisfying our ideological demands, either directly or indirectly. They cannot be simply excluded from the realm of "expression," however, for in many cases, such as kicking an inanimate object out of resentment, confessing one's "unrequited" love to a third party, these expressions are usually thought to be paradigms of emotional expression. But what, then, do they express? What is their function in our emotions and in our lives?

3. Emotions and Magic

> When I am angry about something, I sometimes beat on the ground or against a tree with my cane. But I do not for that matter believe that the earth is guilty or that beating is of any help. "I ventilate my anger." And all rituals are of this sort.
>
> Wittgenstein, reviewing Frazer's *The Golden Bough*

Jean-Paul Sartre calls the emotions "magical transformations of the world."‡ it is an apt phrase, catching precisely the mythological and sometimes irrational demands we impose upon ourselves and upon our world. I "fall" into or out of love, and my world is "transformed" as dramatically as if the world had been struck by or saved from catastrophe. Yet, objectively, nothing has changed. Or I find myself oppressed by superior powers, but instead of rebelling, I silently accuse and condemn, viewing myself as a victim and a martyr for a noble cause. Again, nothing has changed, objectively. The power of the emotions, this "magical" power referred to by Sartre, is the ability to alter our surreality and constitute and reconstitute it according to our personal needs.

Where direct and effective action is impossible, the ideology of the emotion requires a cautious and often complex logic. The imagination is called in to scheme and conspire, and strategy replaces direct action. The employee who is angry at his boss but in desperate need of his job finds direct expression of his anger impossible. He may then scheme and plot, discovering indirect but effective means of punishing his offensive employer, writing an

‡ *The Emotions: Outline of a Theory*, trans. B. Frechtman (New York: Philosophical Library, 1948). See my "Sartre on Emotions," in Paul Arthur Schilpp, ed., *Sartre*, The Library of Living Philosophers (LaSalle, Ill.: Open Court, 1977).

anonymous letter with well-calculated results, spreading rumors among the other employees, stealing paper clips, or falsifying company records. Such indirect expressions may have the superficially odd consequence of requiring the very opposite of the "natural" or direct expression of that emotion. In anger against a superior, the circuitous route to punishment may involve explicit denial of anger, just in order to set up the offender for his just desserts. In love with an indifferent woman, a man may well find it necessary to express his love with disdain and reciprocal indifference in order to gain the intimacy he seeks. Such inverted expressions do not escape but only extend the logic of the emotions. As more routes to direct expression are closed off, more complex and sophisticated indirect and even circuitous routes will replace them. Superficially, the emotion and its expressions may well appear "irrational"; but once the emotion and its parameters are understood, its expression may well appear to be the best possible strategy under the circumstances. (See Section 4, this chapter.) Supercilious flattery and praise may be just as expressive of anger as a well-placed uppercut to the jaw; a slap in the face may be just as expressive of love as a hug or a kiss. In appropriate circumstances, any action may serve as an effective expression of an emotion.

The real problems arise when there is (or appears to be) no effective expression—either direct or indirect—for the realization of the ideals of the emotion. Reality appears to be intractable and so the emotion settles for a reconstitution of surreality, sometimes confusing a change in one for a change in the other. When effective expression is impossible, the emotion finds itself in a desperate situation; it is unable to realize a set of ideals which it has itself constituted. On reflection, we might well recognize this impossibility and adjust our expectations accordingly. At least we might "rationalize" our failures on some plausible grounds. But prereflectively, our emotions tend to adopt more desperate courses of purely subjective action. Refusing to acknowledge their own impotence and unwilling if not unable to give up their ideological commitments, they further expand their mythology, taxing the imagination, at the same time blocking the lessons of objective reflection. In such cases, the notion of "magic" has a very special relevance in the study of emotions. Where direct and even indirect causal manipulation of reality is impossible, an emotion may well resort to a "magical" objective pretense, the sort that Sartre criticizes in his essay, radically altering one's surreality as if that were sufficient to alter Reality as well.

The emotions often, even typically, give rise to clearly irrational or at least pointless behavior. In anger a man strikes a tree with his cane or stomps his foot on the ground. In grief a woman acts as if her deceased husband were still alive. Our so-called facial expressions are typically pointless or irrational in this sense—the scowling of anger and the wincing of envy, the tear-eyed look of love and the swallowed silence of offended pride. How do pursed lips or drawn eyelids help us rectify the offense that has provoked our anger? How does the withdrawn pouting of resentment help us overcome the oppression we resent? Of course, such expressions may constitute effective and even direct expression in certain circumstances; for example, the reprimanding of young children. But it is clear that they are not usually so effective, rather "only expressions," not effective actions at all.

Pouting and gritting one's teeth, muttered curses or mumbled declarations of love, kicking trees and screaming under the railroad bridge, would seem to be at best degenerate forms of expression. But they, too, have a "logic." Freud, of course, has been our insightful observer of "pointless" and "irrational" expressions. Despite his continual endorsement of the hydraulic model (according to which the expression of an emotion is *caused* by the emotion), Freud saw through its inadequacy as a theory of expression and argued brilliantly that such apparently irrational and pointless expressions did in fact have a purpose or a "meaning." The odd behavior he observed in his patients was not caused by the emotions but was expressive of them, attempts to realize them in the face of impossible obstacles. Of course, there is a sense in which such expressions (but not, therefore, the emotions) are indeed "irrational" and pointless. Instead of beating the tree or striking the ground, we should be beating or striking the person who has angered us. But we have not understood the structure of the emotions in general until we have traced the tendentious and often curious "logic" that connects the emotions to such ineffective and sometimes bizarre expressions.

The man who is angry at the bum in a bar may well settle his anger then and there. The man who is furious with his employer may be forced into devious plots and schemes of revenge. But then there is the man who, despite his anger, refuses to allow himself any effective expression. His anger does not simply disappear, and its demands for punitive vengeance do not disappear either. He may deny himself effective expression, but we may be sure that there will be a good deal of ineffective expression—hateful silences and "poisoned" looks, kicks aimed at trees and bitchy objections aimed at his wife or children, muttered curses in the dark of the office supply closet, silent incantations and damnations, as if to bring down the wrath of some Divine avenging force—or at least to bring down the wrath of the stock market—around the ears of his powerful antagonist. "If looks could kill"—but they don't.

How does one explain the fact that so many common "expressions" of emotion appear to have absolutely no effect in realizing the emotion or in changing the world to suit its particular ideology? The hydraulic model with its metaphorical "venting" of emotion will not do. The anger that restricts its expression to muttered curses is anger that will *increase* in intensity; the love that is brooded upon but not openly expressed is a love that may easily become obsessive. (But how much easier than the concrete trials of a real relationship.) The sorrow that allows itself protracted mourning is the sorrow that will turn to grief, and then to despair, leading to the obsessive and often hysterical rituals that Freud observed in so many of his early patients. We might achieve some temporary satisfaction from kicking a tree or boxing a psychiatrist's desk or screaming under the railroad trestle, but no such satisfaction is consequent on the brooding, pouting, gritted or grinding teeth, the tightness of the eyes and throat, or the gripping contractions of one's fist that are the most familiar expressions of an emotion that is forbidden effective expression.

What characterizes most such ineffective expressions is the fact that they are truncated, degenerate, or displaced versions of just those actions that *could* be effective, rituals which act *as if* one's desire would be fulfilled. Kicking the tree instead of the person who has angered us is an obvious example; so is the resentful muttered curse that might be devastating if actually said to the person resented. Or a desperate lover, sitting across the coffee table from the person he desires, repeats to himself the incantation "Please love me," as if, by magic, the request might be effective. In grief every effort may be made to resurrect the dead person, to act as if (s)he were still alive by repeating rituals and reminiscing over situations in which (s)he plays an integral part.

Occasionally, these various degenerate expressions and rituals might seem to be mere shadows of once effective expressions, "once-serviceable habits," as Darwin called them,[1] thinking that all emotional expressions were of this nature. For example, a once effective childhood strategy for getting one's way—crying, stamping one's foot, or urinating in the least convenient places—may be carried into adulthood where it is no longer effective, even in modified and more sophisticated form—whining and bitching, tapping one's foot or fingers in impatience, using one's physiological needs as an excuse to interrupt conversations. Perhaps the clenching of fists in anger could be argued to be a vestigial remnant of the preparation for a fight that we now deny ourselves; our gritted teeth might be the degenerate and inarticulate shadow of a threat or curse to be uttered, or, if you prefer to be even more Darwinian, the vestigial remnant of the urge to bite one's antagonist. It is true that many if not most of our seemingly "natural" expressions of emotion are more or less habitual and unthinking, but it does not follow that they are not also purposive as such.

Observing the sometimes obsessive and compulsive behavior of his hysterical patients, Freud noticed that the various emotional expressions, seemingly ineffective gestures, rituals, and incantations, could not possibly be discounted or dismissed as mere "habits." They were not only intentional, purposive, and "meaningful," but desperately so. In the outer reaches of despair, we will try anything, no matter how irrational we know it to be. With all medical cures exhausted, the cancer patient turns to a faith healer. Why not? Lying terrified in a foxhole, a young atheist turns to prayer. What could he lose? Our emotions in general, I have argued, are purposive, aimed at the maximization of personal dignity and self-esteem. Their expressions are nothing other than attempts to implement this purpose, by changing the world when and where possible. But often the circumstances that threaten us are or seem to be beyond the range of any effective expression. Yet we express ourselves, not by way of "throwaway" gestures and empty rituals, in order to "ventilate" our emotionally bursting selves, but by way of a last-ditch effort to salvage self-esteem in the face of an unyielding world.

Why should we allow ourselves to indulge in such ineffective behavior? Sometimes, *it is all we can do,* and any attempted action, no matter how hopeless (so long as there is a glimmer of possibility), is better than none. In desperation, we often act irrationally, accepting and even trying courses of action that, in our calmer moments, we can clearly see to be absurd. But, in desperation, what is otherwise seen as "irrational" appears to be the best of all possible alternatives. The young atheist has never believed in God; nor does he have any reason to do so now. But all alternatives exhausted, what if possibly . . . ? Under the circumstances, should we still conceive of his expression as "irrational"? (Which is not to say, as we are so often told, that such extremes of desperation provide us with any *reason* for believing in God otherwise. There are many people who are not atheists *only* while they are in foxholes.)

The logic of desperation is often a logic of the bizarre. In desperation we allow ourselves to believe—or act as if we believed—in magical powers and divine interventions which we would not even consider plausible *objectively.* But in the face of utter impotence, we grab onto the implausible and the irrational as a drowning man grabs onto the slimmest reeds. In desperation and impotence, our emotions often turn to *magic,* mysterious quasi-causal powers that arise from the imagination beyond the bounds of rational belief. Consider, for example, several of Freud's early patients, a woman who performs a bizarre daily ritual as if to relive and redress the failure of her wedding night, many years before. Her husband is dead, yet she takes great and obsessive pains to point out to her maid certain telltale stains on her bedclothes. Similarly, there is the little girl who compulsively rearranges the vases and pillows in her room before going to bed in order to prevent her parents from having intercourse. How can these bizarre behaviors be understood, except on the hypothesis that each accepts some magical connection between these rituals and their desperately desired ends. Of course, on reflection, neither the older woman nor the little girl would claim to *believe* in any such connections. But in the face of the collapse of self-esteem and the frustration of our most powerful emotions, truth, rationality, and common sense are dispensable. (Sometimes desperation is far more satisfying than satisfaction.)

It is often said that such ineffective expressions are "symbolic," "standing in" for more direct and effective expressions that have been suppressed. This notion of "symbolic expression" has the marked virtue of excluding the usual metaphor of hydraulics in favor of the far more helpful model of expressions as *meaningful*. (The conflict between these two is always evident in Freud, who was never capable of choosing resolutely between them.) Moreover, the notion of "symbolic expression" ties in well with our concepts of the *mythology* and *ideology* of the passions. But the notion of "symbolism," so freely bandied about in literature, politics, and post-Freudian psychology and philosophy, is more a restatement of the problem than an analysis of it. Why should one indulge in symbolic rather than in full-blooded and effective actions? We can take a clue from radical politics: A "symbolic action" is often one that is acceptable in spirit, but utterly ineffective in outcome. What, then, is its purpose? Not its real effects, but rather, we may say, its *surreal* consequences. In cases of unquestionable desperation, these ineffective expressions are all that possibly could be done. And then there are those many cases of *pretended* desperation, as in resentment and envy, in self-righteous indignation, and in timid love, where duplicity seems to be the strategy; the desperate and ineffective expression is performed *as if* it were possibly effective while at the same time the subject remains confident that it will not be. A man in a rage kicks a tree instead of his wife as if, by some magical transference ("voodoo"), his wife will feel the pain. In desperation that may be all he *can* do. But in pretended desperation, in order to keep the anger alive, the same man will opt for this utterly ineffective strategy just *because* he knows that it is ineffective. A real injury inflicted would undermine his emotion, perhaps replacing it with guilt. The ineffective expression does not, as in the hydraulic "reality" hypothesis, "release" the anger. To the contrary, it is chosen just *because* it is retained, if not *intensified* as well.*

* For an obsessive patriot, "détente" or protracted conflict is always preferable to resolution or victory.

Our desperate emotional expressions often act *as if*—as if the muttered curses and incantations really might have their literal effects ("Go to hell," "May the very heavens strike you . . ."), as if the substitute fetishes and voodoo representations might really transmit some similar results, as if kissing a letter or a lock of hair of a loved one would actually be sensed by him or her, as if the ritual of mourning actually did keep alive the deceased person. These irrational beliefs and strategies—particularly when practiced by hard-headed and "rational" people—seem surprising. But how often we act, prereflectively, on the basis of prejudices and superstitions that would not for a moment stand up to the scrutiny of reflection. How often we doggedly defend a position—even reflectively—because it is a logical consequence of some emotional investment. And in desperation the defense of these investments to whatever lengths is far more important than the impersonal objectivity of rational belief.

The duplicity of feigned desperation can be unmasked by the following thought-experiment. Imagine yourself, in silent anger, mumbling to an offensive stranger, "Drop dead." And he does. Not being mystically inclined, you dismiss the suggestion that you might be the cause. But there is that eerie lump of guilt, and you can bet that the phrase "Drop dead" will be conscientiously deleted from your vocabulary. Or suppose you found that every time you kicked your desk out of anger with your employer, he registered a severe pain in his right shin. In other words, suppose our ineffective expressions in fact became effective? The truly desperate man, at the end of his hopes, might welcome such inexplicable powers. But the person who is feigning desperation for the sake of the protraction of his emotions would experience a very different reaction. He would come to treat his formerly ineffective expressions as deadly weapons, avoiding them entirely. And here we can see the duplicity of his strategy—to express his emotions ineffectively just because he recognizes the inefficacy of his actions. For him, emotional expression is a form of play, like a child's game, full of pretense yet acting as if it were not pretense, pretending to relieve but in fact only further frustrating and intensifying his emotions. The magical expression of our emotions, as Schiller said of poetry, is a deadly serious form of play. It is not for the sake of enjoyment but rather for the sake of building and reinforcing the emotional structures of one's surreality. It is the double duplicity of a "willing suspension of disbelief" with unyielding continuation of disbelief, the pretense of expression while all the while acting only because it is pretense and ineffective. What is ultimately important is the maintenance and strength of the emotions, not their satisfaction.

In order to secure the emotional structures of our world, we opt for those emotions which are least likely to be satisfied, love for the inaccessible (for movie stars whom there is no danger of ever meeting, for dead or long-lost lovers with whom the realities of reconciliation need never be faced). And then there is "turning the other cheek" in a fight, not out of Christian charity or chivalry or even cowardice, but just in order to leave alive the sustaining and now intensified structures of anger and indignation. It is thus, perhaps ironically, that *the least satiable* emotions are those which define our lives: the frustrated ambition or impossible love affair, the unfaced fear and the unrectified anger, the unvanquished enemy and the irredeemable guilt. Accordingly, our emotional expressions—whether from impotence or unwillingness—will largely consist of ineffective and magical gestures, rituals, and incantations. Only in grave desperation will these magical expressions be accepted at face value, and then only during the crisis for which they are required. But the same magical expressions will be typical of most of our emotions, whose rituals and gestures have become so familiar to us that we too easily dismiss them simply as "irrational" and as "meaningless." It is easier not to know their significance, to view ourselves rather as observers whose actions are irrelevant. We might say of the "magic" of the emotions, as Stanley Cavell has recently said of the "magic" of the movies, "that they function, not by literally presenting us with the world, but by permitting us to view it unseen. This is not a wish for power, . . . but a wish not to need power, not to have to bear its burdens."[2]

4. The Rationality of the Emotions

> . . . as if every passion didn't contain its quantum of reason.
>
> Nietzsche (*The Will to Power*)

> Those oft are stratagems which errors seem.
>
> Pope, "Essay on Criticism"

"I didn't mean it; I didn't know what I was doing. I acted without thinking; I acted irrationally. I was emotionally upset." How often we hear that! And, without attempting a refutation, we sense its falsity, the hollow desperation that accompanies a feeble and half-hearted excuse. "I was emotionally upset": That is the capstone of a cop-out plea of momentary insanity. But we know better; not only did you "mean it," but that single ephemeral "lapse," as you call it, was more full of meaning than the years of labored inhibition that preceded it. You knew *exactly* what you were doing. You seized the precise moment, and you went straight for the most vulnerable spot. You knew exactly where to cut deepest, how to damage the most, and you knew exactly what the consequences would be. You had planned it for years, brooding and in fantasy, privately rehearsing and envisioning its effects in quick forgetful flashes. And yet you think the seeming "spontaneity" of that instant negates those years of strategy and rehearsal. "Irrational?" Nothing you have ever done has been more rational, better conceived, more direct from the pit of your feelings, or better directed toward the target. That momentary outburst of emotion was the burning focus of all that means most to you, all that has grown up with you, even if much of it was unacknowledged. It was the brilliant product of a lifetime of experience and knowledge, the most cunning strategy, and it had the most marked sense of purpose of anything you have ever done. Despite the consequences, can you really say that you wish you hadn't done it?

And yet we hear the platitude, "Emotions are irrational." The emotions are said to be stupid, unsophisticated, childish if not utterly infantile, primitive, or animalistic—relics from our primal past, from our perverse and barbaric origins. The emotions are said to be disruptions, interfering with our purposes in life, embarrassing us and making fools of us, destroying careers and marriages and ruining our relationships with other people before they have even had a chance to take hold. "It was fine, until I got involved," "It would be all right if you didn't feel so guilty about it," or "It was a fine triangle until he got jealous and spoiled it." The emotions are said to disrupt our thinking and lead us astray in our purposes. This is the heart of the Myth of the Passions; the emotions are irrational forces beyond our control, disruptive and stupid, unthinking and counterproductive, against our "better interests," and often ridiculous.

Against this platitude, "Emotions are irrational," it must be argued that, on the contrary, emotions are *rational*. This is not only to say that they fit into one's over-all behavior in a significant way and follow the regular patterns of one's "personality"—that they can be explained in terms of a coherent set of causes according to some psychological theory or another. All of this is true enough. But emotions are rational in another, more important sense. They are, as I have been arguing, judgments, and they are intentional and intelligent. Emotions, therefore, may be said to be rational in precisely the same sense in which all judgments may be said to be rational; they require an advanced degree of conceptual sophistication, including a conception of Self and at least some ability in abstraction. They require at least minimal intelligence and a sense of self-esteem, and they proceed purposefully in accordance with a sometimes extremely complex set of rules and strategies. It is in this sense that I have talked of the "logic" of the emotions, a logic that may at times be quite difficult to follow but a logic which is never undecipherable or "unique" to a single emotion. Even the most primitive emotions, fear for one's life or love of one's mother, require intelligence, abstraction, and "logic" in this sense. Most emotions involve much more, strategies for the maximization of self-esteem that would shame a professional confidence man and a prereflective awareness of psychological intrigue that would impress even Dr. Freud. We often criticize our emotions for their stupidity, their lack of justification, their foolishness, but correspondingly we often acknowledge their right and justification, their astuteness and their effectiveness. Such criticism and praise already presupposes a rational structure, a game of intelligence with strategy and logic which can go well or badly. It is significant that we make no such attempts at evaluation of our headaches and feelings in general. We simply suffer them, or on occasion, feel lucky that one came along at precisely the right time (in order that we may miss the dull party or meeting). But unlike feelings, emotions are rational, presupposing a system of purposiveness, logic, and intelligence that far more resembles the structures of rational action than the phenomena of bodily feelings. (We know what it means to say that one's anger is unreasonable; what would it be to have an "unreasonable" attack of nausea?)

It is often thought that rationality resides solely in reflective thought, in the articulate calculations of a mathematician or a statesman. But we all know well enough to trust certain rational "intuitions"† in ourselves, in a chess strategist or a Napoleon, which seems to dispense with reflection altogether but yet follow an indisputable logic. The rationality of the emotions is a prereflective (or "intuitive") logic, but one which, like all logics, can be brought to the surface upon reflection and rendered explicit. This has not been done, of course, only because it has so long been presumed that the emotions had no logic worth investigating, that rationality lay exposed on the surface and needed only formalization, not exploration. But reflection may itself be quite irrational—ponderous and dissociated ramblings which are rational in form only and whose purpose is strictly antirational, to

† "Intuition" is thought to be mysterious and "ineffable" only because reflection alone is so often taken to be the paradigm of rationality, leaving the realm of unreflected experience and judgment an unprotected field, not only for poets and artists but for every half-witted self-appointed wise man with mystical pretensions. Rationality, however, is not the private domain of reflective judgment, and unreflected experience and judgment are as subject to its canons as the most explicit formulations of philosophy and any other critical discipline. "Intuition" is neither less rational nor less insightful than reflective inquiry, but neither is it "deeper" or more insightful. It lacks the benefit and the critical acumen of reflection, but it is not necessarily therefore impoverished in its insight, nor does it thereby benefit from this lack.

throw us off the track of our investigations and defeat the rationality of the emotions which is at work behind our reflective façade. "Rational" does not mean reflective; "rationality" signifies intelligent purposive activity, whether reflective and fully articulated or not. Contrary to their usual image, the emotions are paradigmatic of such activities.

To say that the emotions have intelligent purpose is not simply to say that they play a significant role in our psychological life; this would be admitted by any number of theorists who would wholly reject our view of the emotions as constitutive and rational judgments. Emotions have purpose in the sense in which our actions have purpose—to get something done, to change something. But in the case of the emotions, much of this "something to be done" and "something to be changed" lies in the realm of surreality as well as in Reality. An emotion changes our view of the world and formulates intentions to change the world. In the case of some emotions, the change may be strictly subjective, for example, in envy and resentment, where there is little action but considerable restructuring of one's views and values, and ineffective but "magical" expressions. In other emotions—for example, fear for one's life—the change that is brought about is wholly directed toward Reality. The envious person, through "rationalization," changes the status of his loss without, "in Reality," changing anything at all. The angry man, through his anger, effects the indictment of his adversary that he insists upon. But in this last case, the subjective indictment is accompanied by a demand for a real indictment as well. The angry man wishes his indictment to be corroborated by actual indictment and punishment, a bolt from the heavens, a punch, or a winning lawsuit. Similarly, a woman in love will not be satisfied with her own attitudes of affection (which by themselves constitute admiration or infatuation but not love), but she will insist upon demonstrating her love with gifts and attention. She will want the world in general to corroborate her affections by providing the best for her lover. Most of all, of course, she will want to take steps to ensure that her affections are returned.

An emotion demands that our world, if not *the* world, be changed. It might be said of every emotion, as Marx said of the bourgeoisie, that it "compels all other [emotions], perceptions, judgments and values, on pain of extinction, to adopt its own mode of perception; it compels them to introduce what it calls Reality into their midst, that is, to become that [emotion] themselves. In one word, it creates a world after its own image" (*Communist Manifesto*, 1848).

The rationality of our emotions turns on their success in maximizing self-esteem through such changes. If an objective change in the world is impossible, a subjective alteration of our world will have to do. But it has been shown that we may refuse to change the world, restricting ourselves to pure subjectivity, for the sake of retaining our emotions. "An idea realized is a bore," wrote Schopenhauer, and we know how true that is of our emotions. Accordingly, an emotion's demand for effective expression in action will virtually always be tempered with our need for the emotion itself. (The difference between "civilized" man and brute that has been such a perennial source of dispute since Rousseau and Freud might be characterized in just these terms; the complex world of civilization is constituted by the delicate balance of effective expression and satisfaction on the one hand and the recognized need for emotional maintenance and suppressed expression on the other. To call the latter "repressed" or "inhibited" or "unnatural" is already to load the case against civilization. What characterizes the brute, on the other hand, is not, as traditionally argued, the "natural richness" of his emotions but rather their poverty and, consequently, their "brutality.")

The purpose of an emotion, like the purpose of an action, is a multileveled affair. There are any number of goals in an emotion, from the very specific ("wanting to see that bastard punished") to the very general ("wanting to think well of oneself"). Ultimately, all emotions have a common goal—the maximization of self-esteem. Between the particular goals in a specific emotion and this common goal one might formulate a crude means-ends continuum; for example, "He got angry about the garbage because he wanted an excuse to punish her for (faultlessly) wrecking the family car, which he was angry about only because he was jealous about her affair with the garage mechanic, which threatened him because it made him feel insecure and unwanted. . . ." But this admittedly crude linear device for displaying the "in order to" logic of our emotions can be misleading. Although all emotions share an ultimate end, their interconnection is rather a network of intertwined and mutually entailing judgments, more like a web than a chain, which constitutes the basic structures of our world.

The intelligent purposiveness of every emotion dictates a certain "logic," abstract in its form but geared in every case to the particulars and "the facts" of the situation. To say that emotions are "abstract" is to say that they are never concerned simply with a particular situation. The particular object of the emotion—what it is putatively "about"—is *usually* the focal point of the emotional strategy and its mythology. It is never the whole concern of the emotion. In most cases, the object represents a particular investment, a particular threat or promise, but it is always concerned with the *significance* of that particular. Sometimes, the object may be merely a convenience, like a lover who is "used" for the sake of self-esteem without any concern whatever for his or her well-being or personality by his or her partner. Similarly, a person might "use" a minor loss as the object of protracted grief as a way of gaining the sympathy of others and as an excuse to feel self-indulgently "sorry for himself." But these are extreme cases. Most of the time, the object of the emotion is a precise and sometimes unique representation of a particular investment of self-esteem, fitting into a more general surrealistic pattern and not easily replaceable by any merely similar object. A lover is both loved for him/herself *and* as a representative of the abstract need for self-esteem. Here one might reverse Freud's famous claims to the effect that generalized desire—for example, the desire to sleep with any number of men or women—is in fact a very specific (but repressed) desire: to sleep with one's mother or father. Forgoing the genetic basis of Freud's model, it can be rather said that the desire to sleep with someone particular (including one's mother or father) is but an instantiation of a generalized desire to elevate one's self-esteem by sleeping with somebody (or other). Of course, as one makes increasingly complex "investments" in the love of a particular person, the generalized desire becomes accordingly more specific, perhaps even obsessive, as the need for self-esteem becomes increasingly invested in a virtually (but never logically) unique object.

Like all strategies, the logic of an emotion keeps continuously in mind its abstract and ultimate purpose—the maximization of self-esteem—and tailors itself to particular objects and situations. The "rationality" of an emotion turns on how well it does this— whether the object of an emotion is an appropriate object for the maximization of self-esteem, whether the emotion is the *best* emotion under the circumstances. And even though all emotions are subjective, the *logic* of an emotion is objective, and to be objectively evaluated. It is a commonly stated half-truth that every emotion has its own logic; the half-truth is that emotions are subjective, dependent upon the particular perspectives and investments of a particular person. But it is also true that most emotions are shared in common by all people, whatever their differences in languages, customs, religion, etc. The logic of the emotions is in no case simply "one's own"; in every case the logic of the emotion, once its parameters are known, is a public affair. Consider the sense one gets watching an inferior film or reading a "dime" novel, where the characters are "unconvincing" ("I can't imagine doing that to someone I really loved" or "She wouldn't have reacted that way"). We recognize these breakdowns in the logic of the emotions, and it will do a screen-writer or author no good to protest that we "don't understand the character." Logic dictates the course that emotions will take, and that is where we expect them to go.‡ Similarly, we criticize our own emotions, in reflection or retrospect, for their foolishness and stupidity, for their lack of justification and unreasonableness, and such criticisms make sense only on the basis of an objective logical structure which we expect our emotions to follow.

Consider any number of Shakespeare's tragedies (compared, for example, with his comedies or with the French classical tragedies

‡ One must temper this expectation, as Philip Slater sarcastically points out in a footnote (in *Pursuit of Loneliness*), by recognizing the unwarranted expectations which we apply to other people and fictional characters but rarely to ourselves. We expect absolute consistency and predictability of emotions and behavior. (An angry man is always angry, a loving man is always loving, etc.) For ourselves, we know that *we* are not that simple. The logic of emotions typically involves contraries (for example, love and hate, resentment and indignation, worship and spite), which only psychological naïveté will confuse for contradictories.

that were their contemporaries). Each plot is driven, not by the logic of events (there are often surprisingly few events*) nor by a pre-established plan or routine (the "fates" in classical drama, for example). The plot is the logic of the emotions of the leading characters. In *Hamlet*, for example, we find a play in which virtually all action has either occurred beforehand, is kept until the final moments of the play, or is merely suggested in passing, as if of little dramatic importance. The drive of the play is in the character of Hamlet himself. But if one summarizes that drive in the usual way, as the tragedy of a man "who could not make up his mind," both the character and the plot are lost. At no point in the play is Hamlet indecisive; at each point of decision, given the circumstances and his own emotional requirements (for example, that his uncle not be murdered without a public demonstration of guilt and an unsalvaged soul before the heavens), the logic followed is unfailing.† It is Hamlet's subjectivity that provides the plot of the play, motivated by his Orestes-like complex and interrupted and given more subject matter by the drowning of his lover and his murder of her father, incidents which occupy remarkably little of his concern if one fails to see the obsessive emotional drive of his sense of vengeance. The play moves solely according to the logic of resentful revenge, necessarily subdued in its effective expression and therefore all the more obsessive. One might argue similarly for *Othello*; Othello's own jealousy is uncomplicated and would by itself make either an extremely dull tragedy or a slapstick comedy; Iago's envy is the intelligence that defines the course of the play. (Othello's jealousy is merely its instrument.)

My intention is not to force a somewhat overpsychologized interpretation of Shakespeare but rather to make a general point about the emotions; the logic and strategy of the emotions, which provides the plot and drive of these tragedies, is extremely "rational" and sophisticated. The emotions are not merely forces or

---

* T. S. Eliot understood well the abstract interests of the emotions: "Only those to whom nothing has ever happened can fail to appreciate the great unimportance of events."

† I've seen the play convincingly formalized according to Baysian decision theory along just these lines by Dr. Sanford Weimer, of Langley-Porter Institute.

feelings of but a single dimension, like pleasure or pain, but rather complexes of judgments with endless logical entailments and complications. In the hands of a genius these entailments and complications can be articulated so skillfully that the subjective validity of this logic is immediately realized. In the hands of a Grade D novelist or movie director, the same entailments and complications can become so bungled that one is forced to recognize the breakdown in logic. So strong is the Myth of the Passions, however, we nevertheless often fail to recognize the essential role of a logic of the emotions. (Even some of the better critics can be caught saying things like "It's somehow unsatisfying" or "It just doesn't work" without attempting to explicate the emotional logic that has gone awry.)

Emotions are rational. Yet no one could deny that through our emotions ("out of anger," "out of love for you, I . . .") we perform some remarkably stupid and destructive acts. And so, despite the logic and strategies of the emotions, it seems necessary to add that, the emotions are often irrational as well. But how can emotions be both rational and irrational? And if all emotions are judgments, complete with a logic and a strategy, what does it mean to say that an emotion is "irrational"?

It is necessary to distinguish two senses of *rationality:* In the first sense, all emotions are rational; in the second, only some are. In the first sense, it is often said that "man is rational"; in other words, he is intelligent, capable of solving geometrical theorems and crossword puzzles, planning the destruction of Victorian mansions to make room for chintzy office blocks, and obtaining coconuts by mail instead of by climbing a tree. To be rational in this sense is to operate with concepts, to formulate plans and strategies, to be able to deal with novel situations. In *this* sense, all emotions are rational.

But to operate with concepts and to formulate plans and strategies is not necessarily to do so effectively. To do so *well* is to be rational in our second sense; to do so badly is to be *irrational.* This second sense of "rationality" is an evaluative concept; it presupposes rationality in the first sense and evaluates our logic and our strategies in terms of their consistency and effectiveness. Clearly not all emotions are rational in this second sense.

But neither are they all—nor are even most of them—*irrational*. The usual conception of the emotions as "irrational" indiscriminately (and thus inconsistently) covers both senses; on the one hand, the emotions are said to be unintelligent and nonpurposive (the mere "forces" of the hydraulic model); on the other hand, it is supposed that our emotions are stupid and shortsighted (as if one could be stupid and shortsighted if he did not have some intelligence and vision to begin with). I have considered at length the thesis that the emotions are universally rational in the first sense, but haven't yet considered in any detail their rationality and irrationality in the second sense. First, it is necessary to dispel a serious misunderstanding which has given rise to the idea that our emotions are virtually always "irrational," at least in the second sense of "rationality."

What are we to say against the accusation that our emotions are typically if not always disruptive, foolish, paralyzing, embarrassing, and against our better self-interests as well as against the interests of those around us—the indictment of the Myth of the Passions? To begin with, the ultimate goal of our emotions—and therefore the standard according to which their success and rationality is to be measured—is a subjective standard: personal dignity and self-esteem, which cannot be measured solely in terms of the "outer" manifestations of our emotions in expression, action, and their consequences. The fact that in many of our emotions we face situations in which we seem impotent or choose to retain the emotion at the cost of its satisfaction, accounts for much of the only apparent irrationality. It is true that, because of our emotions, we often fail to succeed in our stated ambitions and our projects, but as often as not, our emotions recognize a fact which we (reflectively) do not: Our self-esteem lies not in *those* successes so much as in our own subjectivity. In terms of their own ultimate goals, therefore, such emotions may be clearly rational, despite the fact that, in terms of certain *other* standards of success, they may result in failure and foolishness.

It is important not to confuse the rationality of our emotions with the rationality of our actions, even when those actions are expressions of our emotions. For example, a man who finds himself trapped in a degrading job may at some point allow himself the imprudent luxury of "telling off" his employer in uncompromising terms, consequently losing his job, ultimately his home and his family. His anger was based upon the best of reasons, and in fact constituted the only possible view within which he could bear the degradations of his employment. But, in the light of his over-all interests, the "outburst" was irrational. What is often called the "irrationality" of our emotions is rather the faulty timing or inept choice of their expressions. The emotions themselves may be perfectly rational.

Similarly, the charge that our emotions are typically "disruptive" may be dispensed with by noting that it is often not our emotion that is disruptive, but rather the situation which threatens us. I have already argued how it is a mistake to think of the emotions solely in terms of their moments of crisis. But even in those moments of crisis, it is not the emotion that is "irrational." In an emergency situation, our normal responses—both subjective and in action—are inappropriate. It is the emergency itself that is unexpected, unpredictable, and thus disruptive. Of course, with experience, we learn an increasingly sophisticated and adaptive emotional repertoire, and we may well insist that our ability to manage such crisis situations is an important test of the adequacy of an emotional strategy. But the over-all rationality of the emotion surely does not depend solely upon the outcome of such possibly infrequent testing situations. Of course, as I have argued, the importance of our emotions makes them particularly vulnerable to threats and crises. (A man without passion would indeed be "cool"—in fact, downright cold—in crisis situations.) But, once again, this vulnerability only underscores, not undermines, the essential importance of our passions in our over-all sense of self-esteem.

There is an anthropological dimension to this question of the rationality of the emotions: In a society in which "cool" behavior and stereotypic responses are taken to be the paradigms of rationality, it follows that the emotions, by their very nature, would be deemed irrational. But one can evaluate the rationality of this conception of "rationality" (by the same criterion—the maximization of self-esteem) and see how much it is found wanting by the sense of meaningless and absurdity in which it culminates. Think of the crude American sense of "pragmatism," which sees the emotions as interferences with good business sense and "sound" (that is, dispassionate) judgment. It is not in America (or in England) that "reason is . . . the slave of passions." In a society that places taboos on the passions in general—condemns them in men and belittles them in women—it is only to be expected that emotional reactions will run counter to public success and ambitions. There are situations where, naturally, "cool" behavior has a decisive advantage—for example, in the face of danger. "Cool" behavior—our all too common paradigm of rationality—is itself an example of extreme irrationality, for it deprives a person of all those structures which might give his life some meaning and maximize his self-esteem, leaving him only with the subjectively worthless coinage of success and public recognition.

It is clear that, blinded by the Myth of the Passions, we often judge our emotions unfairly, accusing them of irrationality when in fact they are typically our most trustworthy and most rational instruments of self-esteem. Because our emotions are subjective strategies, they must not be evaluated solely in terms of our actions or their consequences, but always in terms of their maximization of self-esteem, which in turn depends on our external successes and failures only to the extent that we have emotionally invested in them. When it is the case that such "external" successes are subjectively self-defeating, the rationality of our emotions must be recognized to be a bit wiser than the supposedly "rational" and "common-sense" strategies which have been forced upon us from the "outside." A seemingly ambitious man may discover, no doubt much to his surprise, that he feels best about himself at precisely those moments in which he is furthest from his stated goals. A woman in love may believe that she desires nothing more than the "complete possession" of her lover, when in fact what she requires is something much more—or much less— the continued incompletion of her love which alone provides those self-esteeming structures of surreality that make the life of the lover ecstatically meaningful. In general, the rationality of our emotions is a complex business whose subjective substance may often be misunderstood from a more "objective" point of view. Or one might say—only half tongue-in-cheek—that it is not the emotions that are irrational; people are irrational.

CHAPTER 7: THE LOGIC OF EMOTION

> To him who looks upon the world rationally, the world in its turn presents a rational aspect.
>
> Hegel, *Lectures on the Philosophy of History*

"The logic of emotion"? If that phrase sounds odd, it is only because the emotions have been so long degraded by the Myth of the Passions and contrasted with the supposedly "divine" powers of reason. But if human reason has proved to be something less than godlike, perhaps the balance of our self-esteem can be restored by demonstrating that our emotions are far more than brute "animal spirits" we have inherited from a prerational past. Freud once argued that he had delivered a great blow to our sense of human dignity by showing that "a man is not even master in his own house"—that is, that our most rational behavior is determined by unknown passions. But if the emotions themselves are our own doings, then perhaps we can re-establish the existential mastery that Freud thought he had denied us. Emotions are not dumb forces beyond our control but judgments we make. As such, they have conceptual and intelligent form and a *logic* that characterizes them, if only we will look for it, once we are no longer misled and distracted by the Myth of the Passions.

I am using the term "logic" as Kant used that term, to signify the employment of categories and concepts. His so-called transcendental logic was the study of those basic judgments and concepts through which, according to his theory, we constitute the world of our experience (for example, "cause," "substance," "possibility"). This study, however, is limited to our constitution of *our* world, surreality, in terms of values and self-conceptions (leaving open the Kantian question of how we come to understand *the* world). As constitutive judgments, our emotions, too, are worthy of a "logical" study, the identification and examination of those fundamental (though surely not "a priori" or "universally necessary") subjective concepts and judgments that provide the structures of the world we *live* in. As such, their reason is never abstracted from action and concern. Their "logic" is never the cold and bloodless calculations that usually deserve that title, but they have a logic all the same, a logic of living. Many emotions have a distinctly moral edge to their judgments —notably anger, shame, indignation, and guilt. My anger, for example, includes an indictment, an accusation. Some emotions, and most moods, project all-encompassing systems of metaphysics; guilt, joy, despair, and depression recast my world in purely philosophical terms of sin and redemption, hope and hopelessness. Our emotions carve out our place in the world; shame "puts us down"; resentment is virtually a confession of inferiority, but an inferiority that has been constituted by the emotion itself. There are the accounting emotions, keeping a ledger on our gains and losses —sadness as an inventory of loss, gratitude and vanity as estimates of gain, jealousy and envy as competitive losses to another's (perhaps deserved) gain. Most emotions are concerned, directly or indirectly, with our relations with other people, the distances we enforce between us and the intimacies we seek, the trust with which we share our experiences and the defensiveness with which we wall ourselves off. At the heart of every emotion is a set of fundamental ontological and evaluative commitments, defining the mythologies within which we live and the ideologies we live with. Every emotion, even the pettiest fit of jealousy or embarrassment or the shortest fling of infatuation or indignation, is a micrometaphysical and ethical system, a bit of philosophy, which it is appropriate for us, as philosophers, to make clear.

The study of emotions is a study of the mythologies constituted by the emotions. With the aid of a slight pun, it might be said that it is a study of "mytho-logic." The emphasis on *myth* underscores our insistence that these are *subjective* judgments and positions, *projections* and *interpretations* with a *personal* flavor. The emphasis on *logic* reminds us that the personal nature of these mythologies in no way implies that they are individually created; the structures constituted by the various emotions are common to all of us. However personal an emotion may be, there is no such thing as a unique emotion, one with structures unknown to the rest of us. The structures of the emotion, unlike the intangible cracklings of a headache, can be explicitly formulated and formalized, like any other logical or conceptual system.

I often meet with the complaint, particularly from my students, that this view of the emotions seems to "rationalize" and, in effect, sterilize them. The reply is that something prone to analysis is not denied its power; it is only when one confuses the analysis for the *analysans* that one should be disappointed, particularly when analysis turns to *anal*-ysis, so concerned with formal niceties that one forgets the subjectively inflammatory subject matter under investigation. Of course no analysis "captures" the emotion, if what we mean by that is that an analytic understanding is sufficient to give that emotion to the analysts. But neither does understanding kill the emotion. The emotions we study are often dead, gathered from the annals of memory or transfixed by the scrutiny of reflection. They will not be given new life by our understanding. The emotions which we are now living and will live in the future will gain in clarity and insight, however; those that will perish from clarity and insight are only those that do not deserve to live. (We may be Athenian in our inquiries, but we will be Spartan in our results.) In this chapter I shall attempt to give a reasonable structural analysis of the "logic" of the emotions.* In the following chapter I shall turn to particular emotions, in order to show how each is defined according to its characteristic judgments. The advantage of this procedure over emotion-by-emotion description is that it acquires a unity which allows us to understand the general structure of the emotions and the "logic" that ties them together and distinguishes them, illuminating the common transformations of one emotion to another as well as the conceptually necessary connections between certain emotions and certain views of the world. The disadvantage, it may be objected, is that it sometimes forces an emotion into a predetermined mold, in which it may or may not fit. This objection would be valid, however, only if the study did not itself presuppose a thoroughgo-

---

* Our procedure here resembles that of Lévi-Strauss's study of *"mythologique"* in the sense that it begins (presupposing a huge body of emotional experience) with a matrix of permutations and combinations of essential mythological and ideological structures or "archetypes," only then turning to look at the frequency and variations of actual strategies and structures of particular emotions.

ing familiarity with the emotions, which we all share from the outset. The analysis itself proceeds only *from* the emotions, comparing and distilling and formulating a theory on their basis.

1. Direction

All emotions are intentional, ultimately "about" both ourselves and our world. Yet it is obvious that the various emotions do not pay equal attention to these two "poles" of subjectivity. Some emotions—for example, indignation—are wholly absorbed in some situation or incident, in this case, someone else's misdeed, with minimal attention to oneself. Others are self-concerned to the point of excluding all reference to the "outside world"—guilt, for example, or that peculiar form of worship whose object is sufficiently abstract that, ultimately, it is only one's own act of devotion that receives any attention whatever. ("It was almost without knowing what she was doing that she set out towards the church, ready to enter into any act of devotion provided only that her feelings might be wholly absorbed, and the outer world forgotten"—Flaubert, *Madame Bovary.*) The first difference between emotions is this crude but useful distinction between what I shall call "inner-" and "outer-directed" emotion (only the metaphor, not the analysis, is Cartesian).

"Outer-directed" (or "other-directed") emotions are about particular situations, objects, or other people. Fear, for example (as opposed to anguish), is typically outer-directed, concerned solely with the endangering state of affairs of a threatening situation or person. It is clear that fear also involves—essentially involves—self-concern, fear of what will happen *to us.* But our attention is directed wholly outward, watching every move of the creature that threatens us and every change in the situation that endangers us. In such situations we are often notoriously unself-conscious, reacting as necessary to the danger but rarely if ever directing our attention to our Selves. (To act skillfully or cautiously is not the same as acting self-consciously.) It is what is "out there" that obsesses us.

Similarly, anger and indignation are often if not usually "outer-directed." Of course, it is *I* (or *we*) that is offended by the situation or by the action of another person, but the attention is solely transfixed upon the "object" of the anger, "*his* having robbed me of my wallet" or "*the fact that* there are not enough seats in the plane for us to sit down." (Thus, the victim of the crime need not be—and sometimes cannot be—present at the trial; the law is not concerned about him, although the crime exists only with reference to him.) Accordingly, indignation (and often anger) presents itself as a matter of selfless principle; "it's not for myself that I am concerned, but rather because of the *principle* of the matter." Such stress on principle is a dynamic strategy to keep the attention focused, not on this particular case, which includes *me*, but on the structure of the case in general, in which I am irrelevant.

In some "outer-directed" emotions, the reference to oneself may be left implicit but obvious. In sadness and sorrow, for example, the concern is solely for the lost person or object, but it is obvious in the very structure of the emotion that it is a loss *to me*, or perhaps "a loss to all of us," but never simply "a loss." There are "outer-directed" (particularly "other-directed") emotions, however, that purposefully and even ruthlessly screen self-involvement, forcing the aim of the emotion to remain *exclusively* on its object. Indignation is often like this, and resentment virtually always. It is strictly "the Other" who is at fault: I have nothing to do with it.

The "inner-directed" emotions take one's Self as their focal point, for example, shame, embarrassment, guilt, remorse, regret, pride, vanity, self-love, self-hate, and "feeling sorry for oneself." Other people or situations may be implicit in such emotions; in embarrassment, for example, it is the "regard" of others that provides the court within which the self-defacing judgment is passed. In pride and shame the "object" of judgment surely includes an accomplishment or misdeed, but the focus is not there but on oneself: It is I who did it. "Inner-directed" emotions may make a display of involvement with others (as in embarrassment), of a sense of superiority (in pride) or inferiority (in shame) compared with others, but the focus or direction of the emotion is always "inward," toward oneself. Even where these emotions appear to be "other-directed" (for example, a mother's embarrassment at the behavior of her daughter, a father's shame at the arrest of his son), "the other" is the object of the emotion only insofar as he or she is identified with the subject (the mother identifying with her daughter, the father identifying with and taking responsibility for his son).

There is a class of emotions that are essentially "bipolar"; they are explicitly judgments of a *relationship*. In a sense, all emotions are bipolar, since all involve, at least implicitly, a judgment of both oneself and another person, a situation, an act or incident. Bipolar emotions, however, require the relationship itself to be explicit in the judgment. In love, for example, there is not simply, as so often supposed, an idealistic admiration of the other person's merits and virtues, or "selfless" concern for their interests and welfare. Nor is there simply the narcissistic self-involvement that cynics have often pointed out. Love essentially involves a judgment of bipolarity—that there is a certain relationship between oneself and the other. It is important to note that this judgment of bipolarity may be accepted by only one party. I may "fall in love" with a person who does not even know that I exist. But I see her in relation to me, and myself in relation to her, whatever she thinks (or doesn't think) of me. Whenever love shifts its focus to one pole or the other, it degenerates into something else—for example, worship (when it becomes "other-directed") or vanity (when it becomes "inner-directed"). The same considerations are true of hatred and jealousy. In jealousy there is a direct accusation, a face-to-face confrontation. (Envy, by way of contrast, keeps its distance, remains more "other-directed.") Anger, typically an "other-directed" emotion, sometimes becomes bipolar, depending upon the relative stress upon the offense vis-à-vis the fact that it is I who am offended. Insofar as anger tends toward indignation, it is strictly other-directed. But anger may also stress the relationship between myself and the other (as in anger over a breach in trust) rather than upon the offense alone. Furthermore, anger may even become inner-directed, when the focus is on *my being offended*, at which point anger degenerates into "feeling sorry for myself."

Pity is also a bipolar emotion. Nietzsche so analyzed it, but with a curious notion that the relationship is of the "master-slave" variety. In any case, pity would also seem to be a bipolar relationship, a certain "feeling-with," literally a *com*passion, or *sym*pathy (cf. *Mit*leiden).

2. Scope and Focus

> If only you love one person with all your heart, everybody seems lovable.
>
> Goethe, *Elective Affinities*

An emotion that is outer-directed may be obsessively narrow, limiting our attention to a single detail or an isolated incident. Or it may expand its scope to include the whole of our surreality, as in a mood. And within that scope, an emotion may focus more or less clearly upon a single item or event; or it may attempt to view the whole with pervasive clarity. (The camera-lens analogy is helpful here.) The scope and the focus of every emotion presupposes both the network of interconnections that define our surreality and the particular incidents that act as "triggers" and causes of our emotion, whether or not they remain in the scope of our attention or as our focus. Anger that defines our lives—for example, open-ended and cosmic outrage at the inequities and injustices of the world—may in this particular instance narrow its scope or focus to include only the hair-breadth difference between two portions of lasagna in an Italian restaurant. Afterward, we may easily dismiss the incident as "trivial" and the anger as "unwarranted," ignoring the vast metaphysically loaded subjective structures that made such a specific reaction possible. On the other hand, anger that is triggered by a trivial incident may be instantly expanded (or overexpanded) to make cosmic judgments about the state of the universe as a whole. An adolescent, turned down for a date, immediately turns his very specific disappointment into a tirade against the insensitivity of women and into a Sisyphusian mythology about the purposelessness of the human quest. But before such pomposity is dismissed as "rationalization," one must remember that the difference between rationalization and expanded scope or general focus may be insight as well as self-deception.

Most often, of course, the scope and focus of the emotions is less than cosmic and more than incidental. We sometimes "love everybody and life itself," but such abstract Romanticism virtually always has a concrete core, a new lover, a few good friends. We occasionally do fall in love with a particular detail of a lover's personality or sexuality; but fetishism, too, is based upon the love of a *person*—not just a particular *aspect* of a person. The focus of most emotions, like the focus of the average camera, has no clear delineations but rather gradations of clarity and vagueness, figure, foreground and background. We love a particular person, but of course we also love that person as an instance of a certain *type* of person. We love certain attributes of that person more than others, and we tend to think more of other people—even love them—because of their association with him or her. Similarly, anger and sadness, fear and resentment, have their varied scope and primary focus, with gradations into excessive detail and obscure if concrete background.

Scope and focus apply in much the same way to inner-directed emotions; it is not simply one's Self, but particular acts or aspects of oneself, that are objects of most emotions. One may be guilty throughout, but usually ashamed only of a particular infelicity, embarrassed only about a particular and usually trivial incident. But any emotion which focuses on the Self will have to include, at least as presupposition if not as background, the world of roles and circumstances within which we define ourselves. Inner-directed emotions also range in scope and focus from the very narrow attention to detail (the blemish on my chin, the stupid comment I made at the library) to the broadest possible views of myself in my world (the anguish of one's own existence in Kierkegaard; the arrogance of self-confidence in Hegel).

3. The Nature of the Object

> Man is the supreme being for man.
>
> Marx, *Early Writings* (1844)

Direction, scope, and focus set the stage, but the specific object is what defines the emotion. But there are many different kinds of objects, some of which are suitable to certain emotions but not to others. Different emotions have different *ontologies* or *categorical* concerns. Some are concerned with the exclusively human; others are not. Moral indignation and romantic love would seem to be more or less restricted to the human, although our mythology and an odd experience or two proves the exceptions to such rules. Fear and sadness, however, are clearly not necessarily concerned with the human at all; one can be afraid of a bear or an avalanche as well as a vindictive attorney or bandits in the suburbs. One can feel sorrow at the loss of a lover or a friend. Some emotions require that their object include an action or an activity and a responsible agent; anger, for example, must be anger at an *offense*. Indignation makes no sense if the blame cannot be levied at someone, and shame, an inner-directed emotion, presumes responsibility on one's own part for some misdeed or mistake. Other emotions do not; love and hate, for example, may appreciate and even be based upon the actions of another person, but they need not be so. Some emotions require only that their object be a conscious creature: for example, one can pity only a creature that he believes to have feelings. (One pities a cockroach or a plant only insofar as he or she believes that cockroaches and plants have feelings.)

Among the most important constitutive judgments of the emotions is the decision whether to treat an object as *human* or not. "Human," in this context, is far more than a descriptive term, delineating a certain recently arrived zoological variation of the apes. We often treat our cats and dogs—and even our automobiles and typewriters—as human, in this important sense, and we find that many members of the species *Homo sapiens* are treated as less than human. To ascribe humanity to an "object" is to delegate responsibility, to decide to treat "it" on a potentially† equal footing with ourselves, as having not only the feelings but rights. (In fact, such treatment includes our dropping the word "object," which designates the inhuman in normal discourse, and insisting upon a purely *personal* vocabulary.) To treat someone as *human* is not yet to treat one as an equal, or with respect, but at least it is a qualitative leap over the treatment of other people that is evident in both the action and the language of prejudice, in which they

† The importance of this qualification will be obvious in Section 5 of this chapter.

are literally conceived of and treated as animals, not just inferiors, but irresponsible creatures without rights rather than *human* beings with responsibilities and rights (and therefore obligations as well).

The judgment of humanity is a judgment of agency and responsibility, of *potential* respect and equality, and the opening up of the doors of intersubjectivity. The judgment of *subhumanity* is a judgment of nonresponsibility, closing off access to respect, equality, and intersubjectivity. To treat an "object" as subhuman need not be degrading. To have pity for a roach or a rhododendron, for example, might even be considered "humane," and amounts only to the ascription of certain sentient states—at least sensitivity to pain. But in pitying a roach or a rhododendron we do not ascribe responsibility to it, as if it ought to have or could have avoided its plight. It is only when human beings are so treated that we consider it degrading. In contempt and loathing, for example, another person is constituted as a "creature" (as a "rat" or a "snake," perhaps). But people *ought* to be treated as humans. (Perhaps animals should as well. One has to hold the line on plants, if for no other reason, because we would deny ourselves a guiltless food supply if we didn't.)

Then there is a third category—the *inhuman*, the rock-hard or jelly-soft substances that constitute the "inanimate" universe. It is worth noting, in this context, that our emotional mythologies often wreak havoc with our more "objective" classifications in our world. If we sometimes err shamefully in our treatment of people as subhuman, we more often act amusingly in our treatment of the objectively inhuman and subhuman as human. This is most dramatically evident in our personifications and animations of the material world. Anger, for example, is an emotion that requires a judgment of humanity, an ascription of responsibility. Yet we often find ourselves getting angry at the weather or a stubborn drawer, at the inconsiderate behavior of our automobiles or our typewriters. In our "cooler" moments, we may well find these personifications laughable, although some of them, for example, the animation of (and even conversations with) a favorite piece of machinery may permeate our lives. The philosophical point, however, is that I can only be angry at the weather insofar as I personify it and treat it as quasi-human, as "Mother Nature." And I might curse the heavens and the universe as a whole, but only insofar as I am willing to recognize some agent to take the blame.‡

Perhaps it would be worth adding a fourth category—the *super*human, which we have included within the "human" (that is, "*at least* human"). In worship, for example, the "object" is respected and ascribed responsibility, but something much more, though it is difficult, if not impossible—as traditional descriptions of the Judaeo-Christian God have proven—to say in other than human terms what this "much more" might be. Love and hate sometimes have "superhuman" components.

The categorical switching between the human, the subhuman, and the inhuman once again reminds one of the "mythological" character of our emotions, constituting the universe according to our personal demands rather than according to the "objective" demands of scientific investigation and knowledge. The judgment between human, subhuman, and inhuman ultimately has little to do with "the facts," which are, at most, objective parameters within which such judgments are made. The fact that this creature is biologically "man" does not make him *human*; the judgment that he is human goes beyond "the facts" to a decision how he is to be *treated*. Similarly, the fact that an automobile or a typewriter can be demonstrably proven not to respond to verbal exhortations and words of praise and admiration need have no binding influence on our emotional decision to treat them humanly. The recently discovered "facts" (or at least evidence) concerning the sensitivity of plants may bolster the judgments of plant lovers, who have insisted upon the need for loving care of their green wards since long before science made such behavior objectively reasonable. But no matter what the evidence, not only plants but animals and even people can be constituted as inhuman and inanimate; how we decide to treat the objects of our emotions is al-

‡ Camus's Sisyphus had the considerable advantage of visible gods upon whom to heap his scorn; Camus, however, supposedly a staunch atheist, attempts to personify his universe in precisely the same way, using the Sisyphus myth as his model. It is this mythological and inconsistent personification and its denial that gives his entire theory of "the Absurd" its paradoxical Christian sentimentality.

ways a matter of our personal needs, never simply a matter of
"the facts."

4. Criteria

"Conscience" speaks to us, but it is our own voice.

Heidegger, Being and Time

Because emotions involve evaluations, they require appeal to
some standards of criteria for judgment. These standards vary considerably, of course; the value of loss in sadness, ascription of
blame in anger, of gain (to the other) in envy and jealousy, of
danger in fear, of suffering in pity, of praise in admiration and
love. But there is a more general consideration which must be
considered first—the status of the criteria themselves. For example,
the criteria for making a judgment may be treated as absolute, as
valid utterly independently of myself and my personal interests
and equally independent of the personal interests of others. In
other words, the criteria might be *moral* criteria, "objective" criteria, whose status is total independence of my own preferences
and those of any other people who are involved in my emotion.
Such Kantian criteria are clearly involved in the emotions of indignation and guilt. They are typically involved in the emotions
of anger and shame. They may be involved in pride (but not in
vanity), in remorse (but not regret), in worship (but not in love).
They are typically (but not necessarily) involved in resentment.

The criteria involved in emotional judgments may be purely
personal. The loss involved in my sadness, for example, can be cal-
culated only by me; the virtues I find in my lover are typically my
personal preferences, even if they are moral virtues. (Were they
vices, I would no doubt admire them equally.) My pity for another depends solely on my calculation of his loss (as a Marxist, I
may find myself incapable of considering the theft of your Rolls-
Royce as a loss at all). My envy depends solely upon my calculations of the competitive value (to me) of the gain of the other. (I
may well envy a gain which I fully recognize to be immoral.)

It is worth noting that personal criteria may not be criteria at all. We sometimes make judgments of an all-encompassing nature which are ultimately *criterionless*. For example, having only been introduced to Professor K., I *know* that I distrust him. My judgment may have been based on certain familiar cues, the fact that he would not look me in the eye or the timidity of his handclasp, but these are surely not my criteria for judgment. Similarly, this judgment may have certain origins in my past—for example, the marked similarity between Professor K. and the instructor who unfairly failed me in a freshman philosophy course. But, again, this surely is not my criterion for making the judgment. Having once passed judgment, I may then go on to look for concrete evidence that the judgment is well founded, or proceed to look for tell-tale signs with which I can persuade you to make the same judgment. But such evidence and proceedings come after the judgment, not before. Such "criterionless" judgments are basic to many emotions (which are thus rightly said to be "uncritical"). The judgments of virtue and vice involved in love and hate (as opposed to those in worship and anger) are criterionless. We sometimes love or hate someone prior to our having good reason for doing so (thus we "fall in" love); the reason may come afterward. Similarly, the judgments of inferiority and superiority that are to be found at the foundations of such emotions as resentment and pride are criterionless; the evidence follows. Not all personal judgments are criterionless, of course. Sorrow and fear, jealousy and pity, for example, are typically based upon the most rigorously formulated personal criteria.

There is a third category of criteria, which becomes evident when one considers the emotion of embarrassment. My embarrassment is not a failure by moral standards. I may well be embarrassed by an act which is wholesomely moral; for example, I rip my pants digging out a quarter for a street-corner Santa Claus, or I heroically attack and vanquish a supposed thief, or I may find upholding a moral principle in a den of thieves. Yet embarrassment is not simply failure in my own eyes. It is the gaze and opinions of others that embarrasses me. The same act which I might freely perform while alone or in different company embarrasses me in *this* company. Thus, we must distinguish a third sort of criterion, one which depends upon the opinions of other people, but is not "objective" or moral. We may call it "interpersonal." It is apparently the same sort of criterion that functions in vanity (as opposed to pride). Vanity is a (sometimes obsessive) concern for others' opinions of us which we need involve little moral sense or personal taste.

5. Personal Status

Love does not seek equals; it creates them.

Stendhal, *De l'Amour*

Within the realm of humanity (as opposed to the subhuman and the inhuman), we are continuously jockeying for position, seeking approval and acceptance and striving to "better" ourselves. At the same time, we judge and evaluate our peers, encouraging them or "putting them down." Most importantly, we search for our equals, who will be our friends. We also seek superiors, who will be our idols and our consciences, and inferiors, who will be our lackeys and feed our egos as agreeable "yes-men" and foils with whom we can salvage faltering self-confidence. If this picture sounds unflattering, we need only take an honest look at ourselves, at our constant and sometimes desperate search for support and security, for proof of our personal worth or at least compensation for our weaknesses. I do not want to say that all our dealings with others are competitions for status and "deals" for mutual security and support, but we shall have no chance at all to understand the logic of the emotions if we do not appreciate the central role such competitive judgments have in our personal lives. Ideally, we might well insist that all persons *ought* to be judged as equals, but we are surely fooling ourselves if we think this abstract ideal is in fact instantiated in our everyday emotional judgments.

There are emotions which *require* equality. Romantic love is a most important example. I might fall in love with a movie star or a princess, but insofar as I love her (as opposed to adoring or worshiping her), I must see her as my equal. Because love constitutes our equality with those whom we admire, it is consequently an emotion which *elevates* self-esteem more effectively than any other. Hatred, however, shares this ability with love (by consti-

tuting ourselves as equals of a powerful enemy and by contrasting
our own heroic goodness with the enemy's hateful badness; whatever else might be said against it, hatred is a powerful source of
self-confidence and a sense of mission). Anger is also an equalizing
judgment. An adult allows himself to become angry with a child
only to the extent to which he is considered as an adult. Similarly,
jealousy is an emotion between equals. The same judgment, "He's
got what I want," applied to unequals, results in envy or contempt. Pity is a perplexing example here: Nietzsche considers pity
an emotion which judges the other as an inferior. In fact, he takes
that to be the purpose of this emotion. But it would seem that
Hume was closer to the truth here; pity is often an emotion between equals. It is "fellow-feeling," "feeling-with." One might
argue that one can pity inferiors, or one might argue even that
one can pity only inferiors. It is true, of course, that one can pity
another only when he or she (or perhaps, it) is in a sorry state
while one is himself in a relatively satisfactory state. But this judgment of fortune and misfortune is possible only within the framework of a more general judgment to the effect that the parties are
of equal stature.

There are emotions which take the other to be decidedly
superior—for example, adoration and worship, resentment and
envy. There are emotions which take the other to be decidedly inferior—for example, despising and cherishing. (It is symptomatic
of a male-dominated society that a man might well cherish his
woman but a woman is much more likely to adore her man.
Similarly, one might well cherish his cat or his car, but he could
hardly be said to adore either.) If one considers a vengeful triad of
negative other-directed judgments, resentment, hatred, and contempt, it can be seen how similarly negative judgments of the
other take on an entirely different cast depending on the judgment of personal status of oneself vis-à-vis the other. Resentment
is an impotent and timid, even if all-consuming, complaint against
a superior who as likely as not does not even recognize the ill feeling below him. Nietzsche aptly uses the tarantula to exemplify resentment. Its vicious appearance and poisonous bite, its constant
stance of defensiveness and backward and sideward retreating
movements, its ultimate cowardice and fear of actually attacking,
all exemplify the impotent fury of resentment. Hatred, on the

other hand (with which resentment is often identified, the latter parading as the former, for obvious reasons of status), is essentially an attitude of equality, even where the hated figure is a powerful and objectively superior person. The superiority of contempt, on the other hand, makes action and revenge a matter of indifference. ("Why bother with a man I despise?") Fuming resentment attaches itself to the other like a leech while contempt frees itself altogether by constituting the other as utterly insignificant. Hatred, however, often involves a mutual binding with the other that is no less powerful than the bindings of love, engaging in and even welcoming the combat that resentment fears but which contempt finds beneath its dignity.

It is important to stress once again the fact that personal status, like all the structures of our emotional mythologies, is *constituted* in our judgments. However much we may seek and search for friends and equals, ultimately we decide to *make* them such. The criteria we demand that they fulfill are criteria which we ourselves have constituted, and it is not unusual, upon meeting someone who does not fit "our expectations," to change or ignore altogether the same criteria we have so cautiously upheld, seemingly for much of our lives. The same, of course, is true of inequalities. The need to feel superior and the exigencies of defensiveness may often outweigh the embarrassingly small investments of our reflectively most treasured ideologies. Ultimately, however, equality proves to be not only a reflective ideal but the ideal of self-esteem. (The idea that all emotions tend to maximize self-esteem is not the same as the desire of some emotions to constitute ourselves as superior to other people.) But the realization of this reflective ideal requires the seeing through and breaking down of any number of deeply entrenched and stubborn defenses, which have long seemed to find it to their advantage to continue to see the world in competitive terms of "winners" and "losers," superiors and inferiors.

I want to re-emphasize the independence of these judgments of status from "the facts" of the case. It may be conceded that the other person has any number of such "facts" in his favor (success, popularity, power, etc.) but still be judged that, in an unquantifiable (perhaps moral) sense, he is inferior to oneself. Similarly, to judge someone as a superior is to take him as an authority or model, no matter what his failings and weaknesses. (Because he has been judged superior, these failings and weaknesses may become marks of superiority.) And again, to judge someone as an equal—for example, to love, hate, or be angry with him—we need take no account of the fact that he is a servant or a slave, that he is moronic or a coward, that he is, in every "objective" sense, one's inferior. As Stendhal tells us, love (and all emotions) creates (that is, constitutes), not seeks or finds, equals (and unequals).

It is important to remember that a judgment of subhumanity already precludes candidacy for equality. Thus, I insisted, in a previous section, that a judgment of humanity was required for an individual to even be a *candidate* for equality. Thus, the viciousness of subhuman archetypes (applied to other races or classes, to the mentally infirmed, or to the very young or very old) is that it closes off from the outset any possibility of intersubjective communication. (Thus, the liberal policy that anything remotely resembling a human being should be so considered is the only one within which there can be any reasonable considerations of status.)

6. Evaluations

The heart of every emotion is its value judgments, its appraisals of gain and loss, its indictments of offenses and its praise of virtue, its often Manichean judgments of "good" and "evil," "right" and "wrong." In our more reflective moments, we try to minimize such "black-and-white" evaluations in favor of more descriptive, more discriminating, and more "balanced" accounts. (In politics, for example, confrontations of "right" and "wrong" and "good" and "evil" lead only to conflict and wars.) Our prereflective emotions, however, are far more concerned with our own security and esteem than they are with accuracy or fairness. Accordingly, they are often quick and highly oversimplified, judging people, complicated circumstances, or even the universe as a whole with the glib assurance of a chef deciding whether the cream has turned or not. And, as always, our emotional evaluations need have little to do with "the facts." Often the value judgment precedes the facts (we immediately dislike someone, without knowing anything about him; we instantly feel the loss of something that is taken from us, despite the fact that it is utterly useless to us and we have not even noticed it for years).

Our emotional evaluations vary in scope and focus according to the scope and focus of the emotion itself. Many of our emotions are concerned with particular incidents or details—for example, estimates of loss and gain, loss in sadness, possible future loss in fear, gain in gratitude, possible gain in hope and faith. In cases of interpersonal competition, such losses and gains may themselves be strictly competitive. For example, I may be jealous of my rival when he is offered a job despite the fact that I would not have even considered it otherwise. Or I may lose a large sum of money at a gambling table which in fact I have just acquired by the same means. I do not, all considered, suffer a loss; yet I may well feel resentful and envious of the winner of the evening.

Evaluations of loss and gain are, in general, based upon strictly personal criteria. Our emotional evaluations may also be based upon moral or "objective" criteria; human actions (one's own or others') are emotionally judged to be "right" or "wrong," not on the basis of one's personal preferences but on the basis of impersonal laws of conduct. Similarly, evaluations of "good" and "bad" ("evil") are usually based upon (and always defended on the basis of) ostensibly impersonal criteria. There are also those emotional evaluations of particular incidents that are based upon interpersonal criteria, the awkwardness which is constituted in embarrassment, the flattering detail that is flaunted in vanity.

These particular and incidental evaluations are often only the focal point of far broader considerations. A trivial loss (usually in self-esteem rather than a material loss, although the latter easily emerges as the former) may act as the excuse for the all-pervasive condemnation of a situation or another person in resentment or envy. Similarly, a trivial boon may become the focal point of the excessive gratitude and adoration that is the core of several religions. And, most commonly, a small hurt may spark a startling display of anger, apparently all out of proportion to its object, until we realize that it is the *type* of incident that is its object, not the incident itself, what it *signifies* (a personality trait betrayed rather than a single act of discourtesy, a talent or a skill displayed rather than an isolated performance).

Many emotions may be partially distinguished by their differences in evaluative scope and focus—sadness, sorrow, and grief, for example, the first confined to a particular loss, the last more central to the personality and accordingly more traumatic. Similarly, jealousy is more particular, envy more general, shame more particular, guilt more general, hope particular, faith general, fear particular, anxiety general. Many emotions, however, incorporate different-size evaluations simultaneously; I may be saddened by a loss of human life but grateful for its consequences; in envy I value positively the object but negatively its loss, and perhaps even more negatively the person who has taken it from me; in hatred I both condemn and admire my adversary—condemn him as a person but admire him for his powers; in self-righteous indignation I condemn the other and praise myself, just as in devotion, I belittle myself and extravagantly value the other.

The most fundamental value judgments, however, are concerned neither with incidents nor with more general aspects of a person or a situation but with *over-all* evaluations. We walk into a party and immediately feel uncomfortable, defensive, and resentful and we conclude, before we have even sat down, that it is a "bad" party. Perhaps we instead "take a liking to someone," whether because of a certain look in his or her eyes, a dim resemblance to an old friend, or a striking discrepancy between reputation and appearance; or, in the same manner, feel immediate repulsion and distrust; the handshake feels manipulative or clammy, the look uncomfortably seductive or evasive. Such over-all evaluations precede, but are not based upon, any but the most superficial details or incidents. Accordingly, we called them "criterionless"; their justification and evidence comes after, not before.

Yet we are often impressed with the acuity of our "intuitions" in such instances in the light of subsequent experience and reflection. An immediate liking is the foundation for a long friendship; instant animosity is the basis of long enmity. But again, I want to cautiously suggest that such "first impressions" are constitutive of, not prophetic of, the subsequent relationships. Having decided to *like* someone, we seek out their friendship, encourage their virtues, ignore their faults, *build* the trust that we think we have "found." Or, having set the stage for battle, we avidly seek our enemy's vices and weaknesses, not only in preparation for the hostilities to come but as a *post hoc* rationalization for them. Love and hate, in particular, but also resentment, guilt, and most moods, are characterized by the centrality of such over-all value judgments.

It is important to distinguish these over-all evaluations from judgments of personal status; I may despise a certain criminal but like him personally; I may admire or worship a public hero or a god but dislike him immensely. (Thus, the Christian ideal of "love your neighbor" succeeds, with a slight twist of this philosophical point, in defending a ruthless elitism along with its encouragement for indiscriminant interpersonal approval.)

An over-all evaluation tends to "set up," but not entail, more particular evaluations of the same kind; having decided to like someone, we are prone to praise their slightest talents and virtues, quietly passing over or benignly chastising their vices (not "You're beautiful, I love you," but rather "I love you, you're beautiful"). Conversely, we seek out and criticize the vices and weaknesses of our enemies, treating their talents and virtues as unearned gratuities. We can continue to like someone in the face of any number of particular negative evaluations, and we may praise the talents of someone we dislike or despise (though perhaps with a touch of jealousy). This is also true of our sense of self-esteem, "liking ourselves" as opposed to "hating" or even "loathing ourselves." These, too, are criterionless over-all evaluations which need not depend upon any particular details, aspects, accomplishments of facts about oneself. But the lesson to be gleaned from this is of tremendous importance; however often we may *use* such details to pry ourselves up in our own estimation, the key to our sense of self-worth lies in our constitutive judgments, in our bald *decision* to like ourselves. And since, in our often ruthless but equally often uncritical self-images as ideals and nemeses in our evaluations of others, we can understand the common-sense and undeniable link between self-love and our ability to love other people (and self-hatred and the inability to love). What we have decided to hate about ourselves will be precisely what we shall hate in those people who are most like us (and thus usually the most compatible as well).

7. Responsibility

Our emotions involve more than evaluations; they also ascribe responsibility, praise for gains, blame for losses. Anger and indignation, for example, involve not only judgments of loss but also a judgment of blame, an accusation. Someone is responsible for that loss, which thereby, taken personally, becomes an *offense*. Admiration and gratitude, on the positive side, include judgments of praise. Inner-directed emotions also include such ascriptions of responsibility; shame and guilt include judgments of blame, pride (like other-directed admiration) includes a judgment of praise. There are also emotions which have built into them vindications and exonerations; embarrassment, for example, includes the judgment that I am not to blame for the awkward situation in which I find myself. (Thus, "I'm sorry, I couldn't help it" is a fitting expression.) Similarly, in pity I judge that you are not responsible for your suffering (or at least however much you may have contributed to your plight, you are suffering far more than you deserve. Thus, we can see why pity has played such a central role in certain long-standing theological disputes about the nature of human suffering. The "problem of evil," for example, as argued among the eighteenth-century *philosophes*, often centered around the question of pity—and related questions of guilt. Were the people of Lisbon to be pitied for the great earthquake of 1755? Or were they to be seen in terms of some shared cosmic guilt or a master plan for "the best of all possible worlds"? On the other side Nietzsche and several existentialists, who hold a very strong position regarding personal responsibility, tend to look upon pity with suspicion if not derision. How one judges the emotion pity ultimately turns on his metaphysical view of human freedom: "Are we always (or ever) responsible for our own sufferings?"

Similarly, sadness is a judgment of all-around innocence. One is sad over his loss, but the fact that he is sad rather than angry or regretful attests to his willingness to see his loss as blameless. Vanity, unlike pride, ascribes no responsibility to oneself. (One is vain about his appearances, but proud of what he has *done*.) Love and hate are curious emotions here; love often praises virtues while exonerating blame for vice;* hate blames vice while leaving virtue uncommended. Similarly, worship and resentment, which bear some important similarities to love and hate but differ radically in their judgments of status (the latter being paradigms of self-demeaning emotions) are apt to praise or condemn (respectively) any characteristic whatever. (Worship and resentment seem to be directed at the power rather than the results. An object of worship is praised, for example, even if in fact it never *does* anything. The object of resentment is [quietly] abused and blamed for whatever happens, whether its [his/her] actual doing or not.)

Where evaluations are based upon moral criteria, the responsibility involved is moral responsibility; guilt and moral indignation, for example, include strong moral condemnations (of self and others respectively). Shame and anger are more particular and less emphatically moral, but still involve ascriptions of moral responsibility. (It is worth noting the difference with Freud here; he took self-directed anger to be *depression*.) It is also worth noting the important difference in the scope of the blame in anger and shame, on the one hand, and resentment and guilt on the other. It is possible to be angry at a friend and to be ashamed while maintaining self-esteem. Resentment, however, severs all possible intimacy with others, and guilt undermines every possibility of self-esteem. Thus it is that the former emotions are often signs of a healthy moral sensitivity, but the latter often display a pathological extravagance, which is as often as not compensated for by the equally moral but also pathologically self-righteous emotions of indignation, spite, and a curious sense of "innocence" that I shall mention in the next chapter.

8. Intersubjectivity

We may judge another person our equal, and we may like and praise him (her), but yet have nothing to do with him (her). So far, I have said nothing about our emotional *relationships* with others. Our judgments of status and our various evaluations will surely influence and may in some cases determine the parameters

* "Love means never having to say you're sorry"(?!).

of our relationships, but they do not define those relationships as such. For that, an entirely distinctive set of constitutive judgments is required, judgments of "intersubjectivity," of trust and "openness," sharing and association. Love, for example, is not merely an intense liking for another person. It requires, in addition, judgments of equality and intersubjectivity, a sense of trust and a desire to share, that other forms of "liking" (respect, admiration, idolatry, and worship) do not include. Pity, compassion, and sympathy are also emotions of intersubjectivity, but with reservations and a "distance" that is not tolerated in love. In all such emotions, we "open ourselves" to others, allow ourselves to share their experiences and opinions, their world views, and, ultimately, their other emotions. Curiously, this notion of intersubjectivity is also to be found in hatred, in that curious but familiar camaraderie that is shared by bitter enemies. What they share, of course, is their desire to vanquish the other, and their world views are very much mirror images of each other. Accordingly, hatred may often provide a solid foundation of a shared surreality upon which love can build an unusually durable relationship.

Intersubjectivity is familiar to most of us as "team spirit" and a sense of camaraderie and close association. It is the judgment of "we-ness" and shared interests that defines professional friendships and political coalitions, classmates, teammates, and a good many marriages. Perhaps it is possible to constitute an intersubjective relationship in the face of gross inequalities (as in love between parents and children, or in Kierkegaard's conception of faith and devotion), but it is generally the case that equal status will be as much of a presupposition of intersubjectivity as shared experiences and interests. In fact, the sense of "we" that is so essential to the intersubjective emotions exists in at best an unstable compromise with interpersonal conflicts over status. Thus, a team or a marriage is least durable when questions of interests and status confront it from *without*. Familial intersubjectivity is possible just because questions of status do not arise (at least for a period of years).

The contrast of intersubjectivity is defensiveness. Instead of trust, there is suspicion; in place of openness and candor, there is secrecy and inhibition. In place of shared experiences, there is a strong emphasis on privacy. Emotions which take the other to be superior are inevitably emotions of defensiveness. Thus, resentment displays that poisonous cowardice that keeps so much to itself even as its attention is fixated bitterly outward. Fear, of course, has its built-in defensiveness. So does envy, which is well known for its arsenal of excuses, and embarrassment, which by its very nature must be ready to throw the blame elsewhere and plead impotent innocence. Guilt, although it is inner-directed, is typically coupled with defensive postures of outward-facing resentment, indignation, and self-righteousness.

In all emotions in which one constitutes himself as inferior, there is the paradoxical compensation of an arsenal of protective devices, despite the fact that the ultimate source of degradation is oneself. Accordingly, those schizoid emotions involve a curious dialectic of self-contempt and self-righteousness, of bitter inferiority and arrogant superiority. The main weapon of defensiveness, because it *begins* from a position of relative inferiority and impotence, is the psychological fortress, the subjective wall behind which one remains hidden while silently and safely condemning everyone else, turning others' virtues into vices and their own vices into virtues ("Ignorance is bliss"), gauging others' strengths as weaknesses ("The meek shall inherit the earth"), others' accomplishments as ostentations ("He doesn't have to brag about it") and their beauties as vanities ("It's only skin deep"). This reversal of values, which Nietzsche diagnosed as the "transvaluation of values" of what he called "slave morality," defined by resentment, allows those who have judged themselves as inferiors to nevertheless see themselves as superiors. But this two-faced and paradoxical position is always at odds with itself and, in order to maintain its deceptions, necessarily cuts itself off from any other people who do not share their position. Accordingly, these emotions and their defensiveness must themselves remain hidden, often by feigning very different emotions, puffed-up indignation and false pride, pity (which is why Nietzsche was so anxious to attack this emotion), and that familiar false love that is based upon the desperate need for allies rather than upon the intimacy and trust of true love. I shall discuss the vicissitudes of defensiveness in Chapter 12, but it is important to note, even here, that resentment and its relations, like some diseases of historical distinction, have the ability to mask their infirmity by mocking almost any symptoms whatever. The emotions of superiority, when they are not (as they often are) masks of inferiority, also tend to exclude intersubjectivity. Yet their attitude is not one of defensiveness (which is virtually always a sign of inferiority) but *indifference*. However much one may share certain goals with a servant or someone he despises, there will always be that inevitable breach of trust and candor, the need for secrecy and caution, first from the side of inferiority, but then from superiority as well, of necessity, for the sake of its own protection.

9. *"Distance"*

Intersubjectivity is not yet intimacy, although intimacy presupposes the trust and sense of shared interests and experience of intersubjectivity. Intimacy adds to intersubjectivity a "closeness," a strong desire, a need for physical as well as psychological proximity, which turns openness and candor from the mere potentiality of intersubjectivity to the necessity of familiarity. Professional colleagues and classmates, for example, may know little about each other, although it is expected and assumed that they will, *if* the need arises, be forthright and honest about themselves. In friendship, on the other hand, such exchanges of information and experience are essential, and the friendship itself provides the "need" in question. Similarly, a marriage may well be a strong intersubjective relationship, but it may nevertheless possess a certain "distance" which allows husband and wife to avoid, possibly for years or a lifetime, particular knowledge of each other and those shared experiences which are the most (and often painfully) revealing. The intimacy of love *demands* that knowledge and those revelations of shared trauma.

It is often said that love takes the interests of the lover as being more important than one's own; but here again we would rather say that love takes the lover's interests *as* its own. The inverse is true of hatred; it takes the other's well-being as the negation of its own interests. It, too, demands intimacy and finds nothing so painful as distance from its adversary. Just as love desires nothing more than closeness, so does hatred; if "I feel so close to you" is essential expression for the intimacy of love, it is just as applicable, although never spoken, as a formula (not an expression) of hatred. The hostile face-to-face glowering confrontations with our enemies, like the sweet and mutual regards of love, are liberties allowed only to intimates. By contrast, pity, although intersubjective, keeps its distance; contempt and resentment, though both hostile as hatred, do as well.

Emotions of inferiority and defensiveness tend to increase the distance between self and other as much as possible. Resentment keeps out of view (though keeping its oppressor in its sight) always at a safe physical and, more importantly, psychological distance. In envy, unlike jealousy, we would not think of confronting the person envied. Similarly, emotions of superiority, especially when they are masks for inferiority, keep their distance from their "objects." In contempt, for example, repulsion drives us away from our objects; we do not want to be near them.

Several emotions involve a notion of distance which is neither the intimacy of love and hatred nor the impersonal distances of resentment and contempt. The jealous lover may fear but yet will not avoid a confrontation with his rival. Where envy keeps as much distance as possible, jealousy welcomes a confrontation, but forbids intimacy. It holds its rival "at arm's length." Anger shares this need of "an arm's length" distance, careful not to move so close as to regain intimacy and lose hold of the magisterial distance required for its indictment but equally careful not to back off so far that personal confrontation becomes impossible. In pity we feel "with" the other, but at a safe distance; too close is dangerous (suffering and misfortune are easily contagious), but too far is inhuman and cold-blooded.

An extremely awkward set of judgments is to be found in the ascription of distance toward oneself. In a sense, of course, there can be no distance from oneself, and it would be curious to call it "intimacy." Yet there is a phenomenon of self-estrangement, which is common to many of the self-demeaning emotions and something over and above the demeaning itself. In guilt, in particular, one has a strong urge to "escape from oneself," and he looks at himself as an alien presence, taking refuge in the pure subjectivity of a transcendental self or "soul." Such, of course, is the substance of Hegel's classic "unhappy consciousness" and the continuing theme of Kierkegaard's gloomy Christian schizophrenia. To a lesser extent, such a sense of distance may accompany other emotions, for example, embarrassment, in which the desire to escape may be augmented with a fleeting sense of "not being oneself." A similar distance can sometimes be found in vanity and pride, at least in that uncertain form of pride (not self-esteem) mixed with the nagging doubt that "I don't really deserve all of this." Such instances underscore the need to emphasize the fact that the "distances" involved in our emotions need not be taken in literally spatial terms.

10. Mythologies: The Synthesis of Our Emotional Judgments

These various judgments are responsible—each in its own way—for structuring our world, giving it its emphases, its scope and focus, its values and investments, our status and our relationships. But the mere totality of such judgments, like Kant's initial list of "categories of the understandings," is less than the unified structure of our surreality. Our judgments are synthesized and dramatized as what I have called mythologies, the various images and metaphors within which we live. Our mythologies define our conceptions of ourselves, as heroes or as martyrs, as "goodhearted but misunderstood" or as talented but unappreciated, as lovable but unloved, as gallant or as cowardly, as generous or as miserly. In those emotions in which subhuman judgments are involved, there may well be a quasi-animal mythology, treating our enemies as vipers, dragons, and monsters and those we despise as rats, snakes, and trolls. We may view ourselves in terms more appropriate to our pets, as cuddly or as beastly, as spoiled as a pampered cat or as unctuously grateful as a golden retriever. Our mythologies often include supernatural appeals, to fatalism and to various forms of gods and devils, myths of "possession" and the faithful optimism that "it will all work out." Our mythologies synthesize our views as emotional judgments into a coherent dramatic framework, organizing the dull facts of the world into the excitement of personal involvement and meaningfulness.

11. Desires, Intentions, and Commitments

I have argued that every emotion is also an ideology, a set of demands, "how the world ought to be." It is not only an interpretation of our world but a projection into its future, filled with desires which sometimes become intentions and commitments. Our anger demands that the offender be punished; our love requires the efforts of intimacy, the demand that it be expressed through honesty and touch, the desire to do whatever possible for the welfare and happiness of one's lover. Embarrassment wants to hide, jealousy to retrieve, hatred to hurt, and pity demands charity as well as sympathy. Every such desire, however, cannot be expressed in action. Where direct and effective expression is possible, desire turns to intention (and, where matters of principle are concerned, to commitments) and manifests itself in action. But where such expression is not possible, because of impotence or unwillingness, our emotions may adopt a complex subjective strategy aimed not at changing the world, but rather at changing our view of the world, our emotional mythologies and consequently our ideologies as well.

The ultimate end of all of our desires (and consequently our intentions and commitments) is personal dignity and self-esteem. The particular desires of the various emotions depend, however, on the structure of our surreality as determined by our other emotional judgments and "the facts" of the case. In general, mythology of inferiority will involve desires for elevation and security. Mythologies of superiority, on the other hand, are often defensive of their supposed status. Those emotions which involve a loss will be concerned with recouping or compensating for that loss. Emotions which ascribe responsibility to others will involve demands for reward and punishment, whereas ascriptions of responsibility for oneself will involve desire for redemption and taking credit. Emotions which involve liking another person will involve concern for their welfare, whereas those that involve hostility will include desires for harm. Emotions may involve the desire to escape and the desire to embarrass other people. They may involve the desire for approval, for acceptance, for sympathy, or in desperation, for virtually any form of attention. The desires that emerge from a particular emotion may be direct and straightforward, or they may, depending upon circumstances and our other concerns, become extraordinarily convoluted and sophisticated.

12. Power

One of the determinants of desire and intention is power, our ability to perform the actions we wish to perform and to express our emotions. The power we have in fact, however, is not our main concern. That may determine our success in action, but the emotion itself depends rather on our estimation of power. The jealous lover and the envious wallflower may in fact be equally capable of pummeling the Casanova who has stolen the object of their desires. But jealousy includes a confidence that envy lacks. Jealousy welcomes the opportunity of confrontation; envy assumes impotence from the outset. The strategy and expression of jealousy, therefore, tend to be more or less direct. The strategy of envy, by contrast, is virtually always convoluted and purely subjective, giving rise to those syndromes of defensiveness which build a life based upon a possibly false belief in one's own ineffectiveness.

The distinction between "cannot" and "will not" is not as simple as it seems. Objectively, it may be that one cannot perform a certain action; but subjectively there is no action that one cannot resolve to attempt. Don Quixote's battle plans may seem absurd; but that obvious absurdity did not permeate his subjective intentions, and the presumption of power was sufficient to keep him going, despite the inevitable setbacks, and never falling into the syndromes of self-pity, self-contempt, and resentment, which repeated failure so often excuses. Subjectively, we must always prefer a "will not" to a "cannot," and an estimate of impotence must always be suspected of ulterior motives, of surreptitious strategies for self-esteem and an unwillingness to take responsibility for the often vicious syndromes which will follow.

13. *Strategies*

Every emotion is a subjective strategy for the maximization of personal dignity and self-esteem. The "strategy" in question may be minimal; publicly offended, I strike back quickly and effectively, chastising my offender for all to see. But, as we have seen (Chapter 9), self-esteem is often better served through the retention and intensification of an emotion rather than its satisfaction. In such cases, both the strategy of the emotion and the strategy of the expression may become immensely complicated. A woman continues to patronize a shop which she knows has cheated her; her small losses are more than compensated for by the self-righteous satisfaction of her continuing indignation (but, of course, that is not her "reason" for shopping there; rather "because it is convenient" or some such trivial excuse). Or a couple in love refuse every opportunity to "consummate" and express their affections for each other, just in order to keep alive the fantasies of Romantic love and avoid the possibility of a bland future of adjustments and domesticity. Resentment in general is to be characterized by resolute unwillingness to attempt any effective redress of its alleged misfortunes. The strategy of an emotion, in other words, is a strategy of self-esteem, and both the subjective structures of the emotion and its attempted expressions in action must be understood, in each particular case, as devices and tactics to maximize one's sense of self-worth, using whatever circumstantial facts and objects to its subjective advantage.

CHAPTER 8: THE EMOTIONAL REGISTER: WHO'S WHO AMONG THE PASSIONS

What is the difference between shame and embarrassment? Or anger and indignation, envy and jealousy, fear and anxiety, remorse and regret, love and adoration? Why are love and hatred so typically found together? as are pride and shame, pity and anger, guilt and moral indignation—all seemingly "opposite" emotions yet Janus-like twins as well. Why do we consider some emotions more desirable than others—for example, love rather than hatred, gratitude rather than envy, compassion rather than vengeance? On the traditional models of emotion, there is little promise of an adequate answer, since the very idea that the emotions are physiological changes in the body or forces in the psyche or their feeling—like "affects" leaves out the all-important *conceptual* distinctions and connections between the various emotions. Accordingly, such questions about the dialectical combinations and progressions of the emotions, their subtle differences and vicissitudes, have been left to the poets and novelists as an "unscientific" and "merely contingent" set of curiosities, unworthy of the efforts of psychology and philosophy. But every emotion is a (set of) constitutive judgment(s), conceptual in form and thus displaying the "logic" surveyed in the preceding chapter. Each emotion is a characteristic set of such judgments (and desires, intentions, and strategies). The similarities and differences between them are thus differences and similarities in their respective judgments. (In a sense, there are no individual emotions, but only a system of judgments from which we can abstract and simplify and identify certain dominant patterns of judgment by using individual emotion names.[1])

How many emotions are there? Which are "basic"? These are librarian's questions, based upon our obsession for atomism, classification, and bureaucracy. The small list of "basic" emotions that appears in every dictionary and psychology primer—anger, love, fear, hate, guilt, grief, and jealousy—are but the most visible in our society, the most common and admissible structures that *we* single out as representative of *our* surreality. But if one makes only a casual observation of the logical categories studied in the preceding chapter, it can be seen that the search for basic emotions—those from which all other emotions are composed through combination—is essentially misguided. A quick calculation of the number of permutations of various judgments should be sufficient to show that the number of emotions is all but indeterminate, depending upon how finely one is willing to carve up and individuate the small differences between similar emotions. (The French, for example, have many distinctions between the various forms of intimacy that we more cold-blooded Anglicans clumsily summarize with the clearly inadequate concepts of "love" and "like." Similarly, Yiddish has many more concepts of irony and derogation, appropriate to distinguishing the many ways of enduring hardship, concepts which are wholly absent from the language of paradisical South Pacific cultures.) How many emotions are there? As many as we care to distinguish. (Perhaps someone will develop a Dewey decimal system. . . .)

The quest for the "basic" emotions is one of the oldest games in psychology. The Greeks and the medievals played it frequently; the Germans turned it into a "science." The French since Descartes have indefatigably composed their shorter lists of the passions, and John Watson set up the contemporary American parameters of the game with his now famous list of three—fear, dependency, and rage. The quest itself is often but another part of the Myth of the Passions, as if the emotions were but static atoms which could be added together into so many molecules. But which emotions are "basic" is not a fact of "human nature," but a fact about the surreality of some particular people. Notice how many of *our* "basic" emotions are individualistic, how many are defensive, and how many adopt negative evaluations and claims of status as two of their ingredients. There are societies, however, which do not recognize the hostile emotions.* In societies with

* The Utka eskimos. (See, for example, J. L. Briggs, *Never In Anger* [Cambridge, Mass.: Harvard University Press, 1970].) But

authoritarian moral codes, indignation is more "basic" than personal anger; in our relatively comfortable and introspective lives,
depression is in fact more "basic" than fear. (A short walk on
Manhattan's upper Amsterdam Avenue late at night shows us the
difference; it is impossible to be depressed on Ninety-seventh
Street and Amsterdam at 1 A.M.; one just wants to get home
alive.) The relative roles of pride and vanity depend upon the emphasis on the external trappings of individualism as opposed to
the emphasis on deeds and accomplishments. In societies in
which intimacy is restricted to "nuclear" groups of two (and their
offspring), Romantic love and jealousy will be more basic than
those tribal and community roles and responsibilities which are essential in those societies that reject the isolated individualism that
Romantic love and jealousy presuppose. There are no "basic"
emotions, only those emotions which are prevalent—in word or in
fact—in a particular society. (Our own list is not flattering.)

The temptation to reduce all emotions to a single emotion, pair
of emotions, or set of emotions makes it impossible to appreciate
the richness of our emotional lives. Those soft-headed principles
of literary criticism, for example, that take all our emotions as
demands for love, or those cynical moralists who argue that all
emotions are expressions of possessiveness and defensiveness, or
Freud's various imaginative attempts to reduce all emotions to a
pair of conflicting emotions, sex and aggression, love and hostility,
life and death—however elegant and convenient—are unjustifiable
and arbitrary abstractions. In the same vein, the common distinction of "positive" and "negative" emotions must be rejected. I
have already shown that every emotion contains a number of evaluations in addition to several other judgments (for example, status and intersubjectivity) which might be described in such terms.
Many emotions, for example, value one's Self positively and the
other negatively (as in contempt) or vice versa (as in worship) or
judge an object over-all positively but in some detail negatively
(as in anger or betrayal) or judge another person as superior but
at the same time condemn him (as in resentment). It is as if (to

---

they, too, universalize their emotional surreality: "There is only one
ideal, which is applicable to all human beings, Utka or not, over the
age of three or so, the rule of even-tempered restraint."

borrow another analogy from Frithjof Bergmann) we visited an art gallery but were allowed to judge each work only as either "good" or "bad." Our emotions are far more sophisticated—and far more interesting.

In what follows, I have attempted to give a selective index of the emotions, showing how each is composed of the various judgments discussed in the preceding chapter. To avoid falling into the usual temptation of dividing the emotions into certain groups —for example, "positive" and "negative" (e.g., Franz Brentano), "self-centered" and "social" (e.g., A. Maisonneuve), "psychic" and "metaphysical" (e.g., Max Scheler)—I have taken the uncreative but purposefully arbitrary option of putting them in alphabetical order. Both my selection and the analyses that follow are sometimes controversial. (Essentially, I have crammed some five hundred philosophical analyses into the next eighty pages.) Accordingly, I take what follows to be an exploratory effort rather than a finished theory, a spur to empirical and conceptual analyses that psychologists and other philosophers will supply to substantiate or refute my claims. Meanwhile, my primary concern is to demonstrate in some detail how the theory I have formulated can be applied and understood in our constitution of everyday life.

ANGER

> I'll be judge, I'll be jury, said cunning old fury.
>
> Lewis Carroll, *Alice in Wonderland*

Anger and its variations (rage, outrage and furor, irritation and annoyance, being peeved, pissed, piqued, and incensed) always provide at least one entry in every list of emotions, no matter how abbreviated (for example, in every major dictionary, in Watson's short list of three, in most of Freud's formulations). In the current vogue for "self-expression" and "ventilationism," it is virtually always anger which receives central if not exclusive attention. (Pent-up anger is said to poison the personality, and thus should be "let out"; but we hear few such exhortations to honesty concerning the far more poisonous emotions of envy and resentment.) Anger is an ideal example of the emotional constitution of our world, of the judgmental character of the emotions with their ideological commitments. We freely and often judge the "rationality" of anger (its reasonability and warrant, its pettiness or its moral self-righteousness); and it is clear that anger is neither a "good" nor a "bad" emotion,† neither "positive" nor "negative," but depends, in any particular case, upon the circumstances and the individual, the nature of the "offense" and its background. It is for this reason that I have used anger so often as an example and, because it is also the favorite example of hydraulic theorists, behaviorists, therapists, and emotion-as-feeling Cartesian mentalists, it is an ideal test case for any emotional theory.

The key to anger is its judgment of *indictment* and *accusation*. Anger is a judgment of personal *offense*. It often has a moral edge, but need not (thus clouding the distinction between anger and indignation); it is usually outer-directed but may on occasion be turned inward toward one's Self. It is worth stressing the fact that anger is a great equalizer, judging one's antagonist as an equal.‡ To become angry with a child (as opposed to merely irritated) is to treat him (perhaps unfairly) as an adult. To be angry with a superior is to raise yourself to his level ("insubordination," an apt term; "uppity" also). With an inferior, one avoids anger and will more likely be scornful or disdainful, annoyed or irritated. The mythology of anger, more than any other emotion, is a judicial mythology of trial and judgment, crime and punishment. Its judgmental nature is thus the most explicit of all the emotions, with oneself as the court in which indictment and argument, verdict and sentence (but not necessarily the carrying out of the sentence), are all portrayed. Anger is usually direct and explicit in its projection of our personal values and expectations on the world. Anger, whether expressed or not, is our insistence upon our own ideals, even when that insistence is based far more on self-assertiveness or obstinacy than on any commitment to the ideals as such. (Thus we get angry at trivia, which alone does not concern us at all, in order to assert our right to assess and our need for legislative autonomy, much as a magistrate might levy contempt of court charges, not for the nature of a remark or a gesture itself but

† It is, however, listed as one of the "seven deadly sins" in Christian mythology.

‡ Cf. George Bach's *The Intimate Enemy*, which argues that anger is an apt means to intimacy as well as one of its necessary results.

rather only because it was *contempt* of court, a denial of his own authority.) Anger registers our displeasure that the world does not obey our expectations, and displays our desire to punish those who would not obey our demands, no matter how trivial and meaningless, or how indubitably moral and eloquently humane. (It is important, however, not to confuse anger with mere frustration or disappointment; anger, unlike frustration and disappointment, essentially includes a judicial indictment, an offense and condemnation.)*

(ANGER)

1. DIRECTION: Usually outer-directed, sometimes inner-directed or bipolar (depending on the relative stress of "the offense" *vs.* "*my* being offended).

2. SCOPE/FOCUS: As pettily narrow as a person's ability to perceive details ("He can get angry about *any*thing") or as global as the universe itself ("She is angry about *every*thing") but typically about everyday incidents and events. (Trivia are more usually a source of irritation than anger; global and moral offenses the objects of moral indignation, outrage, resentment, or disdain.)

3. OBJECT: *Always* requires a responsible agent as its object (even if it is anger at the weather, anger at a jammed door, or anger at the termites that are devouring one's house).

4. CRITERIA: Usually have a moral edge, but may be personal or interpersonal as well. (Cf. INDIGNATION.)

5. STATUS: *Equal.* (Cf. SCORN, RESENTMENT, CONTEMPT.)

6. EVALUATIONS: Always a negative evaluation, an "offense."

* Cf. Robert Gordon, "The Aboutness of Emotions," *American Philosophical Quarterly*, 1974; and many of Freud's references to anger as "frustration."

7. RESPONSIBILITY: Someone is *blameworthy.*

8. INTERSUBJECTIVITY: Always at least mildly defensive as a counterfactual reaction against the world not being what we judge that it ought to be. As an indictment, always entails some distrust.

9. DISTANCE: "At arm's length"; it may be a means of intimacy and a result of intimacy (see above), but it is never itself intimate. It may bring together people from an impersonal distance, and it may render two people equals, but it is too defensive, too distrusting, and too critical to allow for intimacy as such. At the same time it is never wholly impersonal.

10. MYTHOLOGY: Courtroom or Olympian mythology; oneself as legislator and judge; the other as defendant. Oneself as the defender of values; the other as offender.

11. DESIRE: To punish.

12. POWER: Variable, sometimes capable of direct and effective action, sometimes not. (In the latter case, anger may eventually turn to resentment.)

13. STRATEGY: To project one's values on the world and define the world in one's own terms. Whoever disagrees with those values or fails to act in accordance with them is justly condemned. Thus, anger always has a tinge of self-righteousness (appropriate to its moral edge) *except* in those cases in which the anger is directed at oneself. (See SHAME.)

ANGST (ANGUISH, ANXIETY)

The concept of *angst* is best known for its central role in the contemporary philosophy of existentialism, but it has never been far from the core of the Christian spirit. Its importance in philosophy gives us a clue—that *angst* is more mood than emotion, an all-encompassing attitude toward the world in general rather than a more limited and narrowly focused judgment of particular events or incidents. The concept encompasses a range of emotions and moods, however, which are often distinguished only implicitly—if at all—in the powerful philosophical treatises in which it appears (Augustine, Rousseau, Kierkegaard, Heidegger, and Sartre). Sometimes *angst* means anguish, sometimes anxiety, and sometimes dread. But these terms are not carefully distinguished either, and each of them is also used to cover a range of meanings. Sometimes they are used to refer to excruciating distress or suffering, sometimes to extreme fear, sometimes a special kind of fear—a fear of the unknown, an all-embracing fear of everything—or a fear of oneself, one's own desires, emotions, or identity. In existentialism —particularly in Kierkegaard, Heidegger, and Sartre—the object of this special fear is *"nothingness,"* lack of meaning or justification, but this term, too, has very different significance in these three authors. Moreover, the recent addition and prevalence of the concept of "anxiety" in Freud and psychoanalytic theory has added a further meaning, barely an emotion at all but rather that diffuse and extremely painful discomfort which is a symptom of a disturbing emotion rather than that emotion itself. (See Chapter 6, Section 4.)

There is no consistent usage, but the terminology, in any case, is not what interests us so much as the structural organization of a number of related judgments. I have eliminated from consideration that sense of *angst* (usually anguish) which simply refers to extreme distress and restrict our attention to emotions proper. What one finds is a range of emotions that are akin to fear; sometimes these terms refer only to extreme fear (see FEAR), but they are of interest primarily in their more dramatic existentialist usages—as fear of the unknown, fear of everything, and fear of oneself (or inner-directed fear). (The fear of nothingness requires special diagnosis, not as an emotion so much as a philosophical mistake, rendered prereflectively.) Somewhat arbitrarily, I have distinguished fear of the unknown (which would include, at least for Kierkegaard and Heidegger, fear of the nothingness) as *dread* (see DREAD), fear of everything as *anxiety* (a mood rather than an emotion), and fear of oneself as *anguish* (a usage that most agrees with Sartre's concept of *angoisse*, which may be fear of "nothingness," but always is a fear of *one's own* "nothingness").

(ANXIETY)

1. DIRECTION:	Outer-directed.
2. SCOPE/FOCUS:	Cosmic, as a mood; directed at our world as a whole and more or less indiscriminately toward everything and anything in it.
3. OBJECT:	Everything.
4. CRITERIA:	None necessary.
5. STATUS:	——
6. EVALUATIONS:	Everything is a threat.
7. RESPONSIBILITY:	——
8. INTERSUBJECTIVITY:	Extremely defensive; general and all-inclusive distrust.
9. DISTANCE:	As great as possible; intimacy out of the question.
10. MYTHOLOGY:	The most Baroque-like portrait of hell, with every turn a torture, every creature a devouring monster, every companion a torturer, every space a prison, every move a risk.
11. DESIRE:	To hide, disappear, make oneself secure.
12. POWER:	Absolute impotence.
13. STRATEGY:	A perverted form of self-aggrandizement, often akin to or part of paranoia; a way of focusing the attention of the universe exclusively on oneself. An excuse for unabashed selfishness and lack of consideration of others, demanding their sympathy but accepting no responsibility for what one does with it, or for returning it. Often compensation for guilt or anguish.

(ANGUISH)

1. DIRECTION:	Inner-directed.
2. SCOPE/FOCUS:	The focus may be very precise (for example, Sartre's example of the man walking along the edge of a precipice, his anguish being solely directed to his temptation to jump), but it is often extremely obscure, as in the many different illustrations of anguish provided for us by Freud and his colleagues (as "anxiety" in which the focus is "unconscious," its object unknown).
3. OBJECT:	Oneself, usually very basic fantasies and intentions which are potentially self-destructive or involve degrading oneself as a responsible agent. (Sartre: the object is "our freedom.") In extreme cases (for example, under the influence of a large dose of peyote or LSD) the basis of one's anxiety may be ascription of *super*human powers to oneself.
4. CRITERIA:	Open; one could be anxious about performing an immoral act, an act personally repulsive, or an embarrassing act.
5. STATUS:	———
6. EVALUATIONS:	Negative evaluations of one's own potentiality (as in outer-directed fear).
7. RESPONSIBILITY:	Ascription of responsibility to oneself (potential blame).
8. INTERSUBJECTIVITY:	(Distrust of oneself makes trust of others difficult.)
9. DISTANCE:	———
10. MYTHOLOGY:	Oneself as dangerous and possibly out of control. May be easily embellished with any of a variety of "possession by a devil" images, as if "something will take hold of me and make me do it." Or, more

to the side of existential libertarianism and the Scriptures, anguish may compose a Sartrian or Christian conception of "bad faith" or Original Sin, such that one is always responsible for *whatever* he does, and he knows and fears that he is capable of the most dastardly deeds imaginable. It is because of their heavy emphasis on anguish that Sartre and the traditional church can rightly be accused of a certain "gloominess" and "pessimism" in their conceptions of human nature.

11. DESIRE: To render oneself impotent, to protect oneself (and the world) from oneself.

12. POWER: Potent; that is the source of the fear.

13. STRATEGY: Self-aggrandizement, existential heroism with a diabolical twist. The ambitions of mass murderers and political assassins as well as megalomaniac German philosophers; "I am dangerous" (even to myself, or at least to myself).

CONTEMPT

Contempt is a judgment against another person of the most severe nature; it finds him worse than offensive, rather vile or repulsive. ("Beneath contempt" is an even more extreme version of contempt.) Like *scorn*, contempt constitutes the other as decidedly inferior, if not as some subhuman creature unworthy of human consideration. It is an attitude of extreme superiority on one's own part, which, as always, should make us suspect a certain defensiveness as well.

(CONTEMPT)

1. DIRECTION: Outer (there is an inner-directed analogue; never bipolar).

2. SCOPE/FOCUS: Open. One can be contemptuous of a cockroach or, like Sisyphus, of the gods themselves.

3. OBJECT: Usually, but not always, people (not particular details or aspects of them). Often with a judgment of subhumanity ("You dirty rat"; such a judgment is contemptuous to a person, perhaps not to a rat).

4. CRITERIA: Usually morally tinged (but double-edged with the suggestion that the person or creature in question is incapable of morality).

5. STATUS: The other is markedly inferior to oneself, even subhuman. (It has been suggested that scorn is a judgment of inferior human status whereas contempt is a judgment of subhuman status.)

6. EVALUATIONS: Severe condemnation of the person (or creature) over-all. Extreme dislike.

7. RESPONSIBILITY: It is often suggested, when the other is judged to be subhuman, that he is incapable of responsibility. On the other hand, the basis of a judgment of contempt may well be flagrant *ir*responsibility. In any case, it is a judgment that the other person is less than responsible.

8. INTERSUBJECTIVITY: Defensive in the same sense that one defends oneself from disease. (But cf.: "Familiarity breeds . . .")

9. DISTANCE: As far away as possible.

10. MYTHOLOGY: The other as a vile creature (and oneself, by contrast, as pure and noble). Typical metaphors: The other as a snake, a reptile, an insect, a worm, a spider, as slime or excrement, as degenerate or depraved.

11. DESIRE: To avoid, to not have to see or be reminded of the creature (at least ostensibly).

12. POWER:	Considerable. In impotence, contempt becomes horror. (A roach, for example, is contemptible only because it is so much smaller and harmless. A giant roach, reminiscent of a 1950s' American horror movie, would not be contemptible but horrible.)
13. STRATEGY:	To dramatize one's own standards, whether personal or moral. And to make oneself appear, by way of contrast, superior, powerful, and noble.

CONTENTMENT

Perhaps it would seem that contentment isn't exactly an emotion or a passion as such but rather the *satisfaction* of the emotion and other passions (particularly desires). It should be included, however, in order to stress a central point of our theory. The emotions are not disruptions of our lives, disturbing and traumatic, but durable structures which give meaning to our experience. But it would be absurd to pay exclusive attention to those emotions which constitute our world in terms of conflict and dissatisfaction and ignore moods and emotions of satisfaction. The judgment that one is satisfied is as much a judgment as the judgment that one is not. As an emotion, contentment is an affirmation of a state of affairs, an acceptance of oneself or some aspect of oneself. It is as if to say, "Now my world is as it ought to be" or "I am satisfied with myself." In the revolutionary sense, such emotions have no ideology (in the dubious sense that you might say that a reactionary politician has no ideology); there is no desire to change.

(CONTENTMENT)

1. DIRECTION:	Outer, inner, or (in relationships) bipolar.
2. SCOPE/FOCUS:	Open.
3. OBJECT:	Anything.
4. CRITERIA:	Open.

5. STATUS:	Open (but it is surely a reasonable empirical hypothesis that it is difficult [at least] to be content while judging oneself as an inferior; and the defensiveness that comes with superiority may lead to conservativism and *laissez faire* status quoism, but hardly contentment).
6. EVALUATIONS:	Positive ("Things are as they ought to be").
7. RESPONSIBILITY:	May include praise (as gratitude) or self-praise (as pride).
8. INTERSUBJECTIVITY:	Generally open and trusting.
9. DISTANCE:	Open; intimacy as an easy possibility.
10. MYTHOLOGY:	Ranging from the pointed satisfaction of "good fortune" or pride to the theological gratitude of "grace."
11. DESIRE:	None.
12. POWER:	Irrelevant.
13. STRATEGY:	To accept the world as it is in order to *make* it true that the world is as one thinks it ought to be, not by changing the world, but by changing what one thinks it ought to be. What could be easier? (It is thus that contentment *may* be a "cop-out" as well as a judgment of fulfillment.)

DEPRESSION

The general attitude toward depression is an illuminating example of the overly medical and antihuman Myth of the Passions. In at least two or three articles in various popular magazines and journals across the country, every week, there is an article with a title such as "How to Cope with Depression." It seems never to be worth suggesting that the depression is itself our means of coping, that it is not a matter of "getting over it" but rather a matter of accepting it and *using* it as our own. Depression is treated as a psychic influenza, debilitating and counterproductive, an invasion of a spiritual virus, a "malaise." We are told how to get rid of it, distract ourselves from it, or at least minimize its deleterious effects. "It will pass," we are assured. Don't take its self-depreciation seriously, and don't even consider its sometimes suicidal impulses. "Ignore it; keep busy; get out of the house." Or take a Librium, as you might take an aspirin for a cold.

But suppose depression is not always a medical "problem,"† but rather a window to the soul, a mood that is our most sophisticated and most radical means to shuffling the structures of our lives when they have become intolerable and unlivable. Most artists recognize the power of depression, the fact that, despite its initial debilitating effects, its aftermath is typically a burst of productivity and creativity. And nearly everyone knows not only that a depression tends to linger, but that we tend to keep hold of it, nourish it, avoiding a cheerful friend whose laughter might break the spell, seeking out the solitude of our own rooms where we can indulge in our depression and wallow in it, feeding it with morbid thoughts and self-criticism, formulating our Camusian doctrines of the absurdity and meaninglessness of it all without the objections of good friends, good fortune, or good times. In depression, we (literally) "press ourselves down," force on ourselves the burdens of universal doubt, the Cartesian method on a visceral level. Our depression is our way of wrenching ourselves from the established values of our world, the tasks in which we have been unquestioningly immersed, the opinions we have uncritically nursed, the relationships we have accepted without challenge and often without meaning. A depression is a self-imposed purge. It is the beginning of self-realization, unless it is simply ignored, or drugged away, or allows itself to give in to the demands for its own avoidance—the most extreme of which is suicide. (The least extreme is philosophy.) It is our most courageous attempt to open ourselves up to the most gnawing doubts about ourselves and our lives, that kind of openness that precedes the most clear-headed commitments and the least qualified acceptances of our selves and our lives. To treat depression as a transient illness is to keep our-

† I do not want to deny that depression can be "pathological"; but so can anger, jealousy, envy, grief, love, and even contentment. I only want to argue that it is in itself not pathological but even essential to normal life and "self-overcoming."

selves closed, to avoid "seeing," in Don Juan's peculiar sense, *through* the values and structures which we have uncritically accepted or imposed upon ourselves, which we now find tedious, unlivable, and self-degrading. To reject the depression is to affirm, by default, those same values and structures. The pain of depression can be the pain of self-realization; or it may be only the pain of continuing to accept, equally uncritically and equally unhappily, the very values which have spurred our doubts in the first place.

(DEPRESSION)

1. DIRECTION:	All directions (as a mood), but mainly inward, toward oneself.
2. SCOPE/FOCUS:	Cosmic, as a mood, but again, with the self as its center of focus.
3. OBJECT:	All objects, human and subhuman, but with reference to one's own attitudes and reactions to those objects (whether friends or tasks or trees or gods).
4. CRITERIA:	Primarily personal, but may include moral and interpersonal considerations.
5. STATUS:	A sense of inferiority, laced with defensive judgments of superiority. But depression is not primarily about status (although it may be a question of status —a reprimand or a sense of unwanted identity—that initiates the depression).
6. EVALUATIONS:	Negative all around—the "worthlessness" of everything.
7. RESPONSIBILITY:	Open; typically includes self-blame and guilt; may defensively display accusations of others, but not essential to the mood.
8. INTERSUBJECTIVITY:	Extremely defensive, but mainly against oneself and the insights coming to view. Curiously (that is, on other views of depression), depression often if not typically includes a certain trust of other

people; depression may be an ideal time for a patient to begin psychotherapy; it is our hypersensitivity to other people—rather than distrust of them—that leads us to avoid them when we are depressed. (Cf. ANXIETY and PARANOIA.)

9. DISTANCE: Ostensibly tries to keep as great a distance as possible, but in fact tries to hold everything and everyone "at arm's length," close but not *too* close, a protection against both influence and impersonal meaninglessness. The mood of depression is riddled with these ambivalences, a fact that is easy to understand when we compare it with its philosophical equivalent, Cartesian or methodological doubt, in which everything one believes is doubted but yet still believed. In depression, one's values and ideals, friends and ambitions, are doubted yet held on to, pushed to a distance for perspective and pulled closer lest they recede beyond reach, drawn close for scrutiny but repelled, lest they become too intimate and smother the spirit of ruthless self-inquiry.

10. MYTHOLOGY: "Camus's Myth" (Chapter 1, Section 4); the universe as indifferent and absurd; our tasks as Sisyphusian meaningless chores, our values as vanities, and our hopes as illusions. Ecclesiastes: "All is vanity."

11. DESIRE: Affirmation, but solid affirmation, as opposed to the flimsy commitments and ideologies that one now sees himself as accepting. The search for something absolute and unshakable, an unblemished lover, a heroic task, the ultimate quest. Or at least, something meaningful, absorbing, a good movie (or even a bad movie).

12. POWER: Confused, since, on the one hand, one
                    feels he merely has to decide on this or
                    that in order to accept it, but at the same
                    time, he finds himself "unable" (unwill-
                    ing) to bring himself to any such com-
                    mitment.

13. STRATEGY: To shake oneself loose from the archaic
                    and outmoded sludge of encrusted tasks
                    and values which one now finds worth-
                    less. The method is Cartesian; doubt
                    everything until you find at least one
                    value or task that remains unchallenge-
                    able. (One usually doesn't, since values,
                    like tasks, are commitments and "proj-
                    ects" [in Sartre's terms], nothing that
                    one merely "finds.")

DESPAIR‡

Despair can hold the most intense sort of pleasure when one is
strongly conscious of the hopelessness of our position.

                                                          Dostoevski

Despair has certain obvious resemblances to depression, anguish, anxiety, and dread (*angst* is sometimes translated as "despair" as well). It, too, involves a painful and sometimes excruciating withdrawal from the world, a sense of imminent and
overpowering danger. Despair is a judgment of unhappy resignation, a conclusion of futility, an admission of defeat. One gives up
hope and expectations, often never realizing that those hopes and
expectations themselves are the products of judgments that might
well be re-examined. Men who do not expect salvation do not despair at the loss of it. People who are never taught to hope for political power never despair at the lack of it. Those who were not

‡ The alphabetical sequence itself is getting a bit depressing.
Anger, anguish, anxiety, contempt, depression, despair, and dread to
come with only contentment to spare us. A general point is worth
noting. We have far more emotions that indicate how much is
wrong with our Selves and our world than there are emotions indicat-
ing what is right.

raised on the Victorian fantasies of undying and uninterrupted Romantic love will never be in despair at its implausibility. If contentment is an attitude that accepts whatever it is given, despair is an attitude that always expects more than it can possibly receive. As such, it, too, is a convenient excuse for inaction and stagnation, an emotional steppingstone to the absurdities of Camus's "Absurd," the myth of an unjust and "indifferent universe," not as a method (as in depression), but as a conclusion.

(DESPAIR)

1. DIRECTION:	Outer-directed, but with reference to one's own action.
2. SCOPE/FOCUS:	Usually global and of large scope. Possibly concerned with some specific hope or expectation, but only if it is absolutely central if not definitive of one's life as a whole.
3. OBJECT:	Open.
4. CRITERIA:	———
5. STATUS:	———
6. EVALUATIONS:	Like fear, despair is a negative evaluation of the future, but in this case, as if it were a foregone conclusion. (Fear has it only as a possibility.)
7. RESPONSIBILITY:	One's own innocence. (One denies himself the responsibility of failure—even if it is his own act. After all, the very essence of despair is the alleged fact that success is hopeless anyway.)
8. INTERSUBJECTIVITY:	Despair is a defense (against success, against responsibility) but not particularly defensive. (It has little to do with other people.)
9. DISTANCE:	Despair loves company.

10. MYTHOLOGY:	"Ah, cruel fortunes . . ."
11. DESIRE:	Ostensibly, to get what one hopes for; in fact, not to have to do anything in order to get it, since "it's impossible anyway."
12. POWER:	Utter impotence.
13. STRATEGY:	To close off access and motivation to action and deny responsibility for failure. To give up all hope and expectations in order to see oneself as a victim of fate, to revel in self-indulgence of "feeling sorry for yourself," and to attract the sympathy of others.

DESPISE (no noun form as such): see CONTEMPT

DREAD

"Dread" is also a favorite translation for *angst*, and consequently another staple in the vocabulary of more gloom-minded philosophers. As I have delineated it here (and again, it is the structure of the emotion rather than the ordinary use of the term that interests us), dread is an intense fear of the *unknown*. Accordingly, it ought to be suspected to be anguish (fear of oneself) turned outward. On occasion what seems to be dread may in fact be anxiety (namely, fear of everything, hiding its all-encompassing cowardice under the guise of a single fear of the unknown). There is something curious about a "fear of the unknown," not in those particular cases in which it is some particular unknown (for example, the as-yet unknown murderer of thirteen women in Boston; or the unknown creature hiding in the bushes), but that general unknown so painfully dreaded by Kierkegaard and so obscurely by Heidegger. One begins to suspect that dread is often an emotion of intrinsic self-deception, a refusal to recognize anguish and lack of resolution in oneself by projecting it outward into some void in the world.

(DREAD)

1. DIRECTION:	Emphatically outer.

2. SCOPE/FOCUS: The scope is variable but usually grand if not cosmic. The focus is emphatically unclear (how else could the unknown be assured of remaining unknown?).

3. OBJECT: Unknown, "something-or-other."

4. CRITERIA: ———

5. STATUS: The unknown is often treated as superior, if only because it is unknown.

6. EVALUATIONS: Variable. (God may be dreaded yet still praised and worshiped; a creature in a hole is dreaded and repulsive.)

7. RESPONSIBILITY: None.

8. INTERSUBJECTIVITY: Extremely defensive, but also in desperate need of allies.

9. DISTANCE: Confusion; fear dictates as great a distance as possible; curiosity demands as close a look as possible. Where the "unknown" in question is explicitly linked with God, a dreadful intimacy is commanded as well (the bulk of Kierkegaard's later writings).

10. MYTHOLOGY: "The thing out there in the darkness; and what can I do?"

11. DESIRE: To either get clear or get out.

12. POWER: Impotence.

13. STRATEGY: Mock heroism against the forces of the unknown; an apt excuse for paralyzing curiosity. Unable to face danger by refusing to identify it; wholly occupying oneself in engagement at a distance by trying to understand it. A favorite strategy for scholars: "We know so little; if only we could understand; but of course we can't *do* anything until we do understand."

DUTY

The sense of duty is rarely considered to be an emotion, another gift of the Myth of the Passions. Duty is "rational," not "passionate," the "dictate of practical reason," in Kant's terms, and *opposed* to the whims of inclination. Moreover, the sense of duty is supposed to be a stable law of the intellect, a principle not a passion. But in both of these arguments, one sees the price of our infamous Myth, for the emotions as constitutive judgments may be both rational and durable, principles as well as passions. The sense of duty may often be that "quiet voice of conscience" that beckons to us when we are tempted to cheat or steal,* but on occasion it has that rousing, fervent zeal that one expects of the most violent passions.

(DUTY)

1. DIRECTION:	Inner-directed (although the duties themselves will be outer-directed).	
2. SCOPE/FOCUS:	Variable.	
3. OBJECT:	One's own actions.	
4. CRITERIA:	Moral, "objective," impersonal, and unquestionable.	
5. STATUS:	——— (But may be used as an appeal for superiority.)	
6. EVALUATIONS:	"Right" and "wrong," ascribed to possible courses of action.	
7. RESPONSIBILITY:	One holds oneself responsible for his own action. (As Kant says, freedom and responsibility are the presuppositions of any morality.) One need not hold himself responsible for the principles themselves. (Many persons would attribute	

* The image of conscience as "another voice" and coming from "the outside" is but another example of our continuing efforts to avoid responsibility for our own projections. (This argument is among the most powerful—and the clearest—in Heidegger's *Being and Time*.)

them to God or civil law; Kant would attribute the principles to reason but their affirmation to oneself; Sartre would argue that both the principles and their affirmation are solely one's own choice and responsibility.)

8. INTERSUBJECTIVITY: Duty may command certain forms of intersubjectivity, but it is not part of the emotion itself.

9. DISTANCE: The sense of duty may well be marked in persons of considerable rigidity and incapacity for intimacy and sensitivity, but this is neither part nor consequence of the sense of duty. (They may, however, develop from a common source.)

10. MYTHOLOGY: "And God said unto Moses, thou shalt . . ."

11. DESIRE: To obey.

12. POWER: Ability to obey is a presupposition ("'ought' implies 'can'").

13. STRATEGY: To be *right*. The emotion can be used, of course, in all sorts of ways; right leads to self-righteousness, the authority of one's "objective" moral code allows him to look at those who don't agree as inferiors or moral degenerates. And, as Nietzsche argues in brilliant detail and allegory, certain moralities can be used as weapons against obviously superior forces (arguing meekness to the powerful, charity to the rich). A powerful (if sometimes intolerant) strategy for personal dignity and self-esteem.

ECSTASY: see JOY

EMBARRASSMENT

> He scratched his ear, the infallible resource,
> To which embarrassed people have recourse.
>
> Byron, *Don Juan*

Embarrassment is one of those emotions that give rise to the idea that emotions are transient intrusions into our normal lives. Embarrassment is usually a quickly passing sense of awkwardness. Only rarely do we find ourselves in a situation that is continuously embarrassing, and it is surely a pathological symptom of something or other if a person continues to feel embarrassed about an incident long past. The logic of embarrassment, however, makes the reason for this evident.

(EMBARRASSMENT)

1. DIRECTION: Inner-directed (one is embarrassed for someone else only insofar as he or she identifies with him or her).

2. SCOPE/FOCUS: Particular situations and incidents, usually trivial.

3. OBJECT: One's own actions and circumstances.

4. CRITERIA: Interpersonal; one is embarrassed by the opinions of others or what he takes to be the opinions of others, whether or not they coincide with his own sense of values. (In a cutthroat bar I may be embarrassed to find that I'm the only one in the conversation who has never mugged anybody. It is important that nothing follows from that. I feel out of place, but surely not in the least compelled to go out and change my status.)

5. STATUS: Markedly inferior, but just for the moment and in this particular incident or detail. (I may be embarrassed by a huge

rip in my pants, but I do not consequently judge myself an inferior person, only a person in disadvantageous circumstances.)

6. EVALUATIONS: Negative, of this particular incident or detail.

7. RESPONSIBILITY: I judge myself innocent. (This is what distinguishes embarrassment from shame; had I arrived at the gathering having knowingly worn torn pants, I would be ashamed, not embarrassed, and somewhat concerned about my motives. In the incident that embarrasses me, I had no motives.)

8. INTERSUBJECTIVITY: Defensive.

9. DISTANCE: Embarrassment certainly puts us at arm's length, but not beyond reach of others. Except when the embarrassment is mutual, intimacy is temporarily out of the question.

10. MYTHOLOGY: The unsuspecting victim of a prank, oneself as unwitting clown, entertaining others at one's own expense.

11. DESIRE: To hide.

12. POWER: Sense of helplessness, as if any subsequent action will be a further embarrassment and draw more attention to one's plight.

13. STRATEGY: To shun blame for one's awkward situation, and, in more extreme cases, to entertain others and be the center of attention, even at the expense of dignity (but to the benefit of self-esteem, which is tentatively placed in the others).

ENVY

The chief features of our mores as evinced in our practical existence are ill-will and envy.

Goethe

As one of the "seven deadly sins" (pride, covetousness, lust, anger, gluttony, envy, and sloth), *envy* has been officially recognized as one of the more common if also despicable structures of our world. Unlike anger, envy seems to clearly deserve its place among the unenviable seven, sharing many of their less agreeable aspects: a bit of false pride, a sometimes lustful covetousness, a propensity for gluttony which is unrealized only because of sloth— or fear—of action. Envy is an essentially vicious emotion, bitter and vindictive. Yet it is usually a harmless passion, except to oneself, for again, unlike anger, it is an emotion of marked impotence and inferiority. Envy peers from a distance at what it wants, knowing full well that it does not deserve it, that it cannot obtain it, and its expression is rarely more effective than a "green-eyed" glowering look and fantasies of theft or destruction unfulfilled and untried. Envy is among the very strongest competitive emotions, thus virtually shutting out all possibility of intimacy (except in alliance with fellow losers). It is worth noting that it lacks all moral support (unlike anger or jealousy) and may be wholly willing to admit that the other person *deserves* what he has while oneself does not. Coupled with the fact that the object of envy is virtually always a matter of importance to subjective self-esteem, one may conclude that the envious man is a pathetic man indeed. Why, then, is envy a "sin," rather than pathos? Because it is not merely misfortune, not merely impotence, but self-imposed, self-indulgent, undeserving greed. Once again, Christian psychology is one of the few sources to have anticipated the central doctrine of this thesis.

(ENVY)

1. DIRECTION: Like all emotions, it is implicitly bipolar, here involving a more-or-less direct comparison and competitive confrontation.

But in its overt structure, envy is emphatically an *outer*-directed emotion, concerned wholly with the other and his competitive gain, ignoring conscientiously one's own unworthiness of the object of his greedy desire.

2. SCOPE/FOCUS:

Usually the broader aspects of a person, his skills or good looks, his wife or her husband, his or her life in general. It may focus on some particular detail or incident (like jealousy), but only as the focal point of a larger field of envy. It would make no sense to envy the universe, however (as one might be angry at the universe); so envy has no related mood. (It often, however, shares one with *resentment*.)

3. OBJECT:

"Object" here may be ambiguous. There is the object of desire—a job or a spouse, a life style or a skill—and there is the object of the emotion (the other person). The object of desire may be anything whatever: a material object (money), a distinctly human attribute (for example, a strong sense of duty or an utter lack of guilt), a talent (playing the violin), or a life style (traveling to Europe every month with a different Hollywood star). In a slightly degenerate sense, one can envy nonpersons—birds for their flight, insects for their orderliness, stones for their permanence—since no agency need be ascribed. (Cf. JEALOUSY.) But the object is usually a *person*.

4. CRITERIA:

Strictly personal. (This is one of its main differences from resentment.) We may be envious of illegitimate power or illicitly acquired wealth, deceptively seduced maidens, and ill-gotten goods and unearned honors of all kinds.

5. STATUS: Markedly inferior.

6. EVALUATIONS: Highly positive value placed on the
                            envied object. (No particular evaluation
                            of the envied person; he may be despised
                            or admired as well as envied. The evalua-
                            tion of envy [again unlike resentment]
                            stops short of the whole person.)

7. RESPONSIBILITY: In envy we should talk more of *rights*
                            than responsibilities. In envy the other
                            person is recognized as having a right to
                            the envied object, whether or not he had
                            any responsibility in obtaining it. One
                            does not see oneself as having any such
                            right, only an intense desire, more than
                            likely compounded with a well-rational-
                            ized wish for the revolutionary overthrow
                            of the very system of rights which de-
                            prives him. (Consider the beggar who
                            envies a rich donor; he neither denies the
                            rich man's right to his money (in fact
                            he may admire the work it took to ac-
                            quire it) nor maintains any right of his
                            own. But he would welcome the insurrec-
                            tion that would put that money up for
                            grabs—or, out of spite (envy's more
                            violent sibling), he would welcome the
                            catastrophe that would bring the rich
                            man to poverty.

8. INTERSUBJECTIVITY: Extremely defensive.

9. DISTANCE: Impersonal.

10. MYTHOLOGY: Greedy anarchy; "I know that the present
                            institutions support this state of affairs,
                            but *I want that!*—even if I am unwilling
                            and unable to do anything to get it."
                            ("Start the revolution without me. [I'll
                            loot afterward.]")

11. DESIRE: Greed and covetousness; to steal.

12. POWER: Impotence.

13. STRATEGY: Luxuriously subjective self-indulgence, independent of any sense of ambition or achievement. A defense against all forms of superiority. Typically masked with resentment. ("All that money couldn't possibly let a man enjoy life.") The relationship between envy and resentment is symbiotic; envy seeks to rob the superior man of his virtues and possessions, whereas resentment provides the ideological justification for robbing him. ("If I had all that money, I surely wouldn't waste it on such frivolity. . . .")

EUPHORIA (the mood corresponding to joy): see JOY

FAITH (see also WORSHIP)

Faith has been so often construed as a narrowly epistemic category (a form of belief without the usual requisites for justification) that it has been ignored as an emotion. When it has been treated as an emotion, however (for example, by St. Augustine and Pascal, by Kierkegaard and several contemporary theologians), it has usually been *opposed* to reason and knowledge. Faith, like any emotion, is a judgment, but not a purely epistemic or "cognitive" judgment. The emotion of faith is neither an ineffable "feeling" nor a peculiar form of knowledge.

The analysis of faith inevitably turns to a particular object of faith—namely, God. But it should be pointed out that Faith is not the only variety of faith, that one can place his faith in other people, in the fortunes of the weather or the Massachusetts state lottery, or in himself. In all its varieties, faith is a judgment of power and beneficence. It is closely related to worship, except that worship does not share faith's optimism, and faith, unlike worship, *expects* something in return. Both emotions, needless to say, maintain a certain diminutive stature and passiveness of the Self (except in "faith in oneself"), a self-demeaning posture that may be powerfully compensated by grandiose expectations (the Sun standing still till the battle is over, the walls of a city tumbling down, eternal bliss and life after death).

(FAITH)

1. DIRECTION:	Outer-directed (except "faith in one-self").
2. SCOPE/FOCUS:	Variable, but often cosmic.
3. OBJECT:	Always an agent, either human or super-human, possibly a natural force, appropriately personified for the occasion ("Lady Luck," for example).
4. CRITERIA:	Personal or moral (depending on the object).
5. STATUS:	Inferiority (but without competition).
6. EVALUATIONS:	Extremely positive; great expectations.
7. RESPONSIBILITY:	None for oneself ("innocence" is the usual catchword of faith); responsibility lies wholly with the other.
8. INTERSUBJECTIVITY:	Absolute trust.
9. DISTANCE:	Impersonality, due to the unavailability of the object (but not always; Kierkegaard, for example, equated faith with a dreadful intimacy. And faith in oneself or one's lover or friend may be complicated in this regard, so much so that we may prefer to call such instances of faith "confidence"—a milder and far more autonomous emotion).
10. MYTHOLOGY:	The benign Godhead and the "chosen people."
11. DESIRE:	To be given . . . anything.
12. POWER:	None necessary.
13. STRATEGY:	Compensating for one's own lack of power by teaming up with powerful benign forces. Allows one to acknowledge virtually absolute impotence in himself but yet feel that he is, by proxy, omnip-

otent. This is a very powerful defensive strategy, in the sense that it is capable, as few emotions are, of giving oneself an enormously heightened sense of personal dignity and self-esteem in the face of every objective weakness, failing, flaw, lack of looks, skill, power, money, etc. . . .

FEAR

Fear is one of the least complicated emotions, so much so that it might almost be treated as a negative desire. There is no doubt that most "higher" animals as well as children (and possibly plants, if one accepts certain recent theories) can feel fear. Fear can take any object whatsoever—other persons, the sky's falling, the apocalypse, going bald, walking on cracks in the sidewalk, cats, death, higher telephone rates, and another garbage strike. Fear is a family term covering all shades of that sense of impending danger and comparative helplessness: fright, horror, terror, and panic; apprehension, concern, misgivings, "nervousness," distrust, and awe. (The more sophisticated versions of fear, fear of the unknown [see DREAD], fear of oneself [see ANGUISH], and fear of everything [see ANXIETY], deserve special treatment.)

(FEAR)

1. DIRECTION:	Outer-directed (except for anguish).
2. SCOPE/FOCUS:	Open.
3. OBJECT:	Anything.
4. CRITERIA:	Any (fear of spiders, fear of failure or moral failings, fear of embarrassment).
5. STATUS:	Open (but always with a tinge of at least temporary inferiority). One can be afraid of the resentful sting of an inferior, betrayal by an intimate friend or lover, berating or punishment by a superior.
6. EVALUATIONS:	Strongly negative anticipation of an impending event, state of affairs, etc.

7. RESPONSIBILITY:	Open (it may be fear of retaliation, etc.).
8. INTERSUBJECTIVITY:	Extremely defensive.
9. DISTANCE:	As far as possible.
10. MYTHOLOGY:	Impending catastrophe (not in itself a very interesting mythology, but often embellished with monsters and paranoid fantasies of considerable creativity).
11. DESIRE:	To get away, to avoid or escape.
12. POWER:	A sense of helplessness; power to run, perhaps, but not confident of overcoming.
13. STRATEGY:	Self-protection (perhaps physical survival, but possibly also protection of a self-image, an ambition or career, or protection of a person, situation, or object close to oneself).

FRIENDSHIP

Without friends, no one would choose to live.

Aristotle

As a relationship between two or more people, friendship isn't an emotion. But there is also a "feeling of friendship," which may or may not be fulfilled in actual companionship, and this is an emotion in exactly the same sense in which love or hatred are emotions. (See Chapter 4, Section 7.)

(FRIENDSHIP)

1. DIRECTION:	Bipolar.
2. SCOPE/FOCUS:	A particular person or several persons.
3. OBJECT:	Strictly human.
4. CRITERIA:	Open.
5. STATUS:	Equality.

6. EVALUATIONS: *Like* the other person(s) (as a whole. May either like or dislike particular aspects or details about him/her/them).

7. RESPONSIBILITY: Sense of responsibility *to* the other and *for* the friendship, with expectations (or hopes) of reciprocity.

8. INTERSUBJECTIVITY: Trust—as a matter of principle.

9. DISTANCE: Intimacy.

10. MYTHOLOGY: Castor and Pollux, "brothers" and "sisters."

11. DESIRE: Mutual support, encouragement, etc., enjoyment, and happiness.

12. POWER: A minimal sense of power is required; friendship (as opposed to respect or adoration) can never be merely passive.

13. STRATEGY: Self-expansion, mutual reinforcement, thus literally projecting one's own values and ideas to another and making his values and ideas one's own. Strength in numbers and mutual protection. Overcoming competition and defensiveness ("If you can't lick 'em, join 'em"). Providing an outlet for otherwise inexpressible emotions, thus dealing with them, being forced to reflect on them by an "outside" yet supportive force. (Not all friendships serve to get rid of envy, resentment, impotent anger, and jealousy, of course; just as many serve to mutually reinforce them. But even this reinforcement is an obvious step in the direction of a sense of joint strength and effective expressibility.)

FRUSTRATION

Frustration, like contentment, could be argued not to be an emotion or a passion as such but rather the result of the *lack* of satisfaction of emotions and other passions (primarily desires). But the judgment that one is not satisfied is as much a judgment as the judgment that one ought to be. Frustration as an emotion is a rejection of a state of affairs as personally unacceptable, with a tinge of hopelessness (like despair) but with dogged if also bullish determination. In expressing frustration, we often destroy what we desire, making an enemy where we sought a friend or lover, wrecking an object we sought to possess, ruining a career we wanted to achieve.

Whether we ought to call such behavior "self-defeating," however, depends upon our estimate of the likelihood of success. And it is the very nature of frustration, like so many other vengeful passions (particularly spite and envy), that it would rather destroy what it cannot possess than to simply give it up in despair. But frustration (like spite and unlike envy) has the power to destroy.

(FRUSTRATION)

1. DIRECTION:	Outer-directed (but with reference to one's own desires).
2. SCOPE/FOCUS:	Open.
3. OBJECT:	Any endeavor or hope of one's own.
4. CRITERIA:	Usually personal, possibly moral or interpersonal.
5. STATUS:	Open.
6. EVALUATIONS:	Object is positively desired; one's chances of getting it increasingly negative; the object's destruction is preferable to its continued survival without my possession of it.
7. RESPONSIBILITY:	One's own (but without blame or praise).
8. INTERSUBJECTIVITY:	(No other people need be involved; but one may be defensive about his failure.)
9. DISTANCE:	———

10. MYTHOLOGY:	Moses destroying the tablets: Alexander slicing through the Gordian knot.
11. DESIRE:	If not to obtain, then to destroy.
12. POWER:	Power to destroy, not to possess.
13. STRATEGY:	Saving face; "If I can't have it, nobody will." A desperate display of power in the face of failure. (See SPITE.)

GRATITUDE

Gratitude is an estimate of gain coupled with the judgment that someone else is responsible for that gain.

(GRATITUDE)

1. DIRECTION:	Outer-directed to bipolar, depending on the relative attention devoted to the giver vs. the given.
2. SCOPE/FOCUS:	Open.
3. OBJECT:	Must be a voluntary agent (human or superhuman), though the gift itself might be anything whatever. (There is a degenerate form of gratitude, usually ironic, in which gratitude is expressed to an unwilling giver—for example, a robber thanking his victim, a beef eater thanking the cow.)
4. CRITERIA:	Open.
5. STATUS:	Open. One can be grateful to an inferior (a slave or a servant) as well as a superior (an employer or God).
6. EVALUATIONS:	Positive regarding the gift itself (more or less; one does get useless and even tasteless gifts); positive without qualification (so far as the gratitude is concerned) regarding the act of giving. Open regarding the giver (one receives gifts from enemies and contemptible acquaintances as well as from friends).

7. RESPONSIBILITY:	None on one's own part. Praise for the giver.
8. INTERSUBJECTIVITY:	Open ("What does he want?"; or the gift as amenity).
9. DISTANCE:	Open.
10. MYTHOLOGY:	Being attended to, receiving (like royalty receiving tribute, "gifts of the Magi").
11. DESIRE:	To thank.
12. POWER:	Usually adequate for that minimal desire.
13. STRATEGY:	Little necessary. The judgment alone places one in the dignified position of passively receiving. All that need be required in return is a polite "thank you." One of those emotions that are intrinsically self-esteeming without much strategy at all. (But consider: A "gift" might also be considered rather as a bribe or a seduction, as an offense to one's integrity or as lack of respect for one's ability [as if he could not have gotten it on his own]. Thus, it is still one's judgment of gratitude, not the objective act of giving or the gift itself, that is self-esteeming.)

GRIEF: see SADNESS

GUILT

I declare war on the concepts of guilt and sin.

Nietzsche

More has been written about guilt than about any other emotion (even love). It forms the core of Judaeo-Christian psychology as well as theology; it is the cornerstone of every criminal judicial system and the shady side of every moral theory of duty and obligation; and it is the key to a great number of psychopathological syndromes. Freud and most therapists since have given the understanding of guilt high priority in their psychological researches. Accordingly, I cannot possibly pretend to do this emotion justice in this brief summary, only a basic structural analysis.

It is important to distinguish the subjective sense (the emotion) of guilt from its several objective counterparts. It is clear, for example, that a person may be rightly found guilty of a crime under the law without *feeling* guilty. In a religious context, a person may judge himself to be guilty before God without in fact *feeling* the least bit guilty. And even apart from such legal or religious institutions, a man may *be* guilty (that is responsible and blameworthy) of an act (of omission as well as commission) without *feeling* guilty. It is this "feeling" of guilt alone that is of interest here, not the sometimes morbid pathological manifestations investigated by Freud but those more normal but still overwhelming experiences that are familiar to virtually all of us.

In its most common manifestations, guilt is self-reproach for some misdeed, differing from shame, if at all, only in its intensity and scope. What distinguishes guilt, however, is its ability to encompass the sense of worth of the whole person; in guilt, one does not reproach himself only for this particular transgression but rather reproaches himself *in general*, as if his very existence is an offense as well as any particular action. It includes a sense of inadequacy and despair that is rarely to be found in shame. Moreover, guilt does not *require* any particular offense; as in the doctrine of Original Sin. One's offense need be only his or her own existence (perhaps supported by genetic attributions of guilt—a colonial heritage, oppressor ancestors, or descent through a species that traditionally sinned [symbolically or in fact]). In guilt a man is his own judge, typically a more ruthless and less reasonable judge than any other he could find. He may blame himself for nothing, reproach himself totally. Even where there is some "objective" offense as well and some external judge (whether God or the criminal courts), it is not the external judgment that constitutes the guilt. When one is "guilty before . . . (God, the court)," this indicates only the criteria which a person adopts in his guilt, not its direction or its source. A man is guilty only "before" himself.

(GUILT)

1. DIRECTION: Inner-directed.

2. SCOPE/FOCUS:	Initially, perhaps, a particular incident, but ultimately the whole of one's being.
3. OBJECT:	One's Self as agent, possibly focused to some extent on a particular misdeed or transgression.
4. CRITERIA:	Moral, supplemented with an appeal to external authority, religious doctrine, or the laws of the land. But always an appeal to "objective" moral law in some sense—for example, the Kantian sense in which the moral law is a dictate of reason, the sociological sense in which a moral law is a "law of human decency." Even where "guilt" is used to refer to minor offenses (for example, "feeling guilty for not returning your call"), the implication is that the broken law is of fundamental importance and nonnegotiable authority. (Many such usages, of course, are simply dramatizations of trivial transgressions, by way of apology.)
5. STATUS:	Inferior to everyone (or possibly, everyone [including oneself] is inferior; cf. the doctrine of Original Sin).
6. EVALUATIONS:	Extreme self-dislike and reproach, possibly but not necessarily coupled with the condemnation of some particular act.
7. RESPONSIBILITY:	Extreme self-reproach and blame.
8. INTERSUBJECTIVITY:	Extremely defensive.
9. DISTANCE:	Incommunicative (Except for Confession).
10. MYTHOLOGY:	The doctrine of Original Sin is exemplary. The authority providing the criteria is absolute and unquestionable; the nature of the particular offense trivial; the scope of the indictment encompassing the person as a whole; the weight of the accusation and the demand for

punishment is transferred to the person himself, so that the accusation becomes self-accusation and the punishment self-inflicted punishment. It is the mythology of being a ridiculously inadequate and offensive creature. (Cf. Kierkegaard's *Sickness unto Death.*)

11. DESIRE: To punish oneself, as terribly as possible, short of self-destruction (which would eliminate the possibility for further punishment). To confess and humble oneself, at least before God if not before men. Redemption or escape (from oneself).

12. POWER: Utter impotence to rehabilitate or justify oneself; power only to condemn and punish oneself. (A power, however, that can be turned outward in resentment to accuse and punish others as well.)

13. STRATEGY: Because guilt is ostensibly so totally self-demeaning, it is not at first obvious that it could possibly be a strategy for self-esteem. The Christian church, however, knew better, and saw in guilt a powerful force that could easily be turned to resentment and indignation, a mythology of righteousness in crusades against the pretentions of innocence and "paganism." It is from Freud, however, that one best learns the subtle intrigues of the strategy of guilt. I can only summarize these strategies here, but sufficiently so that, before one guilt is dismissed as "unnecessary" and "self-destructive," its subversive and deceitful strategy must first be recognized.†
The most obvious advantage of guilt is its extreme self-indulgence; it may not

† See, for example, Walter Kaufmann's *Beyond Guilt and Justice* (New York: Wiley, 1973).

be a happy self-indulgence, but happiness is not the goal of the emotions. It is
maximization of self-esteem. And to
prove one's own existence and revel in it,
self-inflicted pain may be the most
effective means. We pinch ourselves to
prove that we are alive; insufferably anonymous persons confess to and occasionally commit horrid crimes, only to prove
their own existence—at whatever cost. In
guilt, one's own existence is the main if
not the sole fact in their surreality. Guilt
allows a person to be utterly selfish,
oblivious to the suffering around him and
the concerns of other people. (After all,
is he not suffering more than any of
them?)

Guilt is also a powerful instrument of
self-defense. Someone criticizes us for a
small moral mishap; we are unmoved. In
guilt we have already so roundly and
thoroughly condemned ourselves that no
particular criticism can possibly strike us
seriously. Having accused and punished
ourselves in advance, we are freed from
the stings of particular guilt. The thoroughly guilty man has an advantage over
all of us; he cannot be found more guilty
of anything, since he has already found
himself guilty of everything. This may
sound like an absurdity—causing oneself
extreme pain in order not to feel any
number of little pains of lesser guilts and
shames, but it has its own logic. A man
more easily adapts to what he inflicts
upon himself; as his own judgment, he
is already committed to it and willing to
live with it. And, in terms of personal
dignity, he always knows, with a tinge of
absurdity, the vacuousness of the charges
—and the painlessness of the pain—he
has levied against himself. He can be sure

of his own judgments; he may not be so sure of the judgments of others.

In *The Fall* Camus's Clamence advises: "Judge that ye not be judged." His self-imposed and criterionless guilt is a paradigm of guilt's strategy; having failed to esteem himself with his sense of worldly superiority, he "falls"—or rather throws himself into the gutter—confessing his guilt to all who will listen. But then we know—and he tells us—that he has not given up his quest for dignity and self-esteem, but has only inverted its strategy. Starting with the axiom that no man is innocent, he who confesses first and most vigorously turns out to be the *least* guilty, consequently the most superior. Here is the genius of the Christian church—and much of psychoanalysis, too. Guilt turns out to be the very opposite of what it seems—a self-indulgent, self-protective, ultimately amoral, and extremely powerful strategy of superiority. Having judged and punished oneself, how easy it is to feel self-righteously superior to all those who have not (particularly those who have the audacity to accuse you of some trivial earthly transgression, as if they were themselves without sin).

HATE

What is so hateful about hate? Of course, it is a dangerous emotion—particularly to its object. It may indulge in the most outrageous cruelties in order to satisfy itself; it is an insatiable passion that poisons the personality and makes us incapable of love or intimacy. Or is it? As the antithesis of love, hatred has gotten the worst press of all the emotions. In the Manicheanism of humanistic psychology, hatred has been cast as the villain of the passions, the scourge of love, the monster to be conquered through the gentility of loving intimacy. But as in love, what passes for hatred is often some very different emotion, usually resentment. Resentment is, by its very nature, insatiable and vicious; hatred need not be. Like anger, hatred has long been the victim of a one-dimensional ethic of suppression, as if every instance of the emotion was proof of a weakness of the personality, a certain malice in the spirit, an unnecessary hostility that ought to be forgiven in the name of love. But to have *ideals* in our world is to open up the possibility of *nemeses* as well. It is not as if we need enemies (as we need friends and lovers), but to have any ideology requires the *possibility* of enemies. There is no love without the possibility of hate. There is no good without the possibility of evil.

Is there evil in our world or not? (Cf. Sartre, discussing his encounter with a New York businessman immediately after the war: "There was nothing more to talk about. I believed that there is evil in the world and he did not.") My point is not to encourage hatred; we would all be better off if there were no need for it. But hatred is not always unjustifiable; there is "healthy hatred" as well as that malice (usually resentment as well) that poisons and emerges as venom. Unlike resentment, indignation, and contempt, and like anger, hatred is an emotion that treats the other on an equal footing, neither degrading him as "subhuman" (as in contempt) nor treating him with the lack of respect due to a moral inferior (as in indignation) nor humbling oneself before (or away from) him with the self-righteous impotence of resentment. There may even be a trust and intimacy in hatred that is to be found in few of the outwardly hostile emotions; it is for this reason that hatred is so akin to love, so easily interchangeable with it, and so inevitably a part of it. As in a Nabokov novel or in a (much milder) Hepburn-Tracy movie, maximum intimacy and intersubjectivity, as well as personal dignity and self-esteem, may sometimes best be found in mutual antagonism.

(HATE)

1. DIRECTION:	Bipolar.
2. SCOPE/FOCUS:	Open, but usually a particular person or persons.
3. OBJECT:	A person (leaving aside "hating spinach," etc.).

4. CRITERIA: Combination of personal and moral, but may be only personal.

5. STATUS: Equality (again leaving aside spinach).

6. EVALUATIONS: Dislike of the person over-all, mixed with respect for his various skills, abilities, manners, personality; possibly respect for *everything* particular *about* him; but not him.

7. RESPONSIBILITY: Mutual responsibility for the relationship. You can't really *hate* someone who is indifferent to you (rather resent him). Carries with it the idea that the person is responsible for who he is.

8. INTERSUBJECTIVITY: The hostility forces you to be alert, of course. But in an important sense, "you can trust your enemies" (in the phrase of a John Birch pamphlet of the fifties); you know *that* they are enemies and accept them as such. Hatred has a shared code of honor that is lacking in other hostile emotions.

9. DISTANCE: Intimacy.

10. MYTHOLOGY: Depending on the kind of respect you have for your antagonist (is he merely opposed to you, or is he a monster, an embodiment of evil, to be overthrown by your heroism?). The mythology may be an Achilles and Hector relationship, both heroes upon whom the eyes of the world are focused, supported not only by friends and dependencies but by the interests of the gods as well. In one's own eyes, the battle with this respected yet hated enemy occupies the center stage of the world; everything around it stops and watches. There is an evident ambivalence in such relationships, between the antagonism and the mutual respect, which might at any point turn to love.

The vanquishing of such an enemy is virtually always followed by a sense of emptiness as well as a sense of elation; it was the enemy that gave one's life its significance; it was his unusual abilities —matched only by one's own—that provided the admirable human foil for one's own heroism.

The second mythology of hatred more resembles George and the Dragon, or, in more modern times, Churchill's exhortations against "the Hun." It is essential to hatred that the opponent be at least as powerful as oneself, a formidable monster, in order that one be capable of displaying his full range of powers over as extended a period of battle as possible. But unlike the Achilles and Hector mythology, the George and the Dragon or Churchill and the Hun mythology casts itself in moral terms as well as personal. This is not merely a battle of equally heroic wills, but a battle between good and evil. Accordingly, it has a moral fervor—and a lack of ambivalence —that the former encounters lack. It, too, however, will be followed by a depression of sorts as well as the elation of victory; it is the presence of evil that allows one to so homogenously and exclusively praise his own nobility and virtue. Once the monster is defeated, one is forced to see the monstrous aspects of himself. Usually he goes off to seek another monster. (See, for example, Archibald MacLeish's play *Herakles*.)

11. DESIRE:	To hurt or demolish; to *win*.
12. POWER:	There can be no hatred in weakness. What is often called "hate" is most assuredly resentment, when it is too timid to fight and is obsessed with the superi-

ority and advantages of the other person. Hate, like love, is an emotion of strength: It requires strength to endure, and it requires strength for its expression. By virtue of this power, of course, hatred allows us to falsely bolster our egos by "hating" abstract and distant (and therefore safe) opponents, much as that familiar "Romantic" variety of love-at-a-distance serves the same end in the same way. Hatred is always power-hungry, for it always desires for both oneself *and one's opponent* to be ever more powerful.

13. STRATEGY: Since hatred already presupposes a large degree of self-esteem, its strategy is to further expand the self through confrontation with the most powerful and hopefully most evil opponents possible. Accordingly, it is natural in hatred to cast the world in black-and-white terms, casting another person, no matter how seemingly similar to oneself, in strictly devilish terms, thus making oneself appear as pure virtue by contrast. And nothing can be more successful toward this end than hatred, particularly when combined with a consuming love as well.

HOPE

Like faith (and charity), hope often connotes a religious context, the hope of redemption and the grand hopes tied to the Faith of Christianity. When Camus, for example, rejects hope, it is this grand conception of hope that he is concerned with. But there are also small hopes, happy but uncertain expectations, around which we build our lives: the hope for healthy children, the hope for peace, the hope for a pleasant flight. Hope is faith uncertain, a passive anticipation of a positive fortune, beyond one's own control but always possible.

(HOPE)

1.	DIRECTION:	Outer-directed.
2.	SCOPE/FOCUS:	From trivial (hope the scotch is J&B) to life-size (hope one's daughter gets into graduate school) to cosmic (hope to go to heaven and for universal peace).
3.	OBJECT:	Open.
4.	CRITERIA:	Open.
5.	STATUS:	Open.
6.	EVALUATIONS:	Positive for possible future.
7.	RESPONSIBILITY:	None on one's own part.
8.	INTERSUBJECTIVITY:	——
9.	DISTANCE:	——
10.	MYTHOLOGY:	Uncertainty without despair, ranging from calculated probabilities to faith and ascriptions of beneficence.
11.	DESIRE:	To get what one desires, without necessarily doing anything.
12.	POWER:	None necessary.
13.	STRATEGY:	Compensation for lack of power, keeping afloat in uncertain times.

INDIFFERENCE

There is that indifference that is merely lack of emotion. ("Am I annoying you?" the gnat asked the bull. "If you hadn't asked, I wouldn't have known you were there," he answered.) But there is also that indifference which is highly motivated and a matter of subjective principle, an attitude of hostility as brutal as hatred and more effective than contempt. From the domestic ploy of not talking to or talking through the person who stands before you to the international diplomatic ploy of not "recognizing" a government that doesn't agree with you, indifference is perhaps the most effective strategy possible for denying a disliked or out-of-favor opponent any role in your surreality, not even giving him or her the recognition of contempt. He or she is too insignificant to be hated, even too insignificant to be despised or treated as subhuman or inhuman; rather, nothing at all, like the gnat on the bull's ear. It is a strategy that Sartre discusses at considerable length in his discussion "Concrete Relations with Other People." It is a "defense mechanism" whose neurotic counterpart Freud often discusses as "denial." Structuring somebody *out* of your sur-reality is as much of a constitutive judgment as the variety of ways of structuring him in. In fact, it takes more effort, since that person's very presence requires enormous ability to ignore and avoid, as if his/her insults and advances not only had no effect but did not even exist at all.

(INDIFFERENCE)

1. DIRECTION: Outer-directed.

2. SCOPE/FOCUS: Usually another person (or should we say, everywhere else but that person?).

3. OBJECT: A person (or should we say, "the nega-tion of a person"?).

4. CRITERIA: Open.

5. STATUS: The other has none (not even inferiority; that is, "beneath contempt").

6. EVALUATIONS: The other is below whatever standard of evaluation one chooses; a serious trans-gression or obscene personality.

7. RESPONSIBILITY: The other is usually blamed for some serious transgression.

8. INTERSUBJECTIVITY: Extremely defensive, but one defends himself against the recognition of the object rather than against the object. (It is essential, for example, that one does not, in indifference, register the slightest de-fensive reaction against the victim. To do so is to destroy the emotion.)

9. DISTANCE: Impersonal (the difference between somewhere and nowhere).

10. MYTHOLOGY:	The pariah mythology, the man whose name is stricken from all records, who is allowed no quarter, no conversation, no attention, not even punishment. (Cecil B. De Mille's Moses? Boris Karloff's Karis?)
11. DESIRE:	That the person really would disappear.
12. POWER:	If one had the power to make the person vanish, the peculiar but brutally effective strategy of this emotion might not be necessary. But, then, there are times when one does not want to give his antagonist even the satisfaction of punishment, thereby giving him the opportunity for martyrdom. Indifference and surrealistic exile is more effective.
13. STRATEGY:	To degrade utterly one who offends you (for whatever reason). To reduce him to such insignificance in your world that nothing he says or does can have the slightest meaning. Such desperate measures often follow betrayed intimacy, when the vulnerability to offense is great and one's ability to defend oneself minimal. In such cases, it is often most effective to deny the existence of the other altogether, not to force oneself into the position of having to stand up to him or her.

INDIGNATION

Indignation differs from anger in the authoritativeness of its criteria and its consequent self-righteousness. This difference, however, leads to others; the sense of the other's objective guilt (as opposed to mere offensiveness, as in anger) may result in viewing him as inferior, further increasing one's own sense of self-righteousness and innocence, increasing the difference between oneself and the other, and breaking down intersubjectivity in the direction of contempt.

(INDIGNATION)

1. **DIRECTION:**   Outer-directed (but with implicit contrast between the immorality of the other and one's own innocence).

2. **SCOPE/FOCUS:**   Another person or persons, the act of person or persons.

3. **OBJECT:**   Human action.

4. **CRITERIA:**   Strongly moral.

5. **STATUS:**   Self as superior; other as inferior.

6. **EVALUATIONS:**   Extremely negative evaluation of other's (others') action. (Indignant that you said that; indignant that Congress passed that piece of legislation.) May spill over to over-all negative evaluation of the person or persons committing that action, but need not.

7. **RESPONSIBILITY:**   Other(s) responsible and blameworthy.

8. **INTERSUBJECTIVITY:**   Very defensive.

9. **DISTANCE:**   Tends to be impersonal, may even approach indifference.

10. **MYTHOLOGY:**   The offended moralist, personally outraged but not for any personal reasons; rather for reasons of principle. (If you insult me, I will be angry; but if you insult my race/religion/country/occupation/etc., I will be morally indignant because of the "principle of the thing.")

11. **DESIRE:**   To punish.

12. **POWER:**   Variable (indignation without power merges with resentment; indignation with power tends to satisfy itself through effective action, like anger).

13. **STRATEGY:**   To avoid focusing on one's personal weaknesses and vulnerabilities and attend to the moral frailties and offenses of others,

thus setting oneself up by way of contrast as comparatively moral, good, pure,
etc.

INNOCENCE

Those who have not insisted, at least once, on the absolute vir-
ginity of human beings and the world, cannot understand the
realities of rebellion and its ravening desires for destruction.

Camus

To be innocent, as to *be* guilty before the law or before God, is
not an emotion but an objective status. But to think of oneself as
innocent, to absolve oneself of all wrongdoing, and to see the
world through innocent eyes—that is an emotion. It is, perhaps,
the dominant passion in Dostoevski's Prince Myshkin of *The
Idiot,* far more self-aware than other-aware (as in love: thus his
often blind and inconsiderate if well-intended interference with
the other characters of the novel). Innocence may or may not be
coupled with indignation, but indignation is a convenient fulcrum
to lift oneself to this self-appointed state of grace. To be innocent
is surely a virtue; but to see oneself as innocent is usually a self-
deceptive pretense (which is not to leap to the opposite extreme—
that of Clamence and Original Sin—to presume that we are therefore wholly guilty!).

(INNOCENCE)

1. DIRECTION:	Inner-directed (perhaps exclusively, as in guilt, perhaps coupled with outer-directed indignation).
2. SCOPE/FOCUS:	Oneself over-all.
3. OBJECT:	Oneself as a human being and as an agent.
4. CRITERIA:	Moral.
5. STATUS:	———— (but may well include sense of superiority to others).
6. EVALUATIONS:	Positive toward oneself and one's acts.

7. RESPONSIBILITY: Absolute self-vindication and absolution ("*Me absolvo*").

8. INTERSUBJECTIVITY: Much more defensive than one would suspect (who is, after all, "without sin" among us?).

9. DISTANCE: ——— (May involve withdrawal; need not [Myshkin].)

10. MYTHOLOGY: The lamb among wolves, the "beautiful soul" (Hegel, Novalis).

11. DESIRE: To remain flawless (to be recognized as such).

12. POWER: None necessary (except, perhaps, the power of self-deception).

13. STRATEGY: Personal dignity and self-esteem in the most direct constitutive action possible; one simply *legislates* oneself as purified and ideal.

JEALOUSY

Jealousy shares envy's "green-eyed monster" status. In fact, as covetousness, it also shares its uncoveted status as one of the "seven deadly sins." There are differences, however; jealousy, unlike envy, sees itself as the equal of the other. Where envy glowers quietly and ineffectively—even unnoticeably—from a distance, jealousy is willing and even anxious for a confrontation. Jealousy, like anger and hatred (with which it is closely related), is an emotion of bipolarity and equality. Unlike envy, jealousy wants the other to face its fabled green eye. Moreover, jealousy is usually confined to a single possession or incident; envy often includes major aspects or even the entire life style of its distant object.

(JEALOUSY)

1. DIRECTION: Bipolar (competition).

2. SCOPE/FOCUS: A particular incident or series of incidents.

3. OBJECT:	Another person's competitive gain.
4. CRITERIA:	Personal (may be interpersonal—for example, in seeking fame or attention).
5. STATUS:	Equality.
6. EVALUATIONS:	Competitive loss.
7. RESPONSIBILITY:	Looks at the other as responsible for one's own deprivation. But like envy, the question of *right* is more important than the question of responsibility; in jealousy, one sees himself as having a right to the coveted object—at least as much right as the other. (In envy one does not see himself as having any such right, which partially explains its sense of impotence.)
8. INTERSUBJECTIVITY:	Confrontational and defensive.
9. DISTANCE:	"At arm's length"; not intimate, not impersonal.
10. MYTHOLOGY:	"You've taken what rightfully belongs to me"; Menelaus confronting Paris.
11. DESIRE:	To get it (whatever "it" is) back.
12. POWER:	One has the power, or thinks he has—at least enough to *try* (otherwise tends to develop into envy or resentment).
13. STRATEGY:	To place one's stamp upon the things of the earth; "This is *mine*"—a conception that makes no sense unless one is willing to recognize the possibility that it can be stolen and one's *right* to take it back by force. (Hegel's, Marx's, and Locke's discussions of the institution of private property are relevant here.) The claim to property (including the now celebrated "territorial imperative") is an instrument of self-expansion—in an obvious and visible way. ("One is what one *has*.") Thus, it is not uncommon that a

person will become jealous over an object (including a human "object," a husband, wife, child, or lover) about which,
competition aside, he or she has little or
no concern whatsoever. It is the claim of
possession that is crucial, not the importance of the object itself.

JOY

The "up-down" metaphors that permeate discussions of the
passions are nowhere more appropriate than in the contrast between joy and depression (where "up" and "down," in the contemporary idiom, are personal adjectives which are virtually synon-
ymous with these two moods). Where depression often seems like
a thick fog, weighing us down such that we cannot reach the
values that sustain us in everyday life, joy is a buoyant breeze that
seems to lift us above the concerns of everyday. If depression
places our world in "brackets" of doubtfulness, joy encloses it
with silvery meanings. These need have no dependence upon particulars and joy, like depression, may well be oblivious to details.
With its more particular emotional counterpart of *delight*, its
more diffuse mood form of *euphoria*, and its more powerful form
in *ecstasy*, joy is that happy passion that renders our world not
only satisfactory but "wonderful." Like contentment, it formulates its values and expectations to conform with the world. As
such, it has no ideology (except the *laissez faire* of the status quo
or utter indifference to change), no concrete ideals or values.
(Thus, it was rightly argued that Timothy Leary's "politics of ecstasy" in the late 1960s were in fact an apolitical distraction and a
"cop-out.") And because it is so ethereal, joy is extremely difficult
to describe or to talk about without slipping into the mush that
such moods freely supply. (How much easier it is to be
hardheaded about the painful muck of depression.)

(JOY)

1. DIRECTION: As a mood, omni-directional.

2. SCOPE/FOCUS: As a mood, cosmic in scope, indiscriminate focus, though perhaps centering on

a core of delight (a new love affair, some spectacular success, or just a sunny day).

3. OBJECT: Everything, but nothing in particular.

4. CRITERIA: None.

5. STATUS: ——— (Question doesn't even arise; except when one *uses* his joy as a weapon, as one uses innocence. But that is no longer joy. See, for example, William Shutz, *JOY* [New York: Grove Press, 1967].)

6. EVALUATIONS: "Everything's *marvelous*."

7. RESPONSIBILITY: Irrelevant (might be mixed with a little cosmic gratitude or pride).

8. INTERSUBJECTIVITY: Open.

9. DISTANCE: Open, depending on mood of other persons. (Joy and depression tend to avoid each other; joy, like depression, tends to seek out and form intimate bonds with itself.)

10. MYTHOLOGY: "Everything's perfect."

11. DESIRE: None, except perhaps to share the mood.

12. POWER: None necessary.

13. STRATEGY: None necessary.

LOVE

And the moral of that is "Oh, 'tis love that makes the world go round."

Lewis Carroll, *Alice in Wonderland*

How can I say so little about love, considering that it is the ultimate goal of our entire theory? Perhaps another book. For the moment, I can only outline the structure of this most desirable of passions, which may easily include ecstasy and joy but unlike them has its eyes focused concretely on the details of its world, includes an ideology concerning how our world ought to be, and is explicitly concerned with the welfare and happiness of other people rather than free-floating and indiscriminate contentment with itself.

Much of what passes for love is not love at all; those passions of dependency and desperate bids for warmth and security—the often resentful ties that bind us without elevating us and set us against each other rather than draw us together. Love is the ideal of all of us; intimacy and mutually elevating equality, complete trust and maximum esteem for both ourselves and others. But how difficult it is to be so vulnerable and trusting, to reject those many temptations to think of ourselves as superior rather than merely equal, to give up the successful defenses and strategies that have worked so well for us in the past. But who can say of him/herself, "I don't want to love" or "I can't love," without the most profound regrets? And so the solution is more often than not a purely nominal love—in fact any number of other emotions parading as love: resentment and jealous possessiveness, anger and hatred expressing themselves indirectly but effectively through the deceptions of tenderness and pretended concern, abstract joy or depression, searching out a virtually anonymous companion, frustration looking for an outlet and guilt seeking solace, if not absolution. But none of this is love, however commonly it may pass for love, and however rare "true" love may be. Love is intimacy and trust; love is mutual respect and admiration; love is the insistance on mutual independence and autonomy, free from possessiveness but charged with desire; love is unqualified acceptance of the other's welfare and happiness as one's own. Nothing else deserves the name. (I am here concerned only with Romantic Love and love between equals, not love between mother and child, man and God, or the love of danger, love of music, or love of chocolate.)

(LOVE)

1. DIRECTION:	Bipolar.
2. SCOPE/FOCUS:	Another person or persons.
3. OBJECT:	Strictly human (possibly an animal or even an inanimate object treated as a person—a pet or a sports car).
4. CRITERIA:	Variable (combination of personal, interpersonal, and moral).

5. STATUS:	Equality.
6. EVALUATIONS:	Over-all admiration for the other; matched by positive feeling about oneself. ("Love begins with self-love.") Positive evaluations about particular features.
7. RESPONSIBILITY:	One takes responsibility for the health of the relationship (and expects the other to do the same).
8. INTERSUBJECTIVITY:	Unqualified trust (without sacrificing autonomy).
9. DISTANCE:	Intimacy.
10. MYTHOLOGY:	The Platonic "made for each other" congruence theory; the ultimate "we," where distinction between separate selves loses all meaning. Sometimes "us against the world" mythology (where the world is constituted as hostile surrounding this island of benignness); more desirably, an ever-expanding sense of "we," ultimately without limitation and including all of humanity (what is best in Christianity). Indiscriminate "love," however, and "love" without intimacy, honesty, equality, or respect are not love at all. "Universal love" is not an isolated superficial attitude, but one that requires the radical overhaul of virtually all of our perspectives and defenses. Perhaps there have been a few men who have achieved it, but it is usually their words and images rather than their subjectivity that has been imitated, and more as a weapon of resentment than an attempt at love.
11. DESIRE:	To satisfy and make happy the other, whose desires one now accepts as one's own (thus simultaneously satisfying and making oneself happy). To be together; to share.

12. POWER: There is no love in weakness. Insecurity and defensiveness make love impossible. Love is an emotion of strength; it requires strength to endure, and it requires strength for its expression. Desire of an inaccessible other is the most common masquerade of love; but desire—no matter how passionate and how embellished with Romantic fantasies—is not love. Love begins when possessive desire is fulfilled or extinguished. (Thus the heretical insight of the "sexual revolution"; "Let's sleep together first, and *then* we'll see. . . .") Nothing makes love so impossible as the protracted teasing and frustration of Victorian "romance"; much better an Oriental prearranged marriage, which has the virtue of beginning with security and is forced to face the existential requirement of a *commitment* to love. Ultimately, love requires more power—more self-confidence and pre-existing self-esteem—than any other emotion. It begins where other emotions would like to be, and from there tries to boost itself higher—through intersubjectivity and intimacy.

13. STRATEGY: With self-esteem already achieved to a large degree, love seeks to expand the Self, maximizing self-esteem through intersubjectivity, but always with personal autonomy and dignity intact and presupposed. Through mutual support and encouragement of the other or others, love succeeds in forming a synergetic subjective empire. Love becomes infinitely expansive and unassailable, subject to collapse and defeat only from the inside, through subversion and the infiltration of doubts, distrust and allegations of inequity. Love is subject to the explosiveness that comes with the unalert and lackadaisical sloth of overconfidence and lack of vigilance ("taking it for granted").

PENITENCE: see REGRET, REMORSE

PITY

"Why are there still beggars?"

Nietzsche

Pity is an extremely difficult emotion, not least because it is a common defensive mask for several vindictive emotions of inferiority, notably resentment. On the one hand, pity (compassion and sympathy) would seem to be an undisputed prerequisite for minimal humanity. A friend or acquaintance—or even a stranger—suffers a calamity through no fault of his own; how are such occasions constituted in our world? Are they blocked and denied ("It's not my problem")? Surely that view is abominable. Should we appeal, after the fashion of the evidently less than wholly compassionate philosophers of the Enlightenment, to some dubious conception of the "best of all possible worlds" in which every such tragedy is but part of some larger benevolent scheme? That is absurd and inhuman. Should we suppose that, despite all appearances, the injured party has brought this all on himself (the current popular theory of "bad karma," which for some barely comprehensible reason seems more acceptable to many people than the equally cruel barbarities of medieval "will of God" theories)? Are we forced, in the name of humanity, to put ourselves in the same boat with the injured, suffer with him (literally *compassion*) or love him just because he is injured, one of the more admirable but less imitable teachings of Christianity? It is important to appreciate the role of a passion that faces the misfortunes of others with involvement yet at a distance, not avoiding them but not wholly absorbing us in their troubles either. This emotion is pity, which is by its very nature a bipolar emotion (obvious in its near synonyms, *com-passion, sym-pathy, Mit-leiden*) but one which balances intersubjectivity with a certain distance, one which may (but need not) recognize the equality of one less fortunate: "There but for the grace of God go I." (One might also pity a half-drowned roach, however, but only through some extravagant theory of reincarnation adopt the above-quoted sentiment.)

Yet one knows that "pity" mixed with glee, "better him than me," that boisterous sense of superiority that sometimes accompanies a meeting with someone truly miserable. (The extra-economic answer to Nietzsche's question "Why are there still beggars?") Pity can also be used as an offense to place someone in an inferior position. "I pity you" can be a powerful insult, much stronger than the condemnation of anger, implying that you are at least an inferior human if not subhuman and depraved. It is this abuse of pity that is unfairly singled out by Nietzsche in his attack on Christian ethics. (Max Scheler, the Catholic phenomenologist, wrote an entire book, *Ressentiment*, in which he distinguishes this resentful and abusive form of ["bourgeois"] pity from the Christian conception of pity as a virtue.) To view a person as inferior on the basis of (or because of) his misfortune (to consider someone who is crippled or retarded, for example, as inferior or as less than human) is surely a repulsive bid for self-esteem, however successful. But the recognition of misfortune as misfortune, the refusal to reject or despise the unfortunate because of one's own fears and insecurities, that is surely the very essence of our humanity. Whether or not we can summon the strength to love our fellow men universally, at least we can face their troubles and share them, not necessarily sacrificing ourselves on their behalf, but at least providing them with the support of respectful equality that costs us so little.

(PITY)

1. DIRECTION: Bipolar ("suffering with"). When it becomes other-directed, the danger is that pity will turn to entertainment, losing its role as compassion and becoming the revolting gawking that one finds at the scene of a motor accident. At the other end, when pity turns inward, it becomes "feeling sorry for oneself," a wholly different emotion which has noth-

ing to do with the suffering of others at all. (A common reaction to serious illness in others, for example, is to become acutely if not morbidly aware of one's own susceptibility to similar illness. This is surely not pity.)

2. SCOPE/FOCUS: Persons, personlike creatures.

3. OBJECT: Some particular misfortune or inability in a person or personlike creature.

4. CRITERIA: Personal (I find it impossible to pity a person for a loss that I cannot conceive as a loss).

5. STATUS: Equality; but then there is that perverted brand of pity attacked by Nietzsche in which the misfortune in question is made the basis for a judgment of inferiority.

6. EVALUATIONS: Evaluation of misfortune, loss, injury.

7. RESPONSIBILITY: Innocence on the part of the victim. It is the undeservedness of the misfortune that calls for pity. Deserved misfortune rather appeals to our sense of justice. We do not pity the suffering villain, unless, that is, the severity of his punishment far outweighs the severity of his offense. (Thus the horrendous inhumanity of those everyday moralists who confuse any degree of desert with whatever degree of punishment.) We are innocent: otherwise, it would not be pity, but remorse or guilt that we would feel.

8. INTERSUBJECTIVITY: Defense is minimal but measurable, as if in the most rational among us there is the lingering suspicion that misfortune is contagious. In Nietzsche's conception, however, defensiveness (through resentment) is the key to pity. In our conception, this is an abuse of pity, not its standard structure.

9. DISTANCE:

"At arm's length"; impersonality is inhuman (resentful pity doesn't mind this at all); intimacy is too uncomfortable. (In love, it is worth noting, pity isn't even relevant. The sense of sharing in love denies the slight defensiveness and distance of pity, makes the loved one's suffering one's own.)

10. MYTHOLOGY:

"There but for the grace of God go I"; this is why the innocence of the victim is so vital to this emotion. (It is empathy that makes pity possible.) There is, however, that medieval conception of misfortune, extensively debated in the "Enlightenment" and still accepted in poptalk as "the law of karma," that insists on seeing all misfortune as deserved. This theory itself, applied as it always is only to *other* people, is an intellectual weapon of resentment. When it is applied to the emotion of pity, it does indeed yield just those results which Nietzsche so despised—the use of other people's undeserved misfortune as an excuse to consider them inferior (and oneself, by the same token, as superior).

11. DESIRE:

To soothe, heal, or at least comfort the other. (As pity turns inward, there may also be an unflattering and ultimately absurd desire to imitate or inflict similar suffering upon oneself. In such cases, look for guilt—or for a distorted and too literal sense of "suffering with.")

12. POWER:

Relative powerlessness. Competent doctors don't pity their patients; they cure them. (Unfortunately, many incompetent doctors don't pity their "patients" either. [After all, they are "patients"].)

13. STRATEGY:

Even in the most humane forms of pity, there is that strongly desirable sense of good fortune on one's own account, in contrast to the misfortune of another. There is also that sense of dignity and self-esteem that comes with every effort at intersubjectivity, however qualified. Pity is such an effort, though a timid one, unwilling to tolerate intimacy and clearly taking advantage of the unthreatening situation of the other person. When pity is combined with resentment, however, the awareness of one's own good fortune becomes ratified by a questionable moral-metaphysical theory and becomes an excuse for a sense of superiority.

PRIDE

Pride is an established conviction of one's own paramount worth in some respect.‡

Schopenhauer, "On Pride"

Pride does not deserve to be a "deadly sin," much less the first on the list. Of course there is that "foolish pride" of traditional literature, usually delegated to confused women and fops of various varieties, but pride is no more essentially foolish than anger or love, jealousy or hope (two of these also being included on the "deadly" list). To the contrary, pride is an emotion which lies close to the heart of all the passions, the subjective demand for personal dignity and self-esteem. It is important to stress, however, that pride is not equivalent to dignity, and it is the possible "foolishness" of pride that distinguishes them. Dignity and self-esteem are over-all subjective attitudes about oneself resultant of the whole of our emotional mythologies. Pride, on the other hand, is tied very heavily to details, particularly our achievements and our objective roles. There is nothing wrong with this, of course, except when clinging to a false conception of ourselves and degrading ourselves on account of it. Pride is a sin only when it is false pride, a bloated fantasy of self-esteem too flimsily tied to a foundation of

‡ Cf. VANITY.

insignificant accomplishments, used more as a weapon in a self-styled bid for superiority than as a straightforward appeal for dignity.*

Ideally, pride and self-esteem complement each other, pride esteeming our objective achievements, honors, and status, with the support of subjective self-esteem. But as I argued in Chapter 4, the subjective and objective views of ourselves are not always in such harmony. The competitive scramble to maximize objective status often buries the subjective sense of oneself altogether. Similarly, a sufficiently powerful sense of subjectivity can easily (but sometimes foolishly or tragically) ignore objectivity, losing itself in its own mythologies and paying little or no attention to the opinions of others or the "ways of the world." Accordingly, a man may have much pride but yet have little self-esteem; and a man can have considerable self-esteem without being proud. Religious men have often aspired to the latter status and it is through such ideals that pride is viewed as a Sin. Most of us are more likely to fall into the trap of the first disharmony: proud of ourselves and our accomplishments, but yet self-demeaning in a manner that is difficult for us to understand. (After all, I've accomplished everything I wanted to do; so why am I depressed?")

The key to the emotion of pride is that it is about our achievements in the world. "False pride" grossly overestimates those achievements, or perhaps even takes credit for something that is not our doing at all. (A person who has taken steps to make himself beautiful or healthy may be proud of his appearance or his health. A person who simply is beautiful or healthy would only be grateful—or perhaps vain—the passive emotional partners of pride. Our frequent confusion of pride and vanity—our calling ourselves proud when in fact we are only vain—is clearly more than verbal slippage.)

* This double meaning of "pride" is evident, for example, in the dictionary (Webster's Third New International), where the definitions fall into two classes, "the state of being proud" and "a sense of one's own worth," on the one hand, and "inordinate self-esteem" and "unreasonable conceit of superiority" and "ostentatious display," on the other. Phrases like "pride and prejudice" don't help its reputation either. (Cf. Spinoza: "Pride is pleasure arising from a man's thinking too highly of himself" [Ethics, Book III].)

(PRIDE)

1. DIRECTION:	Inner-directed (about oneself, but particularly one's visible ["objective"] achievements).
2. SCOPE/FOCUS:	Usually some specific accomplishment or developed skill, possibly ranging to the whole person but always stopping short of complete subjectivity.
3. OBJECT:	Oneself as an agent.
4. CRITERIA:	Open (but usually with interpersonal considerations).
5. STATUS:	Some sense of superiority, but not necessarily competitive.
6. EVALUATIONS:	Highly positive of one's own achievements.
7. RESPONSIBILITY:	One takes responsibility (in praise) for his own works.
8. INTERSUBJECTIVITY:	May result in defensiveness when achievements are challenged and may be used defensively, but not intrinsically defensive.
9. DISTANCE:	——— (One tends to hold oneself at an ostentatious distance—for better viewing.)
10. MYTHOLOGY:	"I did it"; usually personal mythologies of pride are fairly explicit, modeled after our role-idols, mentors, and heroes. No doubt there is often a parent-pleasing quotient present as well. The mythology of pride is the mythology of accomplishment, and what counts as an accomplishment depends on the ambitions of the individual and his own criteria for success (heroism, creativity, prowess, wealth, moral fortitude).
11. DESIRE:	To be recognized for what one has accomplished.

12. POWER:	Open. Of course, one needs power to succeed and achieve in order to do the deeds that he is proud of; but pride itself does not involve this power. The power of pride is its ability to project its success around itself, convincing other people and gaining recognition comparable to one's own opinion of himself. "False pride" refers to the fact that often our estimations of our own achievements are ridiculously more laudatory than we could reasonably expect from anyone else. "Foolish pride," on the other hand, is the sometimes absurd lengths to which one will go to achieve recognition from others (no matter what the accomplishment).
13. STRATEGY:	To maximize subjective self-esteem through the support of external accomplishments and the recognition of other people. Not a bad strategy, except when pursued exclusively. (See Chapter 4, Section 4.)

RAGE: see ANGER, INDIGNATION

REGRET

REMORSE

Regret and remorse are often thrown together, as "sorrow" or as "penitence." The difference between them, however, is very much like the difference between embarrassment and shame—a difference in responsibility. In regret, one does not take responsibility, blaming whatever disappointment is involved on "circumstances beyond one's control" (thus the appropriateness of "regret" in the less than wholly honest transactions of social etiquette). Remorse, however, is more like shame and guilt in its acceptance of responsibility for past injuries to others. It is far more specific than guilt, usually concerning a single incident or action, but far less social and moral-minded than shame, more self-indulgent and less concerned with "objective" criteria for judgment.

(REGRET)

1. DIRECTION:	Inner-directed.
2. SCOPE/FOCUS:	Particular incident, particularly an omission.
3. OBJECT:	An action, not necessarily one's own, or an incident (omission).
4. CRITERIA:	Open.
5. STATUS:	–––
6. EVALUATIONS:	Unfortunate behavior (of one's own).
7. RESPONSIBILITY:	"Circumstances beyond my control."
8. INTERSUBJECTIVITY:	Open.
9. DISTANCE:	–––
10. MYTHOLOGY:	Fatalistic: "An unfortunate thing happened to me on the way to . . . so that I couldn't . . ." A sense of having been prevented: "If only . . ." Regret, even when aimed at a future omission (regretting that one will miss the coronation) acts as if it is a foregone conclusion and already in the past. Sense of being a pawn of schedules, circumstance, or fate.
11. DESIRE:	Not to have missed (or not to miss) anything. (One regrets not having completed high school because of the war; one would like to be shown that he didn't really miss anything, that there was no loss, that it can be made up for without further loss, etc.)
12. POWER:	Open; one can sometimes make it the case that the loss that lies at the basis of regret is canceled. Sometimes he cannot.

13. STRATEGY: Constitution of a loss as beyond one's own control; sense of being a pawn and determined by circumstances is an extremely comforting feeling, ideal in the avoidance of guilt and remorse.

(REMORSE)

1. DIRECTION: Inner-directed.

2. SCOPE/FOCUS: Particular action.

3. OBJECT: One's own past actions, usually harmful to another person.

4. CRITERIA: Open.

5. STATUS: ———

6. EVALUATIONS: Negative, action as harmful, stupid, disastrous.

7. RESPONSIBILITY: Oneself is to blame.

8. INTERSUBJECTIVITY: Open.

9. DISTANCE: ———

10. MYTHOLOGY: Self-accusation and punishment, much like guilt (Jean-Paul Sartre's *The Flies*, underscoring the point that the nagging, buzzing, biting annoyances are self-inflicted).

11. DESIRE: To be pardoned.

12. POWER: None, impotence.

13. STRATEGY: As a sense of particular guilt, it succeeds in warding off censure and punishment from other people by first inflicting it upon oneself. ("He's suffered enough from his own remorse.") An extremely self-indulgent emotion, more concerned with its esteem in its own eyes than with the victims of its folly.

RESENTMENT

> Nothing on earth consumes a man more quickly than the passion
> of resentment.
>
> Nietzsche, *Ecce Homo*

Resentment is the villain of the passions. It is among the most
obsessive and enduring of the emotions, poisoning the whole of
subjectivity with its venom, often achieving moodlike scope while
still maintaining its keen and vicious focus on each of the myriad
of petty offenses it senses against itself. Curiously, it is not one of
the seven "deadly sins" (although envy, its close but more particular companion, is); yet it is surely the deadliest, stagnating self-esteem and shrinking our world down to a tightly defensive constricted coil, plotting and scheming to the exclusion even of pride,
making all trust, intimacy, and intersubjectivity impossible, except
for the always untrustworthy alliances it forms in mutual defense
and for the purpose of expressing its usually impotent schemes of
vengeance. What is most vile about this all-pervasive emotion,
however, is its deviousness. It rarely allows itself to be recognized
as resentment but mocks the appearance and the titles of virtually
any other emotion. Puffing itself up with moral armament, it presents itself as indignation, jealousy, and anger. Refusing to acknowledge its marked sense of inferiority, it portrays itself as
hatred, or even as scorn or contempt for its superiors. Finding itself threatened, it retreats to the punitive humility of guilt and
remorse—but only until the danger passes. Sensing another's vulnerable trust and openness, resentment plays at love, using all the
devices of tenderness and concern to gain control of the other and
to use him or her as an instrument of its own vengeance. A vicious
emotion—the Richard III of the battlements of our souls, rich in
plots and strategies but always battling desperately, without quarter and with little hope from a position of suspicion and inferiority. With few victories of its own, it relishes every misfortune
that inflicts its enemies, through whatever means or circumstances, and whatever their desert or warrant. (The Germans have
an apt word for it, *Schadenfreuden*—joy at the sufferings of
others.) To make its strategy more devious, resentment will be the
first to express pity—but that pity abused by resentment we spoke

of earlier—thus appearing compassionate but in fact only feeding its morbid sense of its own bloated superiority at closer range. Resentment loves misery as company.

I shall have more to say of resentment in the final chapters. It is the paradigm of a well-entrenched emotional strategy that cannot see beyond its own meager self-constituted limitations. The contrast I shall most employ in that discussion will not be the familiar "opposites" of love and hate, which in fact are very much alike, but rather love and resentment, the true polarity of our emotional lives—the first an open and trusting acceptance of intersubjectivity and intimacy, the second a defensive and closed fortress of schemes and maliciousness, its sense of intersubjectivity the perverted Hobbesian notion of a "war of all against all," in which it is "every man for himself," "no one is to be trusted," and "take what you can get."

(RESENTMENT)

1. DIRECTION:	Outer-directed, emphatically, purposefully avoiding attention to one's own attitudes and stature, motives and intentions, infirmities and (lack of) achievement.
2. SCOPE/FOCUS:	Scope—virtually global (the defensive scan of the radar of a terrified animal, watching for danger or advantage everywhere). Focus—keen at every point. Resentment misses little. (Resentful people make excellent guards, police, librarians, school disciplinarians, clerks, detectives, scholars, and baby-sitters.)
3. OBJECT:	Other people, virtually all other people. Possibly also God and his creatures, trees, buildings, stones, laws, rules, successes (other people's), alarm clocks, etc.
4. CRITERIA:	Always tinged with morality, but may be personal or interpersonal in their origins (for example, in envy or through embarrassment). Always claims to be impersonal and disinterested. (Nietzsche

argues that morality itself is the invention of resentment [*Genealogy of Morals*, Essay 1], the objective pretensions of the personal prejudices of weakness, projected in "categorical" and unqualified form for application to the strong as well [to the advantage of the weak, of course].)

5. STATUS:

Intolerable inferiority. Resentment thrives in the dark and moist shadows of the soul, away from direct confrontations with superiors—bosses, members of the "opposite" sex, bullies, and authority figures. It is the sense of intolerable inferiority that drives resentment, forces it to disguise itself and adopt complex strategies—all aimed at overcoming its present status and proving itself at least equal, if not (preferably) superior.

6. EVALUATIONS:

Negative about everything, except the sufferings of others, which it sees as deserved and therefore a mark of its own advantage. Complaints, objections, and venomous bitterness, often couched in highly articulate and intelligent (even brilliant) forms are resentment's way of dealing with its world. Unable to praise itself, it demeans everything else, usually for good reason. (But, then, would we ever lack a good reason—if we were looking for it, for objecting to anything human?)

7. RESPONSIBILITY:

Like the self-accusations involved in guilt, the other-directed indictments of resentment are ill defined and obscure, rarely delineated by any particular offense but rather general enough to apply to virtually any minor offense or questionable achievement. It is worth noting that guilt and resentment are often found together in dialectical form, the guilt feeding one's sense of inferiority and making it all the more imperative that similar blame is projected outward to others, rendering them no better than oneself. When successful, however, resentment may well surpass its own sense of guilt remarkably, adopting that often obnoxious self-righteous sense of innocence that we find in Clamence in *The Fall*, in Kierkegaard's discourses, and in "confessions" of all kinds, a resentful innocence that comes through one's recognition of guilt, as if that alone were sufficient to render a person superior.

8. INTERSUBJECTIVITY: Extremely defensive and untrusting, constantly building fortifications and plotting plots of vengeance. When it does "let others in," we may be sure that they will be others like itself, surely no stronger than itself, and then only for the purpose of a tentative alliance, guarded by mutual distrust and cultish rituals and guarantees.

9. DISTANCE: Impersonal distance. Intimacy is intolerable to resentment; it is too embarrassed by itself, incapable of handling vulnerability, finds it impossible to give up its universally critical stance toward its world, and other people in particular.

10. MYTHOLOGY: The mythology of oppression and siege. "It's unfair!" A sense of being "thrown" into an inferior existence, through no fault of one's own. A view of the world in paranoid revolutionary terms; "If you're not on my side, you must be on the other side"; Hobbesian picture of every person out to kill (physically or symbolically) every other person. Sense of heroic fighting against tremendous and hopeless odds, like Sisyphus "scorning"

the gods, his only weapon his "defiance" (yet a defiance that is strictly subjective, as he continues with his chore). A tendency to divide the world into warring camps, and an obsession with power (which one never has enough of) and with "winners" and "losers."

11. DESIRE:

To destroy one's enemies, all of them, and to be in a position of indisputable and unmatched power and importance.

12. POWER:

Utter impotence, which feeds and frustrates one's megalomaniacal desires to the point of despair and desperation. It is important to note, however, that this sense of power is also subjective, and that resentment may afflict those who have in fact more power than anyone else in the world as well as those who in fact are oppressed. Indeed, it could be argued that resentment and the sense of impotence that will never be powerful enough are more developed in the neurotics who often obtain the most powerful positions in politics than among the politically oppressed, who as often as not have learned to live without power and without concern for it. It is the sense of impotence that is crucial to resentment, the sense of inferiority, and the goal of revenge and control that structures this morbid view of the world.

13. STRATEGY:

No emotion is richer in strategies than resentment. By mocking other emotions, it can adopt the strategies of any one of them, modified to suit its own purposes. As indignation, it can indict and accuse, placing itself in a position of self-righteous moral superiority. As pity, it can relish the sufferings of others and use them, in accordance with its dubious metaphysical world views, as an argument for its own righteousness and superiority. As love, it can slip into the heart of another person and act out the cruel fantasies it would like to express effectively to the world, but cannot. Resentment is like a tarantula (to borrow Nietzsche's metaphor in *Zarathustra*), a solitary and defensive creature, with terrifying appearance but utterly without confidence. Its bite is painful and poisonous, but rarely fatal; it spends most of its time in its hole or walking backward. Resentment builds all of its strategies on a single principle—to *drag the others down*. It seeks absolute self-esteem by default, by proving oneself superior to everyone else, not by changing oneself so much as by holding others back and destroying them. To this end, resentment will employ any means except one: It never considers its starting point, the self-imposed judgment of oppression and inferiority upon which all these malevolent desires and strategies are built. It is here that reflection serves us best, for one has only to see the strategies of resentment to see through them, and to see how unnecessary and self-defeating they are. But resentment itself will do everything possible to block this reflection. It is for this reason it needs to be so obsessive. Who would live in constant losing and demeaning battle if he could choose to live in peace and harmony with others? But it is so easy to say that, and so hard to see it in ourselves.

RESPECT

Respect is toward other people what contentment is to oneself, satisfaction with their achievements and their conceptions of themselves, acceptance of them for what they are, perhaps with admiration and praise as well. But where protracted contentment can mean weakness and stagnation, respect for others lacks the existential demand of self-overcoming. Of course our expectations of others change as our expectations of ourselves change; we develop new friendships and new role-models, new ideals and new dissatisfactions. But changing others is not our business, only changing ourselves. So while contentment should be enjoyed in guarded doses, respect is a workable structure for our dealings with other people in general. Of course, respect need not be admiration, and one should distinguish carefully between merely respecting another person—that is, recognizing him for what he is and takes himself to be—and admiring him—taking him as a model and a mentor, someone to be imitated or taken seriously as a judge of one's own accomplishments and failures.

(RESPECT)

1. DIRECTION:	Other-directed.
2. SCOPE/FOCUS:	Persons.
3. OBJECT:	Another person as an agent.
4. CRITERIA:	Open.
5. STATUS:	Equality (possibly superiority of the other but then including admiration as well).
6. EVALUATIONS:	Positive, ranging from acceptance to admiration.
7. RESPONSIBILITY:	Ascribes responsibility (not all by way of praise).
8. INTERSUBJECTIVITY:	Open (one can respect strangers as well as friends).
9. DISTANCE:	Open (intimacy in friendships, impersonal respect in professional relationships).
10. MYTHOLOGY:	"Different strokes for different folks," "Everyone has to live his own life," "Ultimately, we are all human beings."

11. DESIRE:	Peace and good will.
12. POWER:	——— (Respect and power over the other are in conflict.)
13. STRATEGY:	To maximize intersubjectivity through elimination of hostility and through mutual esteeming.

SADNESS

Sadness, sorrow, grief, and mourning are, like fear, extremely simple emotions, judgments of loss. The difference between them is mainly the severity and scope of the loss and its relative place in our world.

(SADNESS)

1. DIRECTION:	Outer-directed (although it is always *my* [*our*] loss).
2. SCOPE/FOCUS:	Variable, from particular to general (loss of a souvenir, death of a relative, destruction of 95 per cent of the earth).
3. OBJECT:	Open (a thing, a contest, a pet, a friend, a god).
4. CRITERIA:	Personal.
5. STATUS:	———
6. EVALUATIONS:	Estimate of loss (small loss in sadness, large loss in sorrow, traumatic loss in grief, enduring loss in mourning).
7. RESPONSIBILITY:	None (a loss for which one is to blame constitutes remorse, not sadness; a loss for which another is to blame generates anger or jealousy).
8. INTERSUBJECTIVITY:	——— (Can be an opportunity for either openness or extreme defensiveness.)
9. DISTANCE:	——— (Often an opportunity for intimacy —particularly when the loss is shared. But a personal loss might also result in

	impersonality, even to the point of total isolation and withdrawal.)
10. MYTHOLOGY:	The mythology of mourning, "I have lost a part of myself."
11. DESIRE:	To regain what is lost.
12. POWER:	Usually impotence. Sadness is irrational if in fact one has an opportunity to recoup the loss. In mourning, by the nature of the case, one is utterly impotent.
13. STRATEGY:	The strategy of sadness is a benign self-indulgence. The sense of loss is sincere, but the purpose of the emotion is, if but mildly and unobjectionably, "feeling sorry for oneself." (One feels sorry *about*, not *for*, the lost object, as opposed to pity, sympathy, and compassion, in which one feels sorry *for* another.)

SELF-CONTEMPT

SELF-HATRED

SELF-LOVE

SELF-PITY ("Feeling Sorry for Oneself")

SELF-RESPECT, etc.

There is a large class of emotions which appear, at least from their names, to be outer-directed emotions directed inwardly, toward oneself. These emotions are worth some special mention, first because their names are misleading, second because they display a curious schizoid structure not normally shared by inner-directed emotions. In such emotions, in which we "are angry at ourselves," "in love with ourselves," "loathe ourselves," we treat ourselves as if we were "someone else": Accordingly, such emotions are not self-directed in the usual sense, but neither are they other-directed. (And, needless to say, they cannot literally be called "bipolar," even where distinctly bipolar emotions are involved—for example, love in self-love, pity in self-pity, etc.)

Consider the difference between shame and "being angry with oneself." In both emotions, there is the attribution of blame and one's own acceptance of it. At first, it might appear as if the two emotions are identical; but shame has an ideology and a sense of self-control that anger-at-oneself lacks. To be ashamed requires the desire to redeem oneself; to be angry at oneself rather involves a sense of "it's over and done with." It is as if, in the latter emotion, one accepts the responsibility for his past misdeed without accepting the responsibility for its present redressing. It is in this sense that I want to say that such emotions treat oneself as another, for they typically apply other-directed judgments toward themselves *as if* they were not themselves the subjects in question.

Consider self-love, what Freud called *narcissism*, which is so often condemned as an attitude of self-indulgence and extravagant vanity. The classic portrait of Narcissus admiring himself in the reflecting pool, so transfixed by his image that he is oblivious to the world, devoid of desire and incapable of love or respect for others, is an apt allegory for the irresponsible and paralyzing judgments which admire oneself at a distance, as object rather than as subject.† What one "loves" about himself is merely the image of himself, not him*Self*. Accordingly, "self-love" is not love at all, but rather a misnamed species of inner-directed (or self-image-directed) idolatry which has little in common with the bipolar intimacy and mutual sense of desire and respect that characterizes love proper.

Self-pity ("feeling sorry for yourself") has a similar structure; the question is not whether the misfortune which one has suffered is worthy of pity (usually it is), but rather the peculiar attitude of paralysis that accompanies it. What makes this emotion so objectionable is the fact that the person wallows in his misfortune, not only accepts it but buries himself with it, refusing to adopt an ideology to overcome it and get back on his feet. It is not the misfor-

† The French philosopher L. Lavelle has written an extended essay on precisely this sense of philosophical schizophrenia, *L'Erreur de Narcissus* (Paris: Grasset).

tune, but the refusal to "get off one's ass and do something about it" that we find intolerable. The same should be said for self-contempt. In contempt of others, we adopt an attitude of avoidance, as great a distance and as total a separation of our identities as possible. But in self-contempt, one adopts similarly negative attitudes toward himself, with the unacceptable result that one wallows in his self-ascribed repulsiveness just as the man of self-pity wallows in his misfortune —without an ideology, without an attempt to "overcome himself," without attempting to *do* anything about it. In a strange sense, self-contempt carries with it its own perverse sense of self-satisfaction and contentment. Like all forms of "bad faith," it at least includes that passive acceptance and lack of responsibility which—at whatever cost—we so often prefer to the responsibility of our own subjectivity. ("I'm such a horrible, self-centered, impossible, loathsome person, "But what can I do about it? You'll just have to accept me as I am.")

In general, these emotions must be suspected of introducing just this species of "bad faith" and irresponsibility into our self-conceptions. They are all, even self-love and what is so often called "self-respect" and "self-confidence" (which are *not* the same as what we have been calling "self-esteem"), defensive emotions, attempts to salvage our dignity from a distance, as if to prop our images up from behind, as if we ourselves might remain behind the scenes. But whenever a person tries to be either his "own best friend" or his "own worst enemy," one can be sure that his self-esteem is under siege from somewhere. The man who has to "treat himself to a present" is one who finds it necessary to pick himself up by treating himself like someone else (literally, how could one give a "gift" to himself?). The man who pities himself is not the man who will allow himself to overcome his misfortune; he "enjoys" it too much. The man who loathes himself is not the one who will respond to encouragement and advice; he prefers his repulsiveness to his responsibility. And the man who "loves himself" is not the man to whom one turns for friendship, or love, or even the smallest piece of advice or companionship; he is too "wrapped up in himself," ostensibly in adoration but more arguably in defensiveness, to allow the slightest slip of intersubjectivity to pierce his reflective chrysalis.

SHAME

We Germans need not feel collective guilt, but at least we should feel collective shame.

Th. Hess

Shame, like anger and pride, is one of those emotions which are responsible for (as well as responsive to) the structures of moral responsibility which we impose upon our world. Unlike anger, shame is *self*-accusation, and unlike pride, it is an *un*favorable judgment of one's accomplishments. It is more specific than guilt, less vehement than remorse, limited in its scope and not generally self-demeaning, much like embarrassment, with which it is often associated.

(SHAME)

1. DIRECTION:	Inner-directed.
2. SCOPE/FOCUS:	Particular events.
3. OBJECT:	One's own actions.
4. CRITERIA:	Moral (though may sometimes be heavily interpersonal as well, as in embarrassment, when explicit moral criteria are not yet formulated).
5. STATUS:	――― Open (one need not feel inferior because he is ashamed).
6. EVALUATIONS:	Negative.
7. RESPONSIBILITY:	Oneself as responsible and blameworthy.
8. INTERSUBJECTIVITY:	Open. Shame is sometimes a basis for openness (in confession), but may also be a reason for withdrawal and enforced anonymity.
9. DISTANCE:	Open.
10. MYTHOLOGY:	As in anger, shame involves a courtroom mythology, of law and judgment, accusation and punishment. In shame, however, one casts himself in the uncom-

fortable position of defendant rather
than judge, but a defendant who has
openly admitted to his crime and is willing to accept punishment for it.

11. DESIRE:

To atone and expiate (but not necessarily to vindicate oneself).

12. POWER:

Open (unlike guilt and remorse, where
the offense appears to be beyond redemption).

13. STRATEGY:

In small doses, shame is a prod to self-
improvement (a fact which every parent
and educator knows well). Despite one's
actions, shame is not an over-all self-
condemnation. Quite to the contrary, it
is an affirmation of one's autonomy and
responsibility, a confirmation that one
will live by his standards and accept responsibility "like an adult." Although
shame is directly opposed to pride, it is
similarly conducive to self-esteem. But
shame requires considerable strength to
maintain such limited self-accusation and
often gives way to guilt, a more thoroughgoing indictment but for that very reason a more difficult indictment to confirm. Shame in larger doses, we might
say, becomes a self-demeaning emotion,
extremely defensive and impotent, without the ideology of atonement and
expiation that makes it such an important emotion for self-realization. Or, in a
similar bid for a less demanding surreality, shame feigns the innocence of embarrassment, or adopts the posture (and
it is a posture) of self-abuse in "being
angry with oneself," ostensibly similar to
shame but content with itself as shame
could never be. However shame may
seem to be a self-demeaning emotion, it
is in fact one of those emotions most
conducive to self-esteem. It is easy to

"feel good" about yourself when you have
no values, when you refuse to accept responsibility for your actions, or when
you happen not to have done anything
wrong. But self-esteem and personal dignity cannot depend on the happy con-
tingencies of a life without errors or on
the self-deceptive conveniences of amor-
ality and irresponsibility. The ability to
admit and atone for our mistakes is as
essential to wisdom and personal dignity
as the ability to love other people and
share our world with them. In fact,
would it be possible to do the latter without the former? (What kind of a relationship can exist only in the absence of
fights and abuses, errors and offenses?)

SORROW: see SADNESS

SPITE: see RESENTMENT

TERROR: see FEAR

TIMIDITY: see FEAR

VANITY

. . . vanity is the desire of arousing the conviction [of one's own
paramount worth] in others.

Schopenhauer, "On Pride"

Vanity is to pride as embarrassment is to shame. Vanity gladly
accepts its blessings (and may flaunt them as well) but without
being able to take credit for them. But lack of credit no more in-
terferes with vanity's delight in its "gifts" than the lack of blame
in embarrassment renders its situation less awkward. Because of
its awareness of the fact that its objects are matters of debt rather
than desert, however, vanity always carries with it that familiar
defensiveness and sense of impotence which is so lacking in the
(sometimes arrogant) confidence of pride. Vanity is passive where

pride is active, defensive where pride is aggressive. Where pride may flaunt its achievements in the face of opposition, vanity feels compelled to seek the confirmation of others. Thus, where pride often adopts an almost moral tone of autonomy, vanity feels it necessary to flaunt itself seeking approval, not as a sign of strength, but of weakness. (It is worth noting that the myth of Narcissus, in which vanity and self-love appear together, is a Hellenistic myth, formulated long after the heroic age of Greek mythology, when the dangers of pride, not vanity, occupied exclusive attention.) It is often said that vanity is concerned only with what is most superficial about us—fair skin or luxurious hair, the shape of a nose or a mouth—but we can see that such superficiality is symptomatic of a more profound distinction—between those features of ourselves for which we accept responsibility (in pride and shame) and those which merely "happen" to us (in vanity and embarrassment). Vanity, accordingly, is an existentialist's bane—the identification of one's Self in terms of those facts which are beyond our control rather than our ambitions and accomplishments, what we *make* of ourselves. (Question: What does it mean to say that "all is vanity"?)

(VANITY)

1. DIRECTION:	Inner-directed, but with a constant view askance to its audience.
2. SCOPE/FOCUS:	Particular attributes and features, of oneself.
3. OBJECT:	Passive aspects of ourselves, not ourselves as agents or our actions.
4. CRITERIA:	Interpersonal (though possibly with a personal obstinacy as well); dependent on the opinions of others.
5. STATUS:	————
6. EVALUATIONS:	Positive.
7. RESPONSIBILITY:	Not responsible.
8. INTERSUBJECTIVITY:	Defensive because so dependent on the opinions of others.

9. DISTANCE:	A performer's distance—far enough to be viewed. Therefore antithetical to intimacy.
10. MYTHOLOGY:	Narcissus admiring his good looks. Aesop's peacock.
11. DESIRE:	To be envied.
12. POWER:	Impotence.
13. STRATEGY:	A mildly desperate attempt to bolster up self-esteem by using whatever benefits one enjoys—even if not his own doing—to attract the attention and admiration (or envy) of other people. Unfortunately, vanity is rarely successful, since the opinions of others are never a secure base for one's opinions of himself, and particularly since the grounds for appeal in this case are notably decrepit. (Consider Robert Graves's antifeminist title, *Man Does, Woman Is.*) It is always what a person does, pride in accomplishments rather than envy from others for fortunate features, that provides a person with a basis for self-esteem and a sense of dignity.

WORSHIP

Worship is an emotion closely akin to faith, but without faith's confidence. Worship lacks expectations, despite the fact that the object of worship must always be an agent to whom one appeals (even if that "agent" is hiding in a stone statue or a crucifix). In fact, the object of worship is typically disinterested or oblivious to the worshiper, which makes worship a notably self-demeaning emotion. It has its compensations, however, insofar as one identifies himself with the object of worship, which is typically too far away and too unconcerned to deny the identification. In addition to its usual religious contexts, worship (also idolatry and adoration, its milder forms) often appears as a perversion of love, devoid of intersubjectivity and intimacy and perverting the notion of bipolarity. (This is why adoration and infatuation, cherishing and worshiping, do not constitute love.)

(WORSHIP)

1. DIRECTION:	Outer-directed (oneself as utterly insignificant and minimal).
2. SCOPE/FOCUS:	Always particular (unlike faith).
3. OBJECT:	An agent, human or godlike.
4. CRITERIA:	The criteria for choice of object are open, but the object of worship, once chosen, typically becomes the source of moral authority. Thus, one might choose a religion for personal, interpersonal, or moral reasons, but the god he chooses then becomes authoritative. (Kierkegaard's discussion of Abraham's dilemma in *Fear and Trembling* is an admirable allegory for this sometimes confusing relationship between the personal choice and the subsequent authority of a system of values.)
5. STATUS:	Other is vastly superior; by contrast, oneself is utterly insignificant.
6. EVALUATIONS:	Other is praised, whatever one might think of his or her particular powers or attributes. Though generally, as in love, over-all praise tends to result in praise of particulars as well.
7. RESPONSIBILITY:	The other is a responsible agent, but not particularly responsible to the worshiper, which makes this emotion particularly self-demeaning. Whatever expectations one might have regarding the Other, one has no grounds for complaint, whatever the consequences. ("God works in mysterious ways.") When such an attitude is adopted toward another person, the results are spectacularly disastrous.

8. INTERSUBJECTIVITY:	When combined with faith, worship and trust are reconciled. Otherwise, worship is more likely combined with terror and helpless defensiveness (cf. the Old and New Testaments).
9. DISTANCE:	Enormous; in its constitution of the Other as vastly overwhelming, worship makes intimacy impossible (De Beauvoir: "When gods fall, they do not become mere men; they become frauds"). Kierkegaard's conception of a terrifying and fatherly God, however, makes a dubious attempt to reconcile worship and intimacy. Marcel, in a very different manner, attempts to identify Christian belief and mutual intimacy, emphasizing, like Hegel, the notion of Christian "spirit" at the *expense* of the object of traditional Christian worship (namely, a transcendent God).
10. MYTHOLOGY:	Any religion; insignificant man in contrast with the Almighty (or at least the Much-mighty); man with his desperate appeals to a vastly superior and, if not indifferent, then extremely mysterious agency.
11. DESIRE:	To please and appease.
12. POWER:	Utter impotence.
13. STRATEGY:	Worship displays three interconnected strategies, all familiar to us from other emotions. In diminishing one's own significance, one also minimizes his responsibilities and his accountability (as in guilt). In recognizing the vast powers of the Other, one provides himself with a readily available excuse for his failures, a way of projecting all misfortunes outward (though not casting *blame* for them, an interesting paradox never ade-

quately resolved by the so-called problem of Evil). And finally, by identifying with distant forces, one gives himself the impression of grandeur and power, whether or not his appointed "ally" should ever in fact give the slightest hint of concern or willingness to help. Like guilt, the emotion of worship is an emotion which tries to capitalize on self-degradation.

CONCLUSION: LOOKING AHEAD

This essay too is above all a recreation, a spot of sunshine, a leap
sideways . . .

—Nietzsche, *Twilight of the Idols*

Since *The Passions* was published, the subject of emotion has started
to move toward center stage not only in philosophy but in the social
sciences as well. With the turn in ethics toward an emphasis on
character and the virtues, emotions have emerged as a fundamental
ingredient in our assessments and evaluations. In the social sciences,
with the growing concern for such everyday issues as stress and aggression, the emotions have also come into the spotlight, augmented by
some remarkably detailed research on the physiology of emotional
expression and a good deal of international rather than merely intramu-
ral study of emotions. An enthusiastic international research group, the
International Society for Research on Emotions (ISRE), has brought
together two hundred psychologists, anthropologists, sociologists, neurologists, animal behaviorists, philosophers, and historians interested
in emotion, and from them I have learned a great deal and have come
to appreciate better the multidimensional complexity of emotions and
emotional life. In retrospect, the only chapter of *The Passions* that
embarrasses me, or that I would rather rewrite, is the chapter on
psychology and the science of emotion. To be sure, several psychologists have, with evident reservations, agreed with my rather blanket
criticism of a certain so-called "scientific" approach to emotion, but I
have now come to appreciate how varied and conflicted the social
sciences themselves have been on this score and how much we all have
to learn from each other.

With this in mind, I want to leave this book with a plea for cooperation and for a much-needed breakdown of the walls between our disciplines. It is no offense to the profundities of cosmology and the marvels of mathematics to say that there is no subject more fascinating than our own emotions, and what I learned and confirmed for myself in thinking about and writing this book is the extent to which our emotions are indeed creative activities, functions of our thinking (and vice versa), and not merely misfortunes we suffer. We must give up the sometimes tragic and almost always confused antagonism between reason and the passions, as if only insanity and self-destructive obsessions could be truly "passionate" and only the cold-blooded calculations of disinterested reason could be rational. I believe that we should also examine our collective consciousness and those emotions that motivate so many of our current social and political problems—envy, greed, resentment, contempt, false pride, jealousy, and moral indignation, just to mention a few. If our emotions make our lives meaningful, they can also make them mutually maddening. A philosophy of emotions, accordingly, cannot rest content with a general theory, some piecemeal analyses, and a defense of the emotions as such. It must also be, in a rather large sense, therapeutic, a corrective vision, an aid to cultivating the grand emotions and recasting those negative if often brilliant emotions which, as Nietzsche said, drag us down with their stupidity.

In closing, I just want to thank those good philosophers, writers and social scientists from whom I have since learned so much. In particular, I would like to leave this book with a dedication to the memory of Shula Sommers.

NOTES

Preface

1. *Will to Power*, para. 387.
2. Quoted in N. Malcolm, *Wittgenstein, a Memoir* (London: Oxford University Press, 1966), p. 39.

Chapter Two

1. "What Is a Free Man?" in *Man Against Mass Society* (Chicago: Regnery, 1962).
2. *Nicomachean Ethics*, Bk. III.

Chapter Three

1. Most helpful to me have been Magda Arnold's *The Nature of Emotion* (London: Penguin, 1968) but also David Rapaport's now dated summaries in Chaps. 1 and 2 of *Emotions and Memory* (New York: International Universities Press, 1971). Also helpful are the more restrictive collections and studies by D. K. Candland, ed., *Emotion: Bodily Changes, an Enduring Problem in Psychology* (Princeton, N.J.: Van Nostrand, 1962); P. H. Knapp, ed., *Expression of the Emotions in Man* (New York: International Universities Press, 1963); West and Greenblatt, *Explorations in the Physiology of Emotions* (APA, 1960); P. T.

Young, *Motivation and Emotion* (New York: Wiley, 1961); M. L. Reymert, *Feelings and Emotions* (New York: McGraw-Hill, 1950); H. N. Gardiner, Ruth Metcalf, and J. G. Beebe-Center, *Feeling and Emotion: A History of Theories* (New York: American, 1937); C. L. Stacey and M. F. De Martino, *Understanding Human Motivation* (Cleveland: H. Allen, 1958).

2. Rapaport, *Emotions and Memory*, pp. 271, 236.
3. W. A. Hunt, "Recent Developments in the Field of Emotion," 1941.
4. Magda Arnold, *The Nature of Emotion*.
5. Ibid., p. 2.
6. K. Dunlap, "Emotions as Dynamic Background," in *Feelings and Emotions: The Wittenberg Symposium*, ed. M. L. Reymert (Worcester, Mass.: Clark University Press, 1928).
7. For example, Rapaport, *Emotions and Memory*, p. 29: "expression implies here motor as well as physiological change." See also Charles Sherrington, *The Integrative Action of the Nervous System* (New York: Arno, 1947), and William James, "What Is an Emotion?" (*Mind*, 1884).
8. The term is not new. It has been used, for example, by Elliot Aronson, *The Social Animal* (San Francisco: W. H. Freeman, 1972), in a different context.
9. For example, see the recent work of Paul Feyerabend on the affinities of science and witchcraft.
10. E. Leach, *Claude Lévi-Strauss* (London: Collins, 1971), pp. 50, 54–56, 61.
11. *General Psychological Theory* (New York: Collier, 1963), pp. 125ff.
12. Despite his catholic approach, David Rapaport sums up his research strictly in terms of an explicitly hydraulic "discharge" model of the emotions (Emotions and Memory, pp. 267–72).
13. Rapaport, *Emotions and Memory*.
14. D. O. Hebb, *The Organization of Behavior* (New York: Wiley, 1949): "The term emotion does not refer to any kind of special event in consciousness."
15. E. B. Titchener, *Lectures on the Elementary Psychology of Feeling and Attention* (London: Macmillan, 1908), and W. Wundt, *Grundgriss der Psychologie* (Stuttgart, 1920).
16. Sigmund Freud, "Project for a Scientific Psychology," in *Standard Edition of the Collected Works*, Vol. 3.
17. For example, *Outline of Psychoanalysis*, in *Standard Works*, Vol. 20.

18. M. Prince, in Reymert, *Feelings and Emotions*.
19. K. Colby, *Energy and Structure in Psychoanalysis* (New York: Ronald, 1955).
20. C. G. Jung, *The Integration of the Personality* (London: Routledge, 1940), p. 10.
21. *Ibid.*, pp. 19–20.
22. W. McDougall, *Introduction to Social Psychology* (Boston: Luce, 1921), p. 49.
23. W. McDougall, "Emotion and Feeling Distinguished," in Arnold, *The Nature of Emotion*, p. 62.
24. Konrad Lorenz, "The Nature of Instincts," in *Instinctive Behavior*, ed. and trans. C. H. Schiller (New York: International Universities Press, 1957).
25. N. Tinbergen, *The Study of Instinct* (New York: Oxford University Press, 1951).
26. Konrad Lorenz, *On Aggression* (New York: Harcourt, Brace and World, 1966).
27. Desmond Morris, *The Naked Ape* (New York: McGraw-Hill, 1967) and *The Human Zoo* (New York: McGraw-Hill, 1969). Also R. Ardrey, *The Territorial Imperative* (New York: Atheneum, 1966).
28. R. Plutchik, *The Emotions* (New York: Random House, 1962).
29. For example, T. W. Leeper, "The Motivational Theory of Emotion," in Stacey and De Martino, *Understanding Human Motivation*, pp. 657–65, and "A Motivational Theory . . . ," in Arnold, *The Nature of Emotion*, pp. 203–21.
30. For example, R. S. Lazarus, "Emotion as a Coping Process," in Arnold, *The Nature of Emotion*, pp. 249–60: "The fundamental thing that generates an emotion is the cognitive activity of appraisal and the impulse it generates" (p. 253). See also the Schachter-Singer thesis, discussed in Chapter 7.
31. "L'Order du Coeur," *Pensées*.
32. Henri Bergson, *The Two Sources of Morality and Religion*, trans. R. Ashley Audra and Cloudesley Brereton (New York: Doubleday, 1955).
33. Max Scheler, *The Nature of Sympathy*, trans. P. Heath (New York: Shoe String Press, 1970).
34. R. L. Gregory, *Eye and Brain* (New York: McGraw-Hill, 1973); A. Kenny, *Action, Emotion and Will* (London: Routledge & Kegan Paul, 1963); S. Hampshire, *Thought and Action* (New York: Viking, 1960); E. Bedford, "Emotions," in D. F. Gustaf-

son, *Essays in Philosophical Psychology* (Garden City: Double-day Anchor, 1964). Also see Albert Ellis's "Rational-Emotive Therapy," *Psychology Today*, July 1973.

35. For example, the so-called conflict theory; emotions as conflicts of motives or instincts; e.g., in John Dewey, "The Theory of the Emotions," *Psychological Review*, 1894–95, and Gardiner Murphy, *General Psychology* (New York: Harper, 1933).

36. For example, in "Gestalt" theory of emotions as "significant" or "exciting" experiences; e.g., F. Kruger, in Arnold, *The Nature of Emotion*, pp. 97–108, and Kurt Koffka, *Principles of Gestalt Psychology* (New York: Harcourt, 1935).

37. C. G. Jung, *Memories, Dreams and Reflections*, trans. Winston (New York: Pantheon, 1963), p. 83.

Chapter Four

1. William James, "What Is an Emotion?" and *Principles of Psychology*, 2 vols. (New York: Dover, 1890), C. G. Lange, *Über Gemütsbewegungen* (Leipzig, 1887), and James and Lange, *The Emotions* (1922).

2. W. B. Cannon, *American Journal of Psychology*, Vol. 39 (1927).

3. For example, by Marañon in 1924, and recently by S. Schachter and J. E. Singer, "Cognitive, Social and Physiological Determinants of Emotional States," *Psychological Review*, Vol. 69 (1962).

4. For example, R. S. Lazarus, in Arnold, *The Nature of Emotion*, p. 260.

5. In Arnold, ibid., and also Plutchik, *The Emotions*.

6. James, "What Is an Emotion?", p. 23.

7. See J. L. Austin, "Pretending," and G. E. N. Anscombe, "Pretending," in Gustafson, ed., *Essays in Philosophical Psychology*. See also Chap. 7, Sec. 2.

8. See, for example, A. MacIntyre, *The Unconscious* (London: Routledge & Kegan Paul, 1962).

9. "What Is an Emotion?", pp. 28–29.

Chapter Five

1. In S. Hampshire, ed., *The Philosophy of Mind* (New York: Harper & Row, 1966).

2. See, e.g., A. Kenny, *Action, Emotion and Will* (New York:

Humanities Press, 1963). Cf. Robert Gordon, "The Aboutness of Emotions," *American Philosophical Quarterly*, 1974.
3. See Charles Taylor, *The Explanation of Behavior* (London: Routledge & Kegan Paul, 1964), for a telling formulation of these objections.
4. See Jean-Paul Sartre, *The Emotions: A Sketch of a Theory*, trans. B. Frechtman (New York: Philosophical Library, 1948), Introduction and Chap. 1.
5. J. L. Austin, *How to Do Things with Words* (Oxford: Clarendon Press, 1962).
6. For example, Immanuel Kant, in his *Critique of Judgment*, trans. Meredith (Oxford: Oxford University Press, 1952).

Chapter Six

1. *The Expression of Emotion in Man and Animals* (London: John Murray, 1872).
2. *The World Viewed* (New York: Viking, 1971), p. 40.

Chapter Eight

1. Cf. E. Bedford, "Emotions," in Gustafson, *Essays in Philosophical Psychology*, pp. 78ff.

INDEX